D1083219

Orphanages Reconsidered

NURITH ZMORA

Orphanages Reconsidered

Child Care Institutions in Progressive Era Baltimore

TEMPLE UNIVERSITY PRESS

PHILADELPHIA

Temple University Press, Philadelphia 19122
Copyright © 1994 by Temple University. All rights reserved
Published 1994
Printed in the United States of America

The paper used in this publication meets the minimum
requirements of American National Standard for Information
Sciences—Permanence of Paper for Printed Library Materials,
ANSI Z39.48-1984 ⊗

Library of Congress Cataloging-in-Publication Data

Zmora, Nurith, 1950–
    Orphanages reconsidered : child care institutions in progressive
era Baltimore / Nurith Zmora.
      p. cm.
    Includes bibliographical references (p.   ) and index.
    ISBN 1-56639-071-0 (cl : alk. paper)
    1. Orphanages—Maryland—Baltimore—History—Case studies.
I. Title.
HV995.B2Z46   1993
362.7'32'097526—dc20   93-14640

To Arie, Michael, and Tamar

CONTENTS

TABLES

Note on the Methodology

RESEARCHING NINETEENTH-CENTURY dependent children is a complicated task for several reasons. The first is the lack of readily available sources. Because orphanages became extinct, records were very often lost or moved into private hands outside the reach of historians. Even when materials relevant to the subject exist, researchers are often barred from using them because of concerns about confidentiality. In this project the search for materials was sometimes as exciting as the research itself. The Samuel Ready School for Orphan Girls closed its gates in 1977 and placed its rich archives in the special collections of the Langsdale Library at the University of Baltimore. The collection contains children's files, which include every child's family background, health, and educational achievement. The files also contain letters of recommendation received with applications for admission, letters sent to the superintendent by children during their vacations, and correspondence after the children left the institution. The collection includes the board of trustees minute book, letters from the superintendent to the trustees, and many files that shed light on activities in the school during the period. An important source is the *Ready Record*, the bimonthly student publication. Research of these materials was limited only by a request to keep the children's names confidential and to refrain from quoting directly from private letters found in the children's files.

When the Hebrew Orphan Asylum (H.O.A.) closed, its archives were turned over to Associated Jewish Charities, which held them for several decades and then gave them to the Maryland Jewish Historical Society. The collection includes the H.O.A.'s record book, containing information on the children and their families, their health, and when and to whom the children were discharged. It also includes the superintendent's monthly reports to the board of directors. Finally, the minute book of the board of directors from 1911 to 1916 is available to researchers, as are other files containing documents pertaining to the administration of the orphanage. To obtain a better understanding of the children's point of view, I interviewed four graduates of the H.O.A., the last secretary of the H.O.A., the son of one of the superintendents, and one of the social workers. I also interviewed someone who studied at a public high school with some of the H.O.A. residents. The autobiographies of a graduate and a former superintendent helped to clarify some aspects of life in the orphanage.

The materials pertaining to the Dolan Children's Aid Society, or the Dolan Home, as the orphanage was called, are in the Children's Bureau archives of the Associated Catholic Charities of Baltimore. At first, I was allowed to look at the children's record book and the board of trustees minute book, which included quarterly reports of the superintendent. The archives also contain the book that kept track of the trustees' management of Father Dolan's endowment to the Dolan Home. Later, when I returned to look for data from the 1900s, a new administration was concerned about confidentiality and denied me further access. My research on the Dolan Home suffered significantly as a result.

In trying to learn more about relationships between the children and staff and among the children, I was confronted with the problem of interpreting testimony given more than sixty years later. Does it reflect feelings orphans felt as children or feelings they have today? Even when oral history can be supplemented by autobiographies and other written materials, interpretive problems remain. There is also the question of the quantity of testimony. How many interviews are needed to make a conclusive statement about relationships in the orphanage?

Letters in the Samuel Ready School archives were revealing, but did they reflect feelings the children had while in the school or adult attitudes? (Some of these letters were written long after graduation.) Even letters the children wrote to the superintendent when they were students present a problem in interpretation. Children at that time were very respectful toward adults and authority. They might not have dared to criticize either the superintendent or the institution in a letter addressed to the superintendent. A partial solution to these problems is to use a variety of materials as a cross-check on any particular piece of information. For example, I interviewed people only after studying all written materials to get an idea of what life was like in the orphanage. The oral history supplemented and modified what was available from other sources.

In order to provide a social profile of the children in the orphanages, I selected a sample of forty to forty-five children from each orphanage who entered the institution between 1887 and 1890. The Samuel Ready School opened in 1887, and since I was not sure how representative the first sample of forty girls would be, I added a second sample of forty children who entered the orphanage between 1888 and 1900 and whose family names began with the letters A through L. Although I examined eighty children in the Samuel Ready, I followed only the lives of the children from the first sample after they left the institution.

The task of following the children after they left their institutions was difficult. Although I consulted a variety of sources such as city directories, the U.S. Census, court documents, and city archives, I could not trace many of the children. Girls from the Dolan Home and the Hebrew Orphan Asylum could not be traced, probably because they had married and changed their last names. But boys were also difficult to track down, in part because their names were often common. In some cases, they appeared in the 1900 U.S. Census but not in the 1910 U.S. Census. Since the latter is not indexed, without an accurate address, it was virtually impossible to find them. Another difficulty arose because many of the Hebrew Orphan Asylum's children moved from Baltimore to other cities. Only the Samuel Ready School girls were easily traced, because the school archives contain the alumnae register; letters from later years; and entries in the school bimonthly paper, which mentioned the girls in its alumnae column.

Names of interviewees who wished to remain anonymous and names of children at the orphanages have been disguised.

ACKNOWLEDGMENTS

D URING THE years of research and writing of this book, I became indebted to many people who assisted me in the research, criticism, and editing of the manuscript.

I owe the greatest debt to Ronald G. Walters, my mentor at Johns Hopkins University, whose encouragement, advice, criticism, and fine editing sustained me for the past ten years. I also thank Toby L. Ditz for very helpful criticism of Chapters Two and Three. David Allmendinger's favorable comments on the manuscript lifted my spirits when my own doubts crept in. LeRoy Ashby was my reader for Temple University Press. His thorough reading and criticism of the manuscript saved me a lot of time.

Special thanks go to Jack P. Greene for all the help he extended to me and my family.

The Schimmels (Uncle Bill and Aunt Blanche, as my children call them) "adopted" the research from the very beginning. Their generosity could fill a book. They introduced me to many other people who assisted me in many ways—among them, Dr. Louis H. Kaplan, to whom I am indebted for countless favors. I also thank Dr. Shmuel Litov, a dear friend from the Baltimore Hebrew University, and Dr. Levy Smollar, former president of Baltimore Hebrew University.

The Morris Lieberman Fund gave me a small grant to complete my studies. In 1987 the Charlotte Newcombe Dissertation Award (administered by the Woodrow Wilson Foundation) enabled me to dedicate a year to writing. My mother, Olga Ruth Igali, helped whenever she could, and my mother-in-law, Dvora Zmora, provided financial assistance, for which I am deeply grateful.

I also thank the people who graciously allowed me to interview them and those who helped me obtain these interviews: Jeanette

Rosner Wolman, Dr. Milton Reizenstein, Bess Hammet, the late Jacob Beser, Moshe Cohen, and all those who asked me not to disclose their names.

The people in the Interlibrary Loan Department at Johns Hopkins University, particularly Jenny Newman; the Department of Special Collections in the Langsdale Library at the University of Baltimore; the Maryland Jewish Historical Society; the Baltimore Associated Catholic Charities' Archives; the Maryland Historical Society; and the Baltimore City Archives were all of great assistance. Special thanks go to Dr. Thomas Jacklin from the University of Baltimore, who introduced me to the Samuel Ready Archives in the Langsdale Library, and to Barbara Varga, former archivist for the Baltimore Associated Catholic Charities, the Children's Bureau, for opening the archives to me.

I also thank my friend, Milana Isaacson, who generously gave her time to edit the Introduction to this book.

Janet Francendese, Terry Schutz, Joan Vidal, and all the people at Temple University Press did excellent work in preparing this book for publication. Any flaws are mine.

To my husband and best friend, Arie Zmora, I extend my deepest gratitude.

ARLY ONE day in May 1913, two sons of Russian Jewish immigrants sat at the graduation ceremony of City College, a prestigious Baltimore public high school. Both had taken the commercial course and were enthusiastic basketball players. Michael Aaronsohn, who graduated near the top of his class, was a year younger than Wilfred S. (whose name is changed to preserve anonymity) because he completed the program in three years instead of four. Both had worked in the afternoons throughout high school. Michael assisted a janitor, and Wilfred delivered clothes for a tailor. Each lived in a three-story house. Wilfred shared his home with seven other children and with boarders; Michael shared his room with seven other children. Michael had his own bed and slept in a room that was well heated in the winter and ventilated in summer. Wilfred was cold during the winter because the only source of heat in his house was the oven in the first floor kitchen. In Baltimore summers he was hot and sweaty in his room under the roof. Michael did not like the food he ate, although it included meat, vegetables, fresh eggs, and milk, and he had ice cream and candies at least once a month. Wilfred did not recall candy or ice cream from his childhood, but he developed a taste for them as a young adult. Dishes in his house needed little scraping after meals. If one child left some food on his plate, another would eat it. Both Michael and Wilfred used public transportation to go to school but walked home to save the fare. Wilfred would walk barefoot in the summer to avoid wearing out his shoes. He came to school from his parents' home in a crowded neighborhood in East Baltimore. Michael came from the Hebrew Orphan Asylum in the village of Calverton in West Baltimore. Wilfred knew

Michael in school and again years later, when Michael became known as the Blind Rabbi (having been blinded in battle during World War I while trying to rescue friends). Wilfred did not know until 1989, however, that Michael had come to school every day not from his widowed mother's house but from an orphanage.[1]

Historians would label Wilfred's family middle class because they owned their home, although it was mortgaged and shared with boarders. Moreover, Wilfred's father was a tailor with his own shop. Although their income barely met their needs, they were better off than the Aaronsohns. Michael's widowed mother, who had three children, worked at home finishing trousers for a factory, clearly belonged to the "have-nots."[2] Some historians would regard Michael Aaronsohn's orphanage a jail-like institution; they would assume that it was depressing in appearance and oppressive in its overreliance on harsh discipline, rigid routine, and lack of respect for the individual.[3] Both Michael Aaronsohn and Wilfred S. would disagree with such views. Wilfred described himself as a poor child growing up in a family that was struggling financially and paid no attention to its children as individuals: he enjoyed no birthday parties or presents and no supervision of his studies. His mother signed his report card each semester, but otherwise his parents were too busy attending to the large family's basic needs to read to or play with him or supervise his schoolwork. Michael attributes his success in adult life to the upper-middle-class education and culture provided by the charitable institution, noting that he would have had neither had he stayed with his widowed mother.

This book is about the experience of children like Michael in Baltimore orphanages. It is an attempt to understand how such institutions affected the lives of children they housed and educated as well as the families the children came from. By focusing on the population served by these orphanages, this study departs from histories of social institutions that emphasize the roles of agencies of social control; it joins a growing literature that distinguishes between ideological or management objectives of institutions and their accomplishments from the point of view of those served.

Because orphanages for the healthy dependent child are almost extinct in the United States today, one might ask why it is important to examine them now, apart from the value of recording the past. In 1968, when David Rothman wrote his pathbreaking book about

nineteenth-century asylums, which criticizes the government's bureaucratic grip over various groups of dependents, quite a few orphanages still operated in the United States. But by the end of the
1960s, anti-institutional sentiment had forced most of them to close
their gates. In the 1980s, a new awareness of the dependent population, especially dependent children, emerged. This was a result of the
diminished resources allocated to alleviate their distress, the failure of
alternatives to institutions, the growing distrust of professionals who
handle these children, and the increasing numbers of children needing protection. In a recent article on the crisis in foster care, William
Raspberry discussed the results of a survey of the population of dependent children in New York City in 1986 done by the National
Black Child Development Institute. Alice Walker, professor of social
work at Howard University and the survey's principal investigator,
found that contrary to the researchers' expectations, the children were
not trouble-prone adolescents or children of teenage mothers but rather
were children without severe health or behavioral problems who came
from inadequate homes. Moreover, the survey showed that children are
increasingly in need of shelter at younger ages (the mean age in 1986
was seven years) and that they have no homes to which they can return
after a period of institutional help. "Child care professionals," explained Raspberry, "are increasingly overwhelmed, not merely by huge
case-loads but also by the growing gap between present-day problems
and the traditional solutions."[4] The dependent children characterized in
the survey resemble those who once filled orphanages; no wonder that
child care institutions recently began to regain public attention as a
possible solution to dependent children's needs.

Given the present situation, it is not surprising that historians have
begun to reflect on previous periods when children were the focus of
public attention. The most notable was the Progressive Era, when
reformers emphasized the importance of protecting children's health
through adequate medicine, hygiene, nutrition, and labor laws. They
discovered the need for fresh air and play and learned to distinguish
among feebleminded, healthy, and delinquent dependent children. As
a result, the Progressive Era saw multiple innovations on behalf of
children, including the kindergarten and the playground, the industrial school and the gym.

The focus on children stemmed from different ideological and
practical reasons, but reformers agreed that because children were

the future of the nation, the United States should invest in their well-being. Of particular concern was the growing number of children who needed society's aid. The Progressives' studies concluded that there were many causes for dependency; therefore they experimented with a variety of solutions. They recognized that parents' character was not always at fault and that some causes for dependency were beyond parents' control. Industrialization, hazardous conditions in the workplace, and contagious or incurable diseases left some parents unemployed, some handicapped, and others dead. Some breadwinners who were unable to provide for their families despaired and deserted them.

While all reformers agreed that children should be helped and saved from degrading life conditions, they differed greatly on the means to achieve this goal. Even those who believed that dependent children should be taken from their families disagreed on what would be the best environment for them. Some advocated a protective environment such as a child care institution; others favored an alternative family setting—foster care.

Reformers who objected to removing children from their families pointed out that some of these families were functioning well before calamity broke them down. They suggested help to families, in particular the great number of widows with young children who, they felt, could not be blamed for their poverty. The reformers recommended that states be required to grant widows' pensions to help them raise their children at home. The controversy regarding mothers' pensions was part of another controversy among reformers: should relief be public or private? The campaign for mothers' pensions resulted in recognition that public relief for some of the dependent population is just compensation rather than an act of charity, a step on the way to social security and to the idea of a welfare state. Following the logic of preserving the family, some reformers believed that some forms of dependency could be prevented. They supported investment in the neighborhoods in which poor families lived, arguing that improved sanitary conditions and housing as well as provisions for child care, education, recreation, and health care would prevent poor families from slipping into dependency.[5]

Reformers of the Progressive Era had the advantage of initiating reform, creating institutions, and mobilizing others without depending on the government. Although their efforts often resulted in governmental action, many distrusted municipal and governmental efforts.[6] In the 1990s, when the bureaucratic American welfare system is widely criticized, more and more people favor private institutions assuming some responsibility for dependent children. This study of private initiatives during the Progressive Era cannot provide a road map for contemporary reformers, but it sheds some light on paths that were abandoned and questions some of the assumptions about orphanages that have taken root and flourished. Recognizing that historical interpretation is not free from social currents, we must continually interrogate the assumptions and conclusions of historical work. Hence, a key question in this study is: Why do historians and orphans paint different pictures of orphanages? In contrast to orphans like Michael Aaronsohn, Eileen Simpson, and Frances Garate,[7] historian David Rothman, for example, saw the orphanage as symptomatic of an ideological trend that, at the end of the nineteenth century, labeled poor people as deviant and sought to sweep the streets clean of them by shutting them up in institutions, particularly if they happened to be immigrants. Rothman's *Discovery of the Asylum* influenced a school of thought that perceived asylums as a mechanism of "social control" used by society for disciplining its undesired elements. Patricia Rooke and R. L. Schnell extended Rothman's social control interpretation to Canadian orphanages. They contradicted his view that the public did not differentiate among kinds of institutions, such as insane asylums and reformatories, but regarded all as housing deviant and dangerous populations. Rooke and Schnell demonstrated that, in Canada at least, orphanages differed greatly from institutions for sick or delinquent children and suggested that small, private orphanages might be less bleak than large, public institutions.[8] Recently, a more benign view of orphanages has come from LeRoy Ashby, who studied child care institutions that emerged in the Progressive Era as a result of a new sensitivity to the plight of children. Focusing on the managerial level of the "child savers" movement, Ashby looked at the private initiative to "redeem" children and emphasized reformers' religious convictions and their "amateur altruism," without discounting altogether motives of social control, public recognition, and fame.[9] In a somewhat different vein, Susan Whitelaw Downs and Michael W. Sherraden argued that an orphanage was a community's practical solution, rather than an ideological response to an increasing number of abandoned and orphaned children; once established, the orphanage continually adjusted to community needs.[10]

These historical interpretations of child care institutions in the Progressive Era are not entirely incompatible. No doubt some reformers held ideological convictions that included social control while others were pragmatists more concerned with responding to practical problems than with ideology. Some reformers must have seen such institutions as a means toward both humanitarian and social control goals.[11] Their motives are not easily discerned because they left little documentation about their reasons for doing reform work and their public statements were not always consistent.[12] Ultimately, discovering what reformers accomplished and how their institutions functioned is more important than understanding their motives. The history of child saving that focuses on institution founders, managers, and ideological underpinnings tends to omit the actual life of poor people in the era. The users of the institution—the children and their families—are also important to our understanding of past social welfare practices.

Barbara Brenzel focused on the users of an institution for wayward and delinquent girls in the second half of the nineteenth century. She discovered that many parents labeled their children as delinquent to make them eligible for the Lancaster Industrial School, with the hope that their daughters would benefit from the good education and good living conditions there.[13] Using a method similar to Brenzel's, Bruce Bellingham examined the New York Children's Aid Society (founded by Charles Loring Brace) and concluded that sending dependent children to farms in the West was a solution to the problem of unemployment among teenagers in New York City. Most children sent by the society were either looking for a temporary job or had dreams of becoming farmers themselves.[14] Examining children's records, both historians focused on nineteenth-century innovations in care for dependent and delinquent children, and both developed a more positive view of such institutions than their predecessors had.[15]

All of Baltimore's orphanages were private institutions. The three examined in this book did not shelter juvenile delinquents and, as will be shown, did not permit mingling between dependent children and delinquents. They were founded as a response to the needs of the city's various ethnic and religious groups, which had to help a growing number of single parents, mainly women. Two of these institutions bore little resemblance to the similarly named institutions described by Brenzel and Bellingham. Unlike the industrial school Brenzel studied, the Samuel Ready Industrial School for orphan girls in Baltimore did not include wayward girls or delinquents among its students, nor was the Dolan Children's Aid Society a placement agency, as New York's Children's Aid Society was. Despite a similarity of names, child care institutions in this study differ significantly from those in methodologically similar studies.

This book's aims are to show how the three orphanages studied operated, how they provided for the children they housed, and how they affected the children's lives. It seeks to explore the differences among these orphanages in an attempt to understand better the range of possibilities and varieties within one type of child care institution, its failures, and its successes.

Discussions by contemporary social workers and scholars depict orphanages as generally abusive in their treatment of children. They argue that orphanages secluded and isolated the orphans from their families for excessive periods, provided them with inferior education in public schools, and failed to maintain their intellectual, physical, and mental well-being vis-à-vis peers outside the asylum.[16] Contrary to these observations, my study of three Baltimore orphanges shows that orphanages were not monolithic but varied in character, structure, composition, and aims in accordance with a spectrum of factors, such as (1) the needs of their respective communities, (2) their ethnic and religious affiliation, (3) whether financial support received was private or public, and (4) the beliefs, skills, and personalities of the managerial staff. These preconditions helped shape the composition of the orphanage's population and influenced the educational or vocational practices it eventually adopted.

Contrary to the prevailing notion that asylums were secluded institutions arbitrarily managed by authoritarian professionals, my research clearly shows that orphanages were considered integral parts of their communities and that community leaders worked along with superintendents of orphanages to provide adequate physical facilities, food, hygiene, and medical care and to create optimal educational opportunities by emphasizing both academic achievements and individualized vocational training. Orphans received educational advantages they might otherwise not have had.

My findings suggest that successful institutions were run by semi-professionals motivated by strong ethical and religious convictions, who blended strictness and affection in their attitude toward children and applied rules and regulations according to an evenhanded policy. As a result, children had a stable environment and developed self-confidence and pride in their achievements.

Orphanages were also pivotal in rebuilding families by keeping siblings together and encouraging orphans to preserve close ties with relatives. Contrary to common belief, orphanages did not isolate children from the outside world; rather they eased the transition of orphans from the asylum into the community as constructive, self-supporting citizens.

My research suggests several points of interest regarding the evolution of asylums and the history of child care:

1.   Nineteenth-century institutional structures and practices may have been more flexible than previously expected.
2.   Community and professional interests were not necessarily always in conflict.
3.   Institutionalization may not have been a misguided option, and there may be no absolute distinction between "professional" and "institutional" solutions, on the one hand, and "community" ones, on the other.

Orphanages hardly existed before the Middle Ages. In ancient Greece and Rome, orphans were raised by relatives if they came from rich families; poor ones without relatives willing and able to take care of them were enslaved.[17] Among ancient Hebrews, rich orphans paid for their education (but were exempted from taxes and some city and state charges) while poor orphans became the responsibility of the community, which had to place them in homes and ensure them an education and training for a vocation.[18] Christian orders began to build institutions to aid needy children (the poor, the orphaned, the neglected and abused, and those born out of wedlock); many of the orphanages were closed down and the children dispersed during the Reformation.[19] With the French Revolution and the rise of the modern secular state, the government tried to take responsibility for poor orphans, but high costs left room for private institutions, usually run by religious sects that worked side by side with public institutions.[20]

Still, orphanages were not the sole solution to the problem of dependent children at any time in history. Many children were aided at home by charity organizations or stayed with indigent parents in the almshouse. Some were indentured at an early age. During nineteenth-century industrialization, immigration and urbanization increased the number of needy children and, at the same time, decreased the aid and support that families and small communities traditionally extended to them. A reform movement in the 1840s, partly invoked and inspired by Charles Dickens's description of children's lives in workhouses, led to large-scale building of separate institutions for children.[21]

The history of orphanages in the United States reflects that change. During the colonial period few were built in North America. Those established prior to 1800 were founded by religious individuals and groups, usually as a response to a calamity. The first orphanage in North America was opened in New Orleans in 1739 by the Ursuline sisters, who came to open a school in Louisiana. As the eighteenth century continued, six orphanages were established by religious organizations in response to needs in their communities (in Baltimore, Philadelphia, and Savannah, among other cities).[22] The six represented different Christian sects and different ethnic groups who brought from the Old World their own cultures and traditions regarding poor children's welfare and education. During the first three decades of the nineteenth century, fifteen more private orphanages were established in the United States, mostly by Catholics who feared that their orphans would grow up in Protestant households.[23]

Under the impact of industrialization, urbanization, and immigration, the orphanage movement in the United States then grew quickly. It became systematized in the 1830s.[24] While some orphanages in this period were publicly supported by states or cities, nine out of ten were private, with Catholics taking the lead.[25] By the end of the century, criticism of institutions for dependent children was widespread and influential.[26] Orphanages continued to exist for the next five decades, but their number decreased and their population changed.

Owing to the difficulty of placement and the fairly constant large population of dependent children, foster care was an option, but it was not fully used until the 1970s. The number of dependent children who were orphans declined. Full orphans, (children who had lost both parents) were always a small minority in orphanages, which housed primarily half orphans, mostly those who were fatherless. With widows' pensions, social security, and the development of welfare programs during the twentieth century, a large proportion of the orphan population remained at home with relatives or a living parent, and the eradication of diseases like tuberculosis reduced the number of orphaned children in the general population. Thus from the 1920s, orphanages gradually turned into shelters for abused, neglected, handicapped, and homeless children. Although guidelines published in the *Social Work Year Book* of 1929 recommended foster care for handicapped children and institutions for "normal" children, especially older ones, it was easier to find foster care for "normal" children, and therefore the handicapped were often left in institutions.[27]

Orphanages could shape programs and facilities according to the religious, cultural, and economic situations of their communities, as well as to prevailing notions of children's education. In many cases, child care institutions were in the avant garde of education. When during the 1880s, for example, educators argued that school should be relevant to children's experience and should prepare them for future work in industry, child care institutions developed industrial education, which was later adopted by public schools.[28]

Although many programs were innovative, some ideas about dependent children persisted for decades, including the view that they must be separated from the rest of the population and classified into separate groups. The result was that different child care institutions evolved for orphans, the handicapped, the wayward, and the delinquent.[29] This classification remained in effect throughout the nineteenth century and well into the twentieth. It perpetuated the optimism that characterized the reformers of the first decades of the nineteenth century, which led them to believe that raising children in a proper environment would help them become useful citizens of the republic. This faith endured even in the face of pessimistic views of human potential, such as those of social Darwinism in the second half of the century.[30] People who organized child care institutions virtually declared that children could be saved through education and proper environment, regardless of heredity and family history. Classification and separation of subcategories of children in orphanages had to do with fear of exposing innocent children to those experienced in vice and crime. For educators this was a matter of creating a proper environment rather than choosing the "fittest" to be saved. Moreover, ideas regarding children and their needs during the Progressive Era indicate that orphanages' managers and boards of trustees regarded the children in their institutions as their own and provided them with the best they could give.[31]

Even when reformers argued that educating poor children would prevent crime (following the prevailing idea of emphasizing prevention as an answer to urban poverty), they were not thinking negatively but trying to attract support for the orphanage and to prove that the children were victims of circumstances rather than objects for reform.[32]

Classification of orphans determined the populations of orphanages, their aims and achievements, as well as the image they projected in the community. Contrary to other asylums that isolated their inmates from their families and society, the orphanage's aim was to rebuild the family by providing for and educating its children so that they could help their families once they grew up. The orphanage kept siblings together and encouraged children's ties with relatives (see Chapter Five).

It is not possible, however, to speak about "one" orphanage of the Progressive Era even though most orphanages followed Progressive ideology. They also kept distinctive religious and ethnic identities. In order to help gauge the range of diversity within shared Progressive Era practices, this book focuses on three orphanages from different religious and ethnic groups: a German-Russian Jewish orphanage, an Irish Catholic orphanage, and a Protestant orphanage for children of the old American community.

Jewish orphanges were developed in the context of Judaic laws. The community was required to treat orphans and widows with justice and gentle care, to provide for their needs and to take care of the education of orphans until they became independent, regardless of age.[33]

In Jewish communities special institutions for orphans were rare until the seventeenth century.[34] In Europe and the United States during the nineteenth century Jewish orphanages responded to waves of immigrants from Germany (1830–60) and from Eastern Europe (1880–1918) who often succumbed to diseases due to hard work and harsh living conditions, leaving behind orphans for whom the community needed to care.[35]

Each community took responsiblity for its own members, but circumstances sometimes overstressed their capacities. Some limited the number of new dependents, such as immigrants incapable of working, who settled among them.[36] Baltimore's Hebrew Benevolent Society, for example, asked the Philadelphia Jewish community to stop sending its poor to Baltimore. Most communities worked out their differences through negotiations.[37] The Jewish orphanage in Cleveland, for instance, accepted children from Jewish communities in eight midwestern states, each of which participated in the financing of the orphanage. Orphans from Washington, D.C., Virginia, South Carolina, and Georgia were among the children placed in the Baltimore Hebrew Orphan Asylum, which was subsidized by these communities.[38]

Catholicism viewed the care of orphans as an act of charity rather than a matter of law and justice and invested the parish with responsibility for its own people, including care of the needy and dependent.[39] A parish orphanage was in many cases small and supported primarily through the tithe the church collected from its members, a third of which was dedicated to the needy. Although parish priests and lay members organized orphanages, they were run by brothers and sisters from an order affiliated with the parish. Parishes, just like Jewish communities, cooperated in taking care of transients and immigrants, but unlike Jewish communities, parishes were under the control and supervision of the diocese and its head, the bishop, who had final authority over all matters.[40]

Catholic orphanages grew substantially in number during the second half of the nineteenth century due to a growing concern that the Protestant charities were proselytizing Catholic children by placing them in Protestant families.[41] Catholic orphanages, however, did not accept all orphans, even if they were Catholic. The Catholic church maintained children's aid societies that placed Catholic children in Catholic homes, industrial schools, and reformatories. Subsidized payments for these children were helpful in the tight economy of many orphanages. But the expense of building orphanages, maintaining them, and taking care of children was much greater than any state reimbursements.[42] One clever method of financing an orphanage was to locate a boarding school for wealthy students adjacent to the orphanage. The tuition from the boarding school could be used to maintain the orphanage.[43]

The Catholic church had the advantage of superintendents, teachers, and other staff who dedicated their lives to orphans without pecuniary compensation. These workers tended to stay for long periods in the orphanages, thus creating stability and continuity of care. Centralized supervision by the diocese enabled the church to help those orphanages that needed aid most, without the kind of negotiations in which Jewish communities engaged.[44]

Protestant denominations, such as the Lutherans, the Episcopalians, and the Methodists, had their own orphanages. Additionally, nondenominational orphanages were organized by Protestant men and women who did not belong to a particular church; these orphanages were financed by Protestant communities. Lack of centralization weakened the Protestant charity institutions but also gave them independence in shaping their policies, programs, and populations.[45] Protestants expanded classification of children beyond normal and wayward or delinquent to create institutions for talented, motivated children as well as for those who were less intelligent.[46]

The common wisdom at the end of the nineteenth century was that charity should distinguish between the deserving and undeserving poor. While children usually were viewed as innocent victims of circumstances and, therefore, as deserving, the same was not true of their parents. Some orphanages chose to admit only children whose parents were "deserving." Orphanages that selected motivated and talented children screened the children's family background and accepted only those from "respectable" families in which the parents worked, went to church, and provided education for their children prior to the calamity that forced them to seek help.[47] Orphans and half orphans whose parents were vagrants, drunkards, or gamblers could not enter such orphanages, even if they themselves were talented. They could enter orphanages with less ambitious educational programs or seek out children's aid societies that placed them in western farms. This mode of classification discriminated against immigrants' children because their homes were often unstable and their parents frequently changed jobs and addresses, were unemployed for long periods, and were not usually affiliated with one church. The children of immigrants at the turn of the century were accommodated in ethnic orphanages.

Ethnicity crossed religious lines. The Jewish community had German orphanages and Russian orphanages.[48] The Catholic church had

German, Irish, French, and Italian orphanages.[49] There were German Protestant orphanages, and Protestant orphanages for Swedes, Native Americans, and blacks.[50] German immigrants throughout the nineteenth century preserved their cultural heritage and language in their homes and in the educational systems they established. Although they came from different parts of the Austro-Hungarian Empire, in the New World Germans stressed common cultural traits and values. Their emphasis on order, neatness, punctuality, and discipline was noted by contemporaries.[51]

Irish orphanages maintained their sense of ethnicity by teaching the children about Irish heroes who toiled the land in the old country but later emphasized other vocations more suited to cities. The Catholic church, to which most Irish immigrants belonged, built industrial schools, and Irish orphanages sent their children to be educated in them. As a result Irish programs took care of children until they were old enough to send to a farm or an industrial school; they served as orphanages and as placement agencies, although they often bore the name of a children's aid society.[52]

Black orphanages differed from other ethnic orphanages in that some were organized and financed by the Black community while others were established by outside philanthropists. Apparently lacking the resources other orphanages had, they struggled to provide basic needs and were unable to give their children elaborate educational programs.[53]

Some ethnic orphanages organized by outside philanthropists tried to impose the middle-class values of white America. An extreme case was the Cherokee Orphan Asylum in Oklahoma, where Native American boys had to wear suits and the girls long Victorian dresses.[54] In general, the fact that orphanages were built and run by more affluent groups created the potential for class-based conflicts between children's families and the management of the orphanages. Doubtless such conflict occurred. Although immigrants, almost by definition, strove for better lives and aspired to middle-class rank, they sometimes were forced to sacrifice their children's education in order to survive.[55] Yet education provided the means to rise from blue-collar to white-collar jobs and into the middle class. Education also meant adopting middle-class manners and etiquette. To be sure difficulties arose when children returned to their old neighborhoods and poor families. But in giving these children access to education and social mobility, the orphanages gave them the very advantages that their parents probably desired for them. Few children, orphaned or not, who are able to rise above the poverty of their parents can avoid such conflicts.

Few orphanages depended on public money or were organized by the state or city authorities during the nineteenth century, but the number of publicly funded orphanages increased after the Civil War with the establishment of institutions for war orphans.[56] By the turn of the century most states had public orphanages for orphans and for neglected and abused children. Besides fully maintaining public orphanages, states, and often large cities, supported private orphanages that sheltered dependent children, either by giving them lump sums or by paying for each child they sent to them.[57]

The new emphasis on childhood at the turn of the century created a new field of professionalism—child care. Pediatricians, social workers, superintendents of child care institutions, and even architects specializing in child care institutions appeared for the first time. These new professionals called attention to three important elements affecting childhood development: environment, education, and individual needs.[58] Environment meant the neighborhood as well as physical surroundings. Reformers agreed that the best ecological setting was the country with its fresh air and sun, nature, and space to roam freely.[59] The human neighborhood was a subject for debate. Should children be taken out of a crowded neighborhood and raised in a closed institution with children of the same background and circumstances, or should the institution's children be part of a neighborhood, mingling with other children whose families remained intact and were not dependent on the public dole? Those who advocated closed institutions pointed out that dependent children had special educational needs because they often came to the orphanage already behind in school work for their age. Those who objected to closed institutions argued that children from such institutions were not ready to face real life when they were released. Studying together with other neighborhood children in the same school would expose them to life's realities and heighten their awareness of the struggles ahead.[60]

Educational goals were also debated. Should poor children follow an academic course though few of them would reach college, or should they have practical and vocational training? Should they work in their teens? There was no debate about education of talented children; they should develop their talents to the maximum (see Chapter Four). Awareness of the individual child's character and abilities should figure prominently in choosing a vocation. The Progressives stressed the need to pay attention to the individual, and, for them, achieving this goal meant imitating the family unit. Still, vocational education in orphanages was different for boys and girls: boys studied carpentry and printing, while girls were trained in sewing and cooking. Boys who showed above average intellectual ability were encouraged to pursue a college education, while girls with the same talents were directed to normal schools or business schools. Thus, while talented boys pursued careers as doctors, lawyers, and engineers, girls became teachers, nurses, and clerks. Orphanages reflected the prevailing ideology and reality in which women and men had different educational and job opportunities. To be sure, few exceptionally talented girls were sent to college, but few women in the population graduated from college at the turn of the century.

In the Progressive Era, the orphanage became "the anti-institution institution": no longer did children wear uniforms or pursue the same routine and education; individualism marked their appearance and education.[61] This new concept involved the physical accommodations and the way the children lived. The favored model was the cottage system of small detached houses in each of which a small number of children lived with an adult. Institutions that still adhered to the congregate system (all children living together in one building) tried to break up large sleeping quarters into smaller rooms. Finances dictated the orphanages' methods of accommodation, but ideology pushed the Progressives toward respect for privacy and individuality.[62]

As we have seen, orphanages were established around a variety of missions, funding sources, and organizing strategies; their institutional characteristics might include any combination of options—a private institution for girls might be affiliated with an ethnic and religious group and might be partially financed by the public. Within the range of possibilities, then, there was no typical orphanage. The orphanages under study in this book were established to address problems common to late nineteenth-century cities. By examining three institutions with ethnic/religious affiliations that served similar populations in one city, some light can be shed on what children experienced as a result of their efforts.

Chapter One describes the history of the three orphanages researched: the way they were organized and managed, the people who ran them, and the legal and financial status of each. Chapter Two gives a social profile of the orphans and their families. Living conditions, including the buildings, the food, the children's clothes, hygiene, and medical care are discussed in Chapter Three. Chapter Four deals with the children's education, including elementary school, vocational education, religious education, recreation and enrichment programs, and the daily schedule the orphans had to keep. Chapter Five raises the question of relationships within the orphanage between children and staff, staff and the children's parents, and the children and their families, with special emphasis on the relationships among siblings. It also dwells on the relationship between the institution and the community to which it belonged. Chapter Six describes what happened to the children after they left the orphanage: how they entered society again, what difficulties they encountered, and how they fared in life. I close with suggestions about the development of child care and other social welfare institutions.

CHAPTER ONE

The Organization of the Orphanages

B ALTIMORE HAD only private orphanages. Its population in the late nineteeth century was a mixture of ethnic and religious groups, with well-established citizens, newcomers from the rural areas of Maryland, and new immigrants from Europe. Baltimore was a large urban center, a seaport where immigrants arrived, and an industrial and commercial city with rural hinterland. It had the same social problems that plagued other cities in the United States.

Late nineteenth-century Baltimore social reformers were mainly concerned with child welfare and public health. Their achievements in child welfare brought to Baltimore a compulsory education law (1901), a new child labor law that raised the age of eligibility for employment to fourteen (1902), a juvenile court (1902), and a playground movement (1898). Those interested in the different classes of dependent children—such as the orphaned, the neglected and abused, the insane, and the feebleminded—spearheaded the establishment of orphanages,[1] but this was not an innovation of post–Civil War reform. In Baltimore twelve orphanages had been founded between 1778 and 1856, all by religious and ethnic groups (seven were Protestant and six were Catholic).[2] Almost twice that many were established between 1860 and 1910. By 1910 Baltimore had twenty-eight orphanages: twelve Catholic, two Jewish, seven declared Protestant, and seven labeled as private corporations but organized and run by Protestant philanthropists. Race and ethnicity further divided them: six were for Blacks, three for Germans, two for the Irish, and one for Russian Jews. The rest served either the old American community or were parish orphanages and had a mixture of children from various ethnic groups.[3] Thus, Baltimore seems to have had a history of continuous care and interest by religious and ethnic groups in the welfare of dependent children.

Baltimore orphanages always were founded through private initiative and collective volunteer effort that required a long-term commitment. The orphanages in this study were similarly structured but differed in financial status and needs of the community served. All began with a private donation of a building, a lot, or an endowment, or a combination of these. All three were managed by a social and economic elite of their religious and ethnic communities. Administrators had to deal with a variety of people, including parents, children, educators, and the community to which the orphanage belonged, as well as with a variety of responsibilities related to finances, public relations, education, legal issues, welfare management, and building maintenance.

The Hebrew Orphan Asylum

The Hebrew Orphan Asylum was established in 1872 after several attempts of B'nai Brith to build an orphanage had failed. The Hebrew Benevolent Society, a charity organization of German Jews, adopted the idea of an orphanage, and when Dr. Benjamin Szold, William S. Rayner, and Alfred Y. Ulman became involved, the resources for such an enterprise quickly appeared.[4] Dr. Szold, the Conservative rabbi of Oheb Shalom congregation, promoted the idea, and William S. Rayner, a businessman and Reformed Jew, donated the land and the old almshouse building situated on it. The orphanage was located on the outskirts of the city in Calverton Heights, then a small village. Alfred Y. Ulman, a wealthy German Jew, gave the money needed for remodeling the building and preparing it for children.[5]

Just before Szold's father died he instructed his wife to sell the land he owned in order to pay for the education of the most talented of his four children—Benjamin. Unable to give the boy an advanced Jewish education, Benjamin's mother sent him to be raised by an uncle. Szold then came to the United States from Hungary to serve as a rabbi.[6] William S. Rayner's childhood was similar; he, too, was an orphan who received a good general and Jewish education. At the age of eighteen he emigrated from Bavaria, Germany, to the United States, where instead of teaching Judaic studies, he entered the business world and prospered. Both men had lifelong interests in intellectual and cultural activities beyond their daily work, and both were involved in educational and charity work in the Jewish community.

At the end of the first year, when the H.O.A. sheltered and educated about thirty children, a fire destroyed the building. The children who were not injured spent the first few nights in the directors' homes, then were transferred to a rented apartment in downtown Baltimore. Meanwhile, the directors collected insurance money, hired architects, and mobilized the Jewish community to contribute to a new building,[7] a spacious structure that Michael Aaronsohn recalled as "an arresting building in its beauty."[8] Some graduates I interviewed who did not know the building's history thought it was a mansion for Maryland gentry. The building was equipped with the most modern inventions, starting with the heating system, indoor toilets, and well-drained ground. In years to come, the policy of equipping the orphanage with the newest appliances was continued.[9]

What was the aim of the founders? At the opening ceremony for the new building, William Rayner told a large crowd from the Jewish community and city dignitaries that the orphans could have been sheltered in the German asylum, but "children of our faith we intend to raise in our own way to become good American citizens as well as true Israelites."[10] The aspirations of the founders were high. Rayner did not speak of maintaining the new institution but of enlarging its scope and operation. He said,

> I think you all will agree with me that it ought to be our joyful duty and sacred pride not only to maintain the same, but to make it one of the model institutions of this country. I hope the day is not far distant when the endowments and donations will be ample to make it also a first-class institution of learning, where the intelligent youth can not only be instructed in the rudiments but also in those higher branches of education necessary for professional life, and when it will be considered an honor and a high testimonial to have been a graduate of the school of the Hebrew Orphan Asylum of Baltimore.

Rayner, however, had no illusions about the ability of an orphanage to give children parental love and affection. He advised orphans to turn to God "when you find that the love which only a father and mother can bestow is needed for your young and tender hearts; when the cold world has only censure and commiseration and pity for you, but not love." Still, he expected the children to be achievers and to overcome the disadvantages that are often the poor orphan's lot. He advised them to obey their guardians, to be truthful, and above all to have self-confidence. "If you have confidence in yourself," he declared, you will "leave many others who are now apparently your superiors far behind you, and what now seems to be a great disadvantage to you may turn out some of these days to have been for your best." The advice, Rayner stressed, "comes from one who . . . in early youth drank the bitter cup of friendlessness to its very dregs, and who was once like the poorest and humblest of you—an orphan."

Rayner suggested that the Jewish community regard donations as an investment that one day would bear fruit; some of the children in the future would contribute to the welfare of the community, and the rest would serve as the contributors' advocates in heaven. Rayner's speech was compatible with Jewish laws regarding orphans, but it also carried the American ideology of its day. It reminded the Jewish community that taking care of and educating its orphans was a religious obligation that would bring remuneration in the next world; but it also voiced the sentiments of an American Jew who viewed poor children's education as a great benefit for the Jewish community in particular and for American society as a whole. In LeRoy Ashby's words, children in post–Civil War America became increasingly "indispensable in the battle for the nation's destiny." Save the children in order to have a better society in the future was the reformers' belief.[11]

The orphanage's constitution and bylaws described its organization. The members who formed the association, named the Hebrew Orphan Asylum of Baltimore City, were Jews who paid annual dues of five dollars or more. A five-hundred-dollar contribution entitled the donor to life membership. People from other faiths who donated one hundred dollars became honorary members. All members convened once a year in April and elected officers, including a president, a vice president, a treasurer, and twelve directors. While the president, vice president, and treasurer were elected annually, the directors served for two years.

The president's powers included calling and leading meetings, appointing committees, and serving ex officio on committees. He voted only when new officers were chosen, when alterations of the bylaws and constitution were proposed, and when a vote was tied. The vice presidency was a largely honorary office. The treasurer, however, had the important role of accounting, paying the bills and preparing the annual report submitted to the association. The board, which included the president, vice president, treasurer, and directors, met once a month to debate and decide all business regarding the orphanage (including setting the salaries of all employees and filling vacancies on the board until the annual meeting). According to the H.O.A.'s records, these directors served on one or more of five committees: Asylum and Grounds, Education and Library (which addressed everything pertaining to the orphans' everyday life, studies, recreation programs, and library), Indentures and Discharges (which provided employment or industrial training when orphans were discharged from the H.O.A.); Finance, Visiting and Supply (which provided the asylum with supplies and conducted weekly site visits).

The directors were all prominent members of the German Jewish community. In the 1870s they were immigrants who made their way to the United States in their youth and became wealthy. Some had started working at an early age and had little formal education. Others had a Jewish or professional education. What they had in common was not only German Jewish culture and wealth but also social bonds. They belonged to the same German Jewish elite, frequented the same social clubs, and were involved in organizing and financing the community's Jewish institutions. In some cases the ties were fortified by intermarriage.

The "rags to riches" story of the poor orphan who became successful was not unique to Rayner and Szold. Although Henry Sonneborn, the rich clothing manufacturer who owned a chain of stores, was not orphaned, he started working at the age of fifteen. When he reached twenty-three, he emigrated from Germany to the United States with no money in his pocket. The same could be said about Isaac Strouse, another director of the Hebrew Orphan Asylum, or the Schloss brothers, Nathan and William, as well as the Hutzlers, Hamburgers, and Gutmans, all of whom became rich manufacturers and merchants in Baltimore.[12]

What marked this generation of directors was their dedication to the H.O.A. They were rising businessmen with many social and philanthropic obligations, but they spent long years on the board when such service was not merely an honorary position. The directors supervised the administration of the orphanage, determined its general educational program and each child's particular education, and raised funds for the venture. Some founding members remained on the board in the 1900s, and many new members were sons or other relatives of first-generation members. Thus, the Hutzlers and the Hamburgers, the Gutmans, the Friedenwalds, the Rayners, and the Adlers continued to be represented in the 1900s, and new directors tended also to be prominent members of the Baltimore German Jewish community.[13] The second generation of directors differed only in being better educated and representing the professions more than the business community.

Medicine and law were the best-represented professions among the new directors. Doctors had a special place on the board. They closely supervised the orphans' diet and medical care. No fewer than four famous doctors in the Jewish community served on the board during various periods. Besides serving on various committees, the doctors also screened applicants. Lawyers on the board provided the legal advice needed for financial and other institutional matters.

The second generation of directors was educated in the private and public schools of Baltimore and went on to colleges and universities. Most graduated from Johns Hopkins University and continued their studies in their professions.[14] The high level of formal education of the second-generation directors was evident in their attitude toward the orphans' education. There is a correlation between the standards of education for orphans in the 1870s and from 1900 to 1910 and the educational backgrounds of the boards of directors at these times.[15] Although the board's views reflect changing standards of education in the Jewish community and in the United States in general, they also demonstrate that the directors did not see poor orphans as inferior or doomed to minor positions in society. Rayner's belief in education as a vehicle for social mobility seems to have been shared by other directors. Moreover, the success of the directors and their relatively rapid ascent to wealth and high social position probably served as an example for the children.

One wonders whether the directors' business responsibilities and their social and philanthropic obligations left them much time for the orphanage. For example, Dr. Friedenwald, the eye specialist, was a hospital physician, had a clinic of his own, and taught at a medical school. In addition, he was involved in other charitable enterprises, such as the Hebrew Hospital and the House of Consumption, and belonged to social clubs.[16]

Harry H. Levin was the editor of the *Jewish Comment*, the head of Federated Jewish Charities, a principal bookkeeper in a Baltimore business, and a partner in a law firm. Like Friedenwald, he was also a husband and father and was actively involved in a religious congregation.[17] Yet the records show that the directors ran the H.O.A. and that all decisions regarding the children's welfare were subject to their approval. Moreover, the superintendent, chosen or approved annually by the directors, had little liberty in operating the institution and frequently had to consult committees. Often, the superintendent's report to the board mentioned that the details of a problem had already been examined by the relevant committee.[18] The records do not reveal when the board met or whether some decisions were made informally, during visits to the orphanage or at the social clubs to which they all belonged. They do reveal that parents approached the directors when they wanted to admit or release their children and that the directors chose and confirmed all H.O.A. employees.

Their most important appointment was the superintendent, who had to seek reappointment every year. The first four superintendents were rabbis, and the last three were social workers or educators who had previously worked with children.[19] Although the period after 1910, the year in which the first superintendent who was not a rabbi was employed, seemed to mark a departure from previous policy and a new trend toward professionalism, the rabbi's role in the Jewish community was in many ways similar to that of an educator and social worker. Since the children went to public schools, the rabbi's job was to provide supplemental Jewish education. Ministering to spiritual and educational needs in a synagogue was not markedly different from supervising an orphanage. He dealt with adults and children, taking care of administrative and financial as well as educational matters.

The first three superintendents served only short periods, but in 1886 the directors hired Samuel Freudenthal, a rabbi and a doctor of philosophy from Germany, where he had taught in and directed Hebrew schools. In 1865, he immigrated to the United States and served as a rabbi for nineteen years in congregations in Pennsylvania before he became superintendent of the H.O.A. He remained in this post for almost twenty-five years and was responsible for shaping the development of the H.O.A.[20] Dr. Freudenthal was a Reformed rabbi, a passionate preacher, a good teacher, and a disciplinarian; but at the same time he was a kind and warm person, deeply interested in the children entrusted to his care.[21] His work involved not only teaching, preaching, and supervising the children, but also management. He was in charge of all employees, of assigning their tasks and supervising their work. That included kitchen and laundry help, gardeners, janitors, and nurses. He bought the supplies and sold the products of the small farm (mostly calves, which were sold to butchers). The records show that he was involved in every detail of supplying necessities for the children, such as clothes, gym equipment, and medical examinations.

In addition to teaching Judaism and German, he was in contact with the public school and its principal and teachers and monitored each child's progress. He had to take care of the exceptional children who needed special schools and aids—children with weak eyesight or impairments in speaking, hearing, or mobility. He was also in touch with parents, listening to their requests and informing them about their children's progress. In case of sickness, he provided medical care, and he accompanied every child to the doctor or the hospital. In addition he reported to the directors on special events occurring between board meetings. With such a schedule, it seems doubtful that he had time to monitor the children on an individual basis. But Dr. Freudenthal was married and was father to three children who lived in the H.O.A., and his family shared his responsibilities.

Although the wife of a superintendent was not paid separately, his hiring included hers as well. He had reponsibility for the whole operation; she administered to the needs of the girls, supervised the cleaning of the building, and probably also oversaw the laundry, the sewing room, and the cooking.[22] During Freudenthal's superintendency, his daughters also worked at the H.O.A. (although they were not paid separately either). His eldest daughter, Dora, and later, her sister, Ray, were in charge of the preschool children.[23]

Freudenthal's years as superintendent were marked by vigorous debates in the United States about child care institutions and the methods by which children should be raised. During this time the numbers of children in the H.O.A. rose because of the flow of Russian immigrants to the United States. Freudenthal was well aware of changes in the theory and practice of child care, and he suggested improvements both in physical and educational conditions to the directors. His suggestions included requests for an improved playground and a shortened period of institutionalization for girls.[24] His requests show that he was familiar with changes in other Jewish child care institutions, and he urged the board to adopt similar changes. But Freudenthal was also a good administrator who knew the limits of his budget. He did not press for expensive programs and changes all at once and seemed to give more emphasis to educational programs than to physical conditions.

Yet as much as Freudenthal left his mark on the development of the H.O.A., it should be pointed out that he was constantly checked and supervised by the directors. Not all his suggestions were accepted, and his control over important decisions, in regard to both children and the administration, was restricted. The records do not show clashes of opinion, but the fact that his suggestions were sometimes rejected or even reversed, suggests that although he served the longest period of any superintendent, his power was limited. For example, he urged the board to release a girl with a disciplinary problem. Instead, the directors instructed him to enroll her in a business college and keep her in the institution. The fact that he brought children with disciplinary problems to be reprimanded or observed by the directors shows that they carefully monitored his judgment and decisions.

After Friedenthal's death and a short interim period in which an H.O.A. alumnus, a rabbi, filled the position, the directors appointed Dr. Milton Reizenstein superintendent. Born and raised in Philadelphia, Reizenstein had married into the Hollander family, a respectable family among Baltimore German Jews. He had earned a Ph.D. from Johns Hopkins University, which was considered at that time a center of reform and professionalism. Dr. Reizenstein wrote his thesis on the Baltimore and Ohio Railroad, in the Political Economy Department, but he had an interest in psychology and had run the Jewish Alliance Center in New York. This was a settlement house offering extensive educational programs to children and adults. Dr. Reizenstein, a Reform Jew but not a devout one, did not have his predecessor's Jewish education, but that seemed less important in 1910 than it had in 1880. The fact that he was a reformer and a professional social worker trained in economics seemed right for the office. Twice, the editor of the *Jewish Comment* praised the choice of the new superintendent. Reizenstein certainly was a reformer. He immediately suggested changes in both educational programs and facilities in order to modernize the H.O.A. The extensive repairs and changes, which included reassigning rooms, new toilets, baths, and appliances, strained the H.O.A.'s budget. The wish of the superintendent and the directors to adopt recent innovations was not matched by contributions. By that time many projects claimed community attention, such as the Jewish Educational Alliance (a settlement house), consumption cottages, Girls' Home (a house for working girls), Friendly Inn (a temporary shelter for immigrants), and another orphanage, the Betsy Levy Home.[25] Besides the competition for funds, there was a large increase in the number of children in the H.O.A. Occupancy grew from 70 in the early 1900s to 120 in early 1910. When World War I broke out, competition for funds became even greater, although by that time the H.O.A. no longer solicited contributions directly because it was part of an organization that supported all charitable causes of the German Jewish community in Baltimore.[26]

In 1918, Reizenstein left the superintendency. It was rumored that he was forced to leave because he was not handling the H.O.A.'s budget to the board's satisfaction. No doubt, his reforms both in education and physical layout were expensive, as were those of the next superintendent. Michael Sharlitt, another dedicated reformer, powerfully argued for replacing the congregate living arrangements with a cottage system, a change that Reizenstein had recommended and one that required a huge sum of money. Sharlitt, a graduate of a New York Jewish Orphanage, a teacher, and a social worker, left the H.O.A. in only two years to run Cleveland's large cottage-system Jewish orphanage.[27] Ironically, Sharlitt's cottage system materialized at H.O.A. only after he had been replaced by Jacob Kepecs, a social worker who was hired to close the orphanage and establish a foster care system.

The Samuel Ready School

Samuel Ready, a sailmaker and later owner of a lumber business, died in 1871 at the age of eighty-two, leaving most of his wealth to establish an orphanage for girls. There was no indication in Ready's business career of such generosity. He had been a modest and frugal bachelor who lived with his sister's family. In 1864, the retired Samuel Ready asked David M. Perine, who was at that time the register of wills of Baltimore City, to prepare a charter for a girls' orphanage. He chose the trustees who would carry out the plan after his death and obtained approval of the future institution from the Maryland General Assembly, which waived inheritance taxes on Ready's gift. In the sixteen years after Ready's death, the trustees increased the bequest from $370,999 to $554,110. But when they started planning the orphanage, they concluded that the lot at Washington and North Avenues that Ready had designated for it was not suitable. The ground would have drainage problems in the fall and winter because Baltimore lacked a sewage system in the 1880s.

The trustees found and purchased another property in the same area on North Avenue and Harford Avenue, which included sixteen acres of well-drained ground.[28] Then they turned to Colonel William Allan, principal of the McDonogh School, for advice on building and operating an orphanage. Colonel Allan used his own school as a model. Built outside the city of Baltimore by the trustees of John McDonogh's will, the school was also given by a philanthropist for the education of poor children; although it was not solely committed to orphans, about 90 percent of the boys on its premises were orphans or half orphans.[29] Colonel Allan's twenty-three-page recommendation is an interesting document that reveals an ideology shared and endorsed by the trustees.

Having given few specifications about the kind of institution he wanted (except that it would serve orphan girls), Ready left the trustees free to mold the institution. Pointing out that the city already had satisfactory institutions that provided basic education for destitute girls, Colonel Allan advised selectivity; he supported an orphanage for healthy orphan girls, with "fair ability," from good, industrious families. Labeled the "worthy poor," these were girls from families that slipped into poverty as a result of sickness or death of the breadwinner or caretaker and that were organized, industrious, and independent before calamities brought them to poverty and dependency. In addition to a general education, the school should give these girls a good vocational education that would enable them to be self-supporting when they graduated. Allan advised the trustees not to invest in new buildings, but rather to remodel the existing ones, which were large enough to lodge about thirty girls and staff. The most important decision, he stressed, was choosing the right superintendent and teachers to run the institution.

The trustees proceeded according to Allan's guidelines. They hired as superintendent Miss Helen J. Rowe, then principal of the Female High School in Frederick County and an experienced teacher in her early forties with a strong personality. She was hired in 1886, a year before the orphanage opened, so that she could study other child care institutions before formulating a program for the Ready School. While the buildings were being remodeled, Rowe visited schools and orphanages in Philadelphia, New York, Boston, Cleveland, Xenia, Cincinnati, and Coldwater (Michigan). Her reports reveal the issues that preoccupied the trustees and the superintendent—the curriculum, the nature of vocational education, and living accommodations for the girls.

They also give a critical description of the orphanages and schools that Rowe visited. It is clear that the trustees' intentions were to combine the best programs and accommodations and form a model institution. The new superintendent also spent time in Washington, D.C., studying Bureau of Education reports on educational institutions. Finally, she also paid a long visit to the McDonogh School, learning how it operated from Colonel Allan.

The thorough preparation for the opening of the orphanage ended when the trustees and Rowe decided how the institution would be advertised and candidates selected. By that time the trustees respected Rowe's opinions and accepted her judgment. She recommended a female colleague from her school in Frederick as a teacher and vehemently objected to the suggestion that a man should help her in running the institution. She preferred a housekeeper rather than a matron for fear that the latter would challenge her authority. In all educational matters that came to be debated in the first year, her opinion seems to have prevailed. Her correspondence with the trustees is always very respectful, her tone confident, as she suggested rather than asserted her view. The correspondence with the trustees reveals only a few cases in which Rowe's opinion was not fully accepted.[30]

The trustees of the Samuel Ready orphanage were respected gentlemen of the old Baltimore upper class. They belonged to the same commercial and social circles, and some of them were neighbors.

Like the directors of the Hebrew Orphan Asylum, these people viewed their involvement in philanthropic work as part of their obligation to society. Also like the H.O.A.'s directors, they served on the board of "the Samuel Ready" for decades or until their death, and their sons frequently followed in their footsteps.[31] For example, on August 24, 1942, Blanchard Randall, a trustee, died at the age of eighty-six. The obituary in the *Baltimore Sun* the same week described Mr. Randall as a representative of a generation of gentlemen that were passing away. "Baltimore has changed vastly and even fundamentally in the last fifty years," it declared. "But side by side with the new Baltimore the old intimate Baltimore persisted and would not give in. Mr. Randall represented that old intimate town." Blanchard Randall was a man from the county who became a merchant in Baltimore, succeeded in the export business, and moved from business into finance. The *Baltimore Sun* article compares his career to that of other well-known Baltimore merchants—Dr. John Stevenson, William Patterson, Robert Gilmor, Johns Hopkins, and Enoch Pratt. Blanchard Randall shared other characteristics with this elite: "He had a sense of his obligation to the community which had profited him, and he paid the debt in philanthropy and in constant civic endeavor."[32]

John E. Hurst, the vice president of the National Exchange Bank and a director of the Board of Trade, the Eutaw Savings Bank, the Mercantile Trust and Deposit Company, and other financial companies, was another Samuel Ready trustee. Like several of his colleagues, he had a strong church commitment, being described as "an active member and vestrymen of St. Peter P. E. [Protestant Episcopal] Church."[33] E. Glenn Perine, a trustee from 1864 to 1915 and for a long time secretary and treasurer of the Samuel Ready, was a stock broker who had retired from business at the age of thirty-six. He came from a prominent Baltimore family and was a vestryman and treasurer of the Protestant Episcopal Church of the Redeemer.[34] Wilton Snowden, a lawyer and banker and once president of the Samuel Ready, lived on Cathedral Street, as did Glenn Perine and John Hurst.[35] Like the H.O.A., the Samuel Ready also had representatives of the professions on its board: Charles H. Latrobe, a well-known civil engineer in the city who also designed the orphanage, and Dr. Daniel C. Gilman, the first president of the Johns Hopkins University.[36]

The board of the Samuel Ready, not as large as the H.O.A.'s, had between five and seven members at a time. Although they had a great influence on the policy of the institution, they left day-to-day decisions to Rowe and, once the institution was stabilized in terms of staff and recruitment, took a back seat. They convened formally twice a year to hear Rowe's reports, to prepare an annual report for the governor, and to select new candidates and make reappointments for the following academic year. Decisions that had to be made between meetings were referred to the secretary, who contacted the trustees. While the trustees left many decisions regarding the children to Rowe, they controlled finances, investing the money Samuel Ready left and overseeing expenditures. Every decision involving an expenditure had to pass through the board.[37]

The Dolan Children's Aid Society

In 1847, three ships carrying Irish immigrants fleeing the potato famine docked in Baltimore harbor. The immigrants were starving and plagued with sea fever. Some had died during the trip, some upon arrival, leaving behind about forty orphans. Among the members of the Hibernian Society who came to the newcomers' aid was a Catholic priest, James Dolan, from St. Patrick's Church. Father Dolan borrowed money from an Irish Protestant, Hugh Jenkins, the president of the Hibernian Society, and established an orphanage for boys. Twenty-three years later, when Father Dolan died, he bequeathed two-thirds of his money and property to orphanages—the one he had established for boys from St. Patrick's parish, and a new one for Irish boys and girls from all denominations in the city of Baltimore and neighboring counties. Father Dolan was a devout Catholic but also a very proud Irish-American. His will, in which he also left money to disperse among the poor in his native parish in Ireland, testifies to his strong ethnic ties.[38]

The parish orphanage was given to St. Patrick's Church to organize and manage, but the Irish orphanage would, by Dolan's will, be established and run by the Young Catholic's Friend Society. This was a group of prominent members of all Catholic parishes in Baltimore and neighboring counties who devoted their time to poor children's education, organizing free schools and supplying clothes and shoes.[39]

Father Dolan asked the Young Catholic's Friend Society to use his

own house on Gough Street for the new orphanage, which he designated as a home for children of both sexes between the ages of six
and twelve; siblings were not to be separated.[40] The organization was
called the Dolan Children's Aid Society and aimed to shelter and
educate about thirty children. The Young Catholic's Friend Society
invited the Holy Cross sisters to run the new orphanage. The Sisters
of the Holy Cross were also employed in the St. Patrick's Orphanage
and in the school for girls and boys adjoining St. Patrick's Church,
and they ran an academy and a normal school for young ladies. The
order both cared for the children and educated them because the
children of the Dolan Children's Aid Society went to the parish
school.

The orphanage opened in 1874. Although day-to-day care was left
in the hands of two sisters and a helper, the trustees of the Dolan
Home (as it was soon referred to) oversaw all other aspects of the
orphanage. The roles these trustees filled without pay and in their
free time were similar to those filled by the directors of the Hebrew
Orphan Asylum, with the exception that the nun who served as superintendent of the Dolan Home had fewer administrative responsibilities and devoted more time to the actual care of the children. No
doubt the superintendent had to concentrate on basic necessities because all the children in the Dolan Home were young and there was a
shortage of help to provide for their needs. The sisters' poor record
keeping is evidence of the lack of a secretary to handle correspondence and registration and to keep records of the children's health
and progress in school and of their family situations.[41]

Like the Hebrew Orphan Asylum's directors, the Dolan's trustees
heard requests for admission and release. They also had to place the
children in homes or schools whenever relatives or parents did not
assume those responsibilities. Unlike the H.O.A's children, who were
not sent out to work or study before the age of fourteen, the children
of the Dolan Home left the orphanage at the age of twelve. In some
cases, a court had declared their parents unable to care for them and
the trustees had to find other homes for them, sometimes before they
were twelve, in order to facilitate their adjustment to a new family
situation. The result was that the trustees either had to employ an
investigator to look for homes and supervise the welfare of the children or to perform these tasks themselves. The fact that they looked
for such houses in the countryside, among Catholic farmers, compli-

cated their task. The admission and release procedure in the small orphanage of about thirty children included complicated correspondence with courts, parents, other orphan asylums in the city, farmers, and priests who could help verify information as well as write letters recommending children, parents, and foster parents (see Chapter Two).

The secretary of the Dolan Home, who was in charge of correspondence, was the only member of the board of trustees who was reimbursed for his services, and the payments were small enough to suggest that he was merely compensated for his expenses. Unlike the Samuel Ready or the H.O.A., the Dolan Children's Aid Society did not have enough money to provide an office for the secretary or the treasurer. The endowment left by Father Dolan was mainly city land that he owned and collected rent from. (In Baltimore land and buildings may be owned separately. Some people own their home but pay "ground rent" for the land.) The scattered lots were leased to different people, and the trustees were required to maintain the leases; they could not sell the lots. The treasurer had to hire a rent collector and also to solicit contributions because the money from the endowment was insufficient to maintain the orphanage.

Even the oversight of the superintendent and the sisters was more complicated than in the other two orphanages. The final authority for the sisters was the mother superior of the Order of the Holy Cross, not the board of trustees. The mother superior sent the sisters to their mission and could ask them to leave. When she did not approve of conditions in the orphanage, she openly threatened to withdraw her nuns. The trustees found themselves more than once in conflict with the sisters on questions regarding both the children's welfare and the administration of the institution. For example, that the Dolan Home had children of both sexes "thrown together" was problematic for the sisters and was contested by the mother superior. In this case, Dolan's will specifically provided for siblings of both sexes, although the trustees also admitted children without opposite-sex siblings. The sisters' complaints ended when the trustees provided more rigid segregation within the house.

The trustees of the Dolan Home, who were representatives of the Young Catholic's Friend Society drawn from all Catholic churches in Baltimore, met every three months to hear the superintendent's report and to approve the budget, but they had an Executive Committee that met frequently in the interim.[42] The trustees were, as one might expect, prominent Catholic laymen.

Dr. Ferdinand E. Chatard, a well-known Baltimore physician, was president of the Dolan Children's Aid Society from 1885 to 1900. He was born in Maryland to a family of French origin, and both his father and his grandfather practiced medicine. Dr. Chatard served as a trustee of the Dolan Home after 1877 and at the same time as a trustee of St. Mary's Female Orphan Asylum. He was also president of the board of managers of both St. Agnes's Sanatorium and St. Joseph's Hospital and a member of the state medical and chirurgical faculty and the clinical society and the Maryland Academy of Sciences.[43] Michael A. Mullin, the next president of the Dolan Children's Aid Society, was a lawyer in the city and president of the Maryland Bar Association in 1908. At various times he was a member of the state legislature and the city council and was examiner of titles. He was a reformer involved in the civil service reform movement and a member of the board of St. Mary's Industrial School for boys and the Houses of the Good Shepherd, important Catholic child care institutions in Baltimore.[44] The board also had among its members an engineer, E. J. Codd, who had his own company; James R. Wheeler, who was president of the Commonwealth Bank; a liquor dealer, Simon I. Kemp, who was a prominent Irish Catholic who sat on the board of the almshouse and St. Mary's Industrial School for boys; and other businessmen who appeared frequently in the society columns of the Catholic press.[45]

In composition, the boards of trustees of the Dolan Children's Aid Society, the Samuel Ready, and the H.O.A. were similar, they had representatives of the professions: physicians, attorneys, engineers, and businessmen. Members were involved in their communities, contributing time and money to charities, and were devout members of their religious congregations. Although many of them had been born in Maryland, they tended to preserve their ethnic ties in addition to their religious affiliations. Thus, the German Jews, those who were immigrants and those who were second-generation immigrants, moved in the same social circles, spoke German, and identified themselves partly at least with the Germans of Baltimore.[46] The same is true of the Irish Catholic board members of the Dolan Children's Aid Society, who celebrated St. Patrick's Day as an important holiday and were active members of the Hibernian Society. The board of the

Samuel Ready, as we have seen, was equally determined to help children of its own group, the old American stock, long resident in Maryland. The trustees were an elite who lived in comfort and had servants at home; they sent their children to colleges and universities at a time when only a few could afford such an education. They belonged to the most prominent social clubs, and their names appeared in the society columns of newspapers.

The Philanthropic Community

On the surface these elites seem to have moved in different circles, each according to its religious and ethnic affiliation, in a divided city. However, orphanage trustees from different ethnic and religious groups knew and helped each other at the turn of the century when the city was still intimate. Some were active in other reform movements in Baltimore. For example, David Hutzler, once president of the H.O.A., was involved in Federated Charities (a centralized organization in Baltimore, successor to the Charity Organization Society), as was Thomas F. Hiskey, a trustee of the Dolan Children's Aid Society.[47] Some were partners in businesses and financial institutions. The board of the National Exchange Bank of Baltimore included John E. Hurst, a Samuel Ready trustee, and Eli Oppenheim, a director of the H.O.A. On the board of Central Savings Bank in 1910 were Wilton Snowden, president of the Samuel Ready School, George W. Corner, Jr., whose father was a Samuel Ready trustee, Thomas Foley Hiskey, a Dolan Children's Aid Society trustee, and Eli Oppenheim from the H.O.A's directors.[48] These men also directed city-sponsored relief institutions and served on several boards of charities and institutions of their religious denominations.[49] The fact that the same people were chosen to direct different kinds of organizations shows that they regarded such service as a civic and religious obligation. And the involvement of their families—second and third generations as well as wives—in charitable causes further indicates that they viewed the work as important, valuable, and transcending ethnic and religious lines.[50]

Long-term commitment was a source of stability, provided continuity of care, served as a model of civic responsibility to the community, and underscored the importance of philanthropic work. These men and women were also able to establish strong ties with contributors, volunteers, and the business community—connections that helped the orphans to find jobs and scholarships for further studies when they left the orphanage. Such commitment also, however, introduced the danger of preserving existing conditions without adopting beneficial reforms. It was the role of the superintendent to push for necessary changes. Continued adaptation of the orphanages to the latest innovations in child care (discussed in subsequent chapters) shows that the superintendents and the trustees were sympathetic to improvements whenever finances allowed.

The trustees of the three orphanages were preoccupied mainly with finances. Whether the institution had an endowment or depended on contributions, the trustees had to plan the budget, invest the money, and control expenses. It was not accidental that the majority of the trustees in all three institutions were businessmen.

Financial Management of the Orphanages

The Samuel Ready School was the wealthiest and most secure of the institutions because it had a large endowment. Wise investments made by the trustees during the years between the death of Samuel Ready and the opening of the institution yielded profit and changed the nature of the endowment, which was initially mainly income from land in the form of ground rent.[51] In 1910, the financial report showed that income from investment of the original capital came almost equally from two sources: ground and house rentals, and bank interest. The grounds and houses were investments that yielded profits only over a long term. In the short term, mortgages, taxes, and maintenance had to be paid for. The houses of the nieces of Samuel Ready, for example, according to his will were left to them for life and required allocations of money for repairs and taxes. But the overall value of the assets of the Samuel Ready endowment increased during the years 1886 to 1910 more than 50 percent as a result of the investment in land and houses: from about $550,000 in 1883 to about $845,000 in 1910. The report of 1910 also shows that the interest paid on money invested in banks covered the expenses of the orphanage and the negative balance from investment in land and houses, leaving a cash balance of about four thousand dollars. In other words, the diversification of investment that the trustees pursued was calculated to achieve two goals: to cover all expenses and to increase capital at the same time.

The Samuel Ready had, by that year, an overall income of about $60,000 from grounds, houses, and interest. Of this sum, about $27,000 came from a bank deposit and the rest from rent. The expenses of the trustees were about $55,000, of which only $18,000 (about 33 percent) was related to the operation of the orphanage. The rest were payments for acquiring, maintaining, and improving capital. Of the $18,000, about $3,000 was office expenses, which included the salaries of the treasurer, the secretary, and the collector. The office administered the endowment as well as served the orphanage. Dividing this sum ($3,000) between the orphanage's direct expenses and the endowment's administration and adding all the sums spent on the children would give an estimate of the total spent directly on the orphans.

In 1910, there were seventy-five children in the school and the direct expenses were about $16,500 annually (about $220 per child). The expenses for the institution included provisions, servants' wages, salaries of the principal, teachers, and matron, clothing, fuel, repairs to buildings, the engineer's wages and boiler room expenses, supplies for the school room, repairs to furniture, doctor and dentist fees, telephone costs, and repairs to the organ and pianos. There were also expenses for maintaining the garden, including day laborers' wages, lawn mowers, and repairs for the gardener's house. The gardener was also the engineer and basically was in charge of maintenance work in the school.

In 1902, one of Samuel Ready's nephews wrote a letter to the editor of *The American* in response to an article in the newspaper on the Samuel Ready School. The letter bitterly complained that although Samuel Ready had wanted to benefit poor orphan girls, the institution bearing his name was not a shelter for waifs but a school for a few fortunate competitors who were educated at a price of $500 per person a year.[52] The school was selective, although records show that it served only poor orphans, but the cost of an education there was not $500. Moreover, the actual cost of $220 annually per child was reasonable in comparison with costs at other child care institutions.[53] The direct costs of the orphanage in 1888, the first year the school operated, were about $250. The garden and repairs on the house cost proportionally more because the institution was just beginning. Yet the girls at the Ready School in 1910 enjoyed far better conditions than the girls in 1888.[54]

The reason for the difference in standard of living was the contributions of trustees. They had contributed new buildings, special rooms for vocational education, a new dormitory, and a new library. By donating the costs of such improvements, the trustees were able to save endowment money for expanding educational programs and raising standards of living without increasing the annual cost of the orphanage.[55]

The Dolan Home was also financed by an endowment, but as the introduction to its Minute Book reveals, the revenue derived from it amounted to "very little more than seven hundred dollars per annum" in 1874, when there were only thirteen children in the orphanage. The situation did not improve much in the years to come. The report from October 5, 1890, gives the finances of the Dolan Home for the previous six months. The income was $1,164, and the expenditures were $647.61. Of that sum the treasurer gave the sisters $471. The rest was $159 paid by parents whose children were boarders and $14 in donations. The sisters also solicited contributions of food from the Lexington Market worth $70 for that period. Adding the sums and dividing them by thirty-eight, which was the average number of children staying at the home at that time, shows that the orphanage spent about $20 per child for half a year, or $40 annually. This sum was the direct expenditure for food, clothes, school books, light, and fuel, and it included the salary of the hired servant. The sisters' salaries, administration, school expenditures, and medical care were not included in the budget. These items were covered by other institutions and organizations that provided the services. For example, the parochial school that the children attended was financed by the parish of St. Patrick.[56] There were no doctors' fees in the budget and no administration expenses except $20 every three months, paid to the treasurer, for stamps, telephone bills, and other office expenses. Even for the time, the Dolan orphanage's expenditures were very low. By comparison, the cost for clothing and fuel at the Samuel Ready School for the same year (forty children in 1890) were equivalent to the Dolan Home's entire budget. Even if we consider that the Dolan Home sheltered only young children who most probably consumed less food than teenagers and who wore uniforms, the sum per child is still very low.

The Hebrew Orphan Asylum did not have an endowment. The building and the lot had been donated and were free from debt; but operation of the orphanage depended on contributions from people of all walks of life in the Jewish community. People left legacies or donated money in memory of a family member. This money was invested, and the H.O.A. received some of the benefits of an endowment because the investment yielded a steady income.[57] Another source of income was members of the H.O.A. Association. Many were from the wealthy German Jewish community, but less affluent Jews and former alumni also paid annual fees.[58]

The Purim Association also helped to raise funds. Traditionally, during Purim food was sent as a present to the poor. The Jewish community of Baltimore used that holiday for soliciting money for its two main charitable projects: the Hebrew Hospital and the Hebrew Orphan Asylum. Money raised by a Purim ball was given alternately one year to the hospital and one year to the H.O.A. Although the Purim Association was a separate organization, many of its members were members, directors, or former directors of the H.O.A.[59]

Another organization that helped cover the H.O.A.'s expenses was the Hebrew Orphan Asylum Ladies Aid Society. This organization included women of the German Jewish elite in the city, many of whom were directors' wives and other female relatives. They took it upon themselves to supply the orphanage with clothes and linen by collecting membership fees used to purchase materials and by donating their time to sew the clothes. Once a week these women entered the asylum followed by chauffeurs carrying portable sewing machines. The women also provided refreshments and entertainment for holidays and special occasions and were responsible for sewing lessons at the H.O.A. When a girl graduated and needed vocational education and a home, these women provided for her until she no longer required their help.

The H.O.A. received other contributions of services and supplies on a regular basis. Every month, the superintendent's reports recorded contributions received, which included meals, food treats, toys, and games. Clothes and sports outfits also frequently appeared on the list, as well as books for the library or money given to purchase them. Presents given on Hanukkah and prizes at commencement were also part of the donations received.

Volunteering was another form of contributing to the H.O.A. The teacher who taught vocal music and organized the choir donated his time, as did the tutor who helped some of the children prepare for high school. The stenography and typewriting teachers, as well as those who taught musical instruments, were all volunteers. Jewish newspapers gave the H.O.A. free subscriptions, and the directors transported the children in their automobiles when they made excursions outside the orphanage. These donations represented the Jewish community at large. Although many of the monthly contributions came from the directors and their families, some came from alumni and nonmembers of the H.O.A. association. Some contributors supported the H.O.A. for decades. For example, Michael S. Levy, owner of a large straw hat factory, donated hats for the children every spring and also subscribed to the association. But Levy was not a director of the H.O.A. In fact, he donated a building to the Russian Jewish orphanage named after his wife, the Betsy Levy Home. Like the men who gave to the Samuel Ready School, Bernard Cahn donated an addition to the H.O.A. that became a gymnasium; William S. Rayner gave a piece of property to enlarge the playground; and Bertha Rayner Frank, Rayner's daughter, built a manual training school at the asylum in her husband's memory.[60]

The Hebrew Orphan Asylum was a community project dependent entirely on community support. The Dolan Home leaned on some community support (St. Patrick's Church) and on a small and insufficient endowment and supplemented its income by taking in boarders—children whose parents needed the orphanage as a temporary shelter and were able to pay some money toward their keep. The Samuel Ready School had a large endowment and enjoyed large contributions from its trustees and their friends. (Samuel Lyon donated a hall in the name of his deceased wife, and the Eaton family donated a library to the school.) Differences in endowment and patterns of giving make it difficult to compare conditions in the three orphanages on the basis of per capita expenditures alone. The annual budgets included different items in each orphanage, there is no way to calculate the value of volunteer work and donations, and expenses do not indicate the quality of services provided.

An examination of the superintendents' salaries in the three institutions reveals the limitations of comparing budgets. The superintendent's salary at the H.O.A. in 1883 was $1,242, the superintendent of the Samuel Ready in 1887–88 received $900, and all the sisters at the Dolan Home in 1890 including the one serving as superintendent received $100 each per year ($4 more than the washwoman's salary). The superintendent of the H.O.A had fifty-one children under his charge. Miss Rowe, the superintendent at the Samuel Ready, had forty children to look after, and the sisters of the Dolan Home had thirty-eight. The differences in the number of children under care are not significant. There were however, significant differences in roles assigned to each superintendent. Helen Rowe was principal of the school besides running the orphanage. Dr. Freudenthal of the H.O.A. and Sister Chlotilda, the superintendent of the Dolan Home, took care only of the religious education of the children. Freudenthal's salary covered the services of his wife, who was a matron, and his daughter, a kindergarten teacher. Assuming that a salary of a superintendent should be between $800 and $900, the two sisters of the Dolan Home would cost, had they been properly paid for their services, about $1,200 (for superintendent and matron). That sum alone would bring the cost of maintaining a child in the Dolan Home to $70, and adding medical and educational costs would probably bring the amount to $100 per child annually. Deducting the school expenditure at the Samuel Ready from the annual budget would bring the sum spent on each child there below $200. In other words, comparing conditions in child care institutions on the basis of annual reports does not necessarily give accurate results and does not reflect the reality of the children's lives there. Having an endowment sometimes can isolate an institution from the community and deprive it of broad-based support. An institution dependent on donations and contributions from a community is not necessarily poorer than an institution with a large endowment.

Besides monitoring day-to-day operations, outlining goals and programs, and taking care of the finances, the trustees dealt with legal problems regarding the orphans and the orphanage and with questions of guardianship, protected children after they were placed out, and secured legacies given to the orphanages. A representative of the institution had to appear in court when someone left a bequest to the orphanage. Sometimes a donor would leave a property or shares of a property, stocks or bonds, or a sum of money. In each case the will had to be affirmed by the court and then executed. In some cases execution took years and required repeated visits to the court.

One such case appears in the court records under the file of *Mary Loretto Russel* v. *Board of Trustees of the Dolan Children's Aid Society, as well as the Trustees of St. Patrick's Home and School.* The Russel family demanded that the court provide for the family's orphans before it granted money to an institution. Michael Mullin, the trustee of the Dolan Home who appeared before the court in 1904 and 1905, did not see the end of this litigation. It did not conclude until 1922, when the trustees finally persuaded the court to order the family to sell the property bequeathed to it and give the orphanage its share of the legacy.[61] Not all legacies were contested in court, and not all disputes lasted so many years.

Orphanages and the Court

Finances were not the only matters that required the trustees presence in the courtroom. Sometimes they had either to sue a child's guardian or to defend the right to keep a child in the orphanage. In 1908 a relative turned to the court to force the H.O.A. to release Milton to her custody. Although the Juvenile Record Book of 1908 is missing and the details of the case are not clear, the court did not grant the plaintiff her wish and the child remained in the custody of the H.O.A. Such cases were infrequent because the trustees of the H.O.A. were reluctant to fight relatives in court. In 1918, when the H.O.A. refused to release Jacob after investigating his home because it feared neglect of the child and his schooling, Jacob's father threatened to snatch him without permission. He claimed that other families had snatched their children and not been brought to court. In this case the child was not released, but the fact that his brothers and sisters returned to the parents who were not considered fit shows how rarely the trustees fought over a child's custody.[62]

In the Samuel Ready this kind of litigation was absent. Whenever a parent asked the school to return a child, the answer from the trustees was prompt release, regardless of legal documents that entitled the institution to full custody. Both the Samuel Ready School and the H.O.A. were very strict about accepting only children who were legally committed to an institution, but they differed in the policy of returning children to families. The H.O.A. investigated the homes and returned children to complete custody of their relatives only if the trustees were convinced that the family could fully provide for the child. When families requested a child's return but an education and economic well-being were not secure, the H.O.A. released the child but retained legal rights. Children committed through the juvenile court could only be released through a court order.[63] While the H.O.A. and the Samuel Ready School strictly followed all legal requirements, the Dolan Home, at least in the 1890s, was laxer. The sisters, who received boarders as well as children committed through the court, sometimes failed to secure the proper legal papers. When the three Sandler brothers were transferred to St. Mary's Industrial School, they were refused admission because the legal papers the sisters sent with them were worthless and did not relinquish legal authority. When children were sent for adoption by rural families, the adoptive parents and the institution signed a contract drafted by the Dolan Home, but the trustees found that the contract was not binding in court. In 1896 the trustees ordered the sisters to register the children carefully with the correct legal documents, and they themselves drafted a new contract for adoptive parents. The Minute Book of the Dolan Home shows that the trustees needed to go to court to defend children's rights and to sue relatives who failed to fulfill their agreement with the home.

Other legal matters included annual reports. The H.O.A. had to report annually to the Hebrew Orphan Asylum association. The orphanages also had to give annual reports to the governor because the state exempted orphanages from taxes and also contributed toward the H.O.A. and the Dolan Home's maintenance.[64]

THE THREE institutions, the Dolan Home, the Samuel Ready School, and the Hebrew Orphan Asylum, had much in common: each was founded as a result of private initiative, and each was administered by prominent community leaders. The three, however, differed greatly in their organization, their finances, and their management. The Irish Catholic orphanage, the partially endowed Dolan Home, the poorest among the three, was under the central authority of Baltimore's Catholic archdiocese. But its trustees and staff, which divided all responsibilities regarding the orphanage among themselves, belonged to two different church organizations and had to negotiate their relationships. The fully endowed orphanage, the Samuel Ready

School, had paid staff and treasurer but unpaid trustees who left the day-to-day management to the staff. In the community-based Jewish orphanage (the H.O.A.), with paid and voluntary staff, the volunteer trustees had tight control over decision making. Thus, the more an institution was dependent on community support, the more control the board of directors or trustees exercised. The orphanage that relied heavily on community funds had resources equal to and sometimes greater than the fully endowed orphanage. Quality of care, however, cannot be solely determined by the amount of money each institution spent for its charges.

The superintendents of these institutions were educators, but not all were trained in social work. Directors or trustees were experienced managers whose responsibility for the financial and legal affairs, as well as supervision of the educational programs of their institutions, required a broad range of knowledge and skill. They drew upon their expertise as lawyers, doctors, engineers, educators, and financiers to run the orphanages. Thus, along with the educators, they committed many years of service to the orphanages' administration, assuring continuity in institutional policy, community ties, and care of the children in their charge.

CHAPTER TWO

A Social Profile of the Children

HIS CHAPTER discusses the variation among the populations of
the three orphanages. It provides a social profile of the parents
and the children, the circumstances that led children to enter the
orphanages, the length of time they stayed, and the reasons why they
left, as well as an account of the institutions' policies in regard to
admission and discharge. The social profile is based on a sample of
129 children who entered the orphanages between 1887 and 1890.

When Michael Aaronsohn's mother was widowed, she had no job,
little knowledge of English, no relatives in the United States, and
three small children to support.[1] At the turn of the century city employment of unskilled women like her was limited to industry and
domestic service.[2] Some factory work could be done by taking in
piecework at home (a practice used mostly in the garment industry),
but other types required going to the factory. Similarly, domestic service meant either living in the employer's house as a maid or a governess, or working at home by cooking and cleaning for boarders or
taking in laundry. For women with children, working outside the
home was rarely an option because the low wages earned did not
cover the expenses of child care. In addition, Italian and Jewish
women, in particular, were reluctant to work in other people's homes
whether they had children or not.[3] Aaronsohn's mother chose to do
piecework for the garment industry in Baltimore.

Taking in piecework meant a long day of work at meager pay, in
addition to running the household. Widows who tried to do both
housework and piecework were overworked and exhausted. Moreover, they were not able to monitor their children's activities closely.
Aaronsohn's mother continually had to interrupt her sewing to locate
her active, six-year-old boy. Finding Michael in a dangerous situation

after a long search, she decided to place him and her daughter, both young, school-age children, in the Hebrew Orphan Asylum. She kept the youngest boy at home. Her story resembles not only other immigrant women's experiences but also those of poor, single, native-born American women. While long-established American residents could rely on an extended family, and sometimes could send their children to live with relatives, this option was limited because relatives preferred to take either the very young, in a kind of adoption, or teenagers who were capable of looking after themselves and earning their living. School-age children (ages six to fourteen) were usually sent to orphanages.

Poor widowers seeking care for their school-age children faced the same choices. Although they were breadwinners, they did not earn enough to employ housekeepers, and they lacked the time and training to run their households well.[4] Poor, single parents with several children, school-aged and younger, were the backbone of orphanages and very often their raison d'être.

Parents who needed child care institutions turned to their church or ethnic group through ministers, rabbis, or charity organizations.[5] But nonaffiliated poor parents who did not have information or connections to any particular group turned to judges. Before juvenile courts were established at the turn of the century, justices of the peace sat in police stations and decided cases involving children whose parents claimed they could not provide for them. The judge had the power to commit a child to an orphanage.[6] Many parents or relatives voluntarily committed children, either through a religious or ethnic organization or through the court,[7] but some children came to orphanages through a court's order without their parents' consent (see Table 1). These children, listed in orphanages' records as "abandoned" or "neglected," were committed as a result of intervention by judges and societies for prevention of cruelty to children.[8] Child-saving reformers expected parents to comply with the era's standards of care for children. If they did not, their children could be removed from the home and placed in child care institutions. Thus, vagrants who allowed their children to beg in the streets or parents who ran houses of "ill fame" or had "bad habits" (another expression that implied sexual deviancy) were targets of investigation by child-saving agencies, and some children with these backgrounds were committed to orphanages as well.[9] A small fraction of the orphanages' popula-

TABLE I   Individuals or Agencies Placing the Children

Individual/Agency	Dolan	H.O.A.	S.R.S.	Total	% of Total
Unknown	I	—	—	I	.8
Court	3	—	—	3	2.3
Institution office	II	4	—	I5	11.6
Placing society	7	—	—	7	5.4
Relatives	22	41	40	103	79.9
Total	44	45	40	129	100.0

tion, about 13 percent (see Table 2), were full orphans or children abandoned by both parents.

Between 1887 and 1890, roughly the same number of children entered the three orphanages, but the number of families from which they came shows a wider range. Forty girls from twenty-nine families entered the Samuel Ready School between November 1887 and January 1889. Forty-five children from nineteen families were admitted to the Hebrew Orphan Asylum (H.O.A.) between January 1888 and January 1889. In the Dolan Home in 1890, there were forty-four children from thirty-four families. Most entered during 1889 and 1890.[10]

The Baltimore sample of 129 children is representative in terms of ethnicity, religion, and gender of the general population of orphanages in the United States. The 1890 census of benevolent institutions detailed the birthplace of parents of dependent children in child care institutions. The proportion of foreign- to native-born was almost two to one (of 106,836 parents, 28,042 were native-born, and 53,168 were foreign-born, with 25,626 of unknown origin). The largest foreign-born group was the Irish, which comprised half of all foreign-born parents. The next largest group was the German, and though considerably smaller, the third largest group was the Russian and Polish together.[11] Parents of children in the three institutions discussed here represented the same range of ethnic groups. For such parents in Maryland, the proportion of foreign-born to native-born was similar to the aggregated numbers in the United States (1,352 were foreign-born, 873 were native-born, with 766 of unknown origin).[12]

The 1890 census shows that in Maryland there were more girls

TABLE 2   Reasons for Children's Admission

Reason	Dolan	H.O.A.	S.R.S.
Both parents dead	8	2	4
Mother dead	3	6	4
Father dead	19	11	32
Parents sick	6	16	—
Abandoned by both parents	1	1	—
Abandoned by one parent	1	17	1
Abused	6	—	—
Parents divorced	3	—	—
Impoverished	3	41	40
In need of temporary care	6	—	—
Unknown	5	—	—
Total	44	45	40

Note: Some children were admitted for more than one reason.

(63 percent) in orphanages than boys, but this is inaccurate because it does not include the populations of three orphanages for boys: the St. Mary's Industrial School, St. James, and McDonogh.[13] Girls and boys were probably more balanced than the census shows, although there might have been a tendency for girls to stay in institutions longer because work possibilities for them were more limited. Reformers also tried to shelter girls from what they perceived as sexual predators. My sample has more girls than boys because the Samuel Ready School was a female institution and the other two had mixed populations. Of the 129 children in the sample, 58 percent were girls and 42 percent were boys.

The three institutions also represented three of the major religious groups in Maryland: Protestant, Catholic, and Jewish. But the sample did not represent the true proportions among the groups: the Protestants were a majority, the Catholics a large minority (37 percent), and the Jews a small minority.[14]

The three orphanages studied were midsized in the range of Maryland orphanages in 1890. Of the thirty-six orphanages, fourteen had thirty to seventy children, twelve had six to twenty-nine children (the majority had about twenty), and seven had more than one hundred (two of these were orphanages for infants).

The Children of the Dolan Home

Children who entered the Dolan Home had to be of Irish descent but not necessarily Catholic, according to the home's charter. However, it is likely that in 1890, all forty-four of the children in the Dolan Home were Catholics.[15] Their age at entry ranged between five and eleven years, with the exception of one girl who was two and a half years old when admitted (see Table 3). They were admitted for a variety of reasons, although for legal purposes they were divided into those committed through a court order and those whose parents requested the Dolan Home to accommodate them as boarders (see Table 2). Fourteen children (31 percent) were boarders: seven girls and seven boys. Twenty-one (48 percent) were legally committed: six girls and fifteen boys. The legal status of nine children (20 percent) is not indicated in the records; most of them were probably committed.[16]

Most of the children were half orphans, and a few were full

TABLE 3   Children's Age upon Entry

Age	Dolan	H.O.A.	S.R.S.	Total	% of Total
3	1	6	—	7	5.4
4	—	4	—	4	3.1
5	6	2	1	9	7.0
6	7	6	3	16	12.4
7	7	6	4	17	13.2
8	9	5	2	16	12.4
9	3	5	4	12	9.3
10	6	4	8	18	14.0
11	3	2	2	9	7.0
12	—	3	9	12	9.3
13	—	1	2	3	2.3
14	—	1	3	4	3.1
?	2	—	—	2	1.5
Total	44	45	40	129	100.0

Note: The average age of entry was 7.5 at the Dolan School, 7.4 at the H.O.A., and 10.3 at the S.R.S.; 15.7% of all the children entered between the ages of 3 and 5, 69.3% entered between the ages of 6 and 11, and 15% entered between the ages of 12 and 14.

orphans; some had both parents living. Of the twenty-two children (52 percent) who had lost one parent, three had lost their mothers and nineteen their fathers. Eighteen children (40 percent) had siblings in the orphanage. Children became boarders usually because of a temporary parental inability to take care of them due to illness, divorce, or a job that required living out.[17] Some of the parents or relatives paid full board, which was four dollars a month. Some paid "a few dollars," some "half board," and some "three dollars." Some parents who put their children in the home as boarders were unable to continue paying their maintenance, but the children's legal status as boarders did not necessarily change. Those committed by the court, however, might also be temporary residents; they could be released if their family showed ability and readiness to take care of them.[18] Children could enter or leave the institution at any time of year, and it seems that every child's individual circumstances were considered with respect to the length of stay in the institution (see Table 4). Some children repeatedly left and reentered the home, according to their parents' financial and occupational situation.[19]

The children's family history and background varied considerably. Some were raised and educated in a two-parent household until one parent died. Others were found begging in the streets or living in a single-parent house described in the Dolan Home Record Book as "improper" because of the parent's "vicious habits." A few children were transferred from St. Vincent's Orphanage, indicating that they were probably born out of wedlock or deserted in infancy.[20]

Of the forty-four children who stayed at the Dolan Home during 1889–90, Adele, the youngest child admitted, came in 1882 at the age of two and a half years. Her mother, a servant, had to live out and left Adele "for a few months" as a boarder at the orphanage, at a cost of four dollars a month. The "few months" turned into years; Adele left the orphanage for the first time at the age of sixteen to live with an aunt. A year later she was released again, to live with another aunt. Adele spent almost fifteen years at the Dolan Home, though she was never legally committed and all the while had a family outside the institution. Her friend, Nellie, also a boarder, came in 1885 at the age of five, and stayed eight years before her father took her. Both the mother of Adele and the father of Nellie were apparently unable to take care of young children and earn a living at the same time. They used the Dolan Home as a boarding school. Some of

TABLE 4　Children's Length of Stay

Years	Dolan	H.O.A.	S.R.S.
under 1	7	15	4
1	6	1	1
2	5	1	1
3	6	3	2
4	4	5	3
5	5	7	4
6	6	1	8
7	1	3	7
8	1	2	5
9	1	2	1
10	—	3	1
11	—	—	2
12	—	1	1
13	—	—	—
14	—	—	—
15	1	1	—
?	1	—	—
Total	44	45	40

Note: The average stay was 3.56 years at the Dolan School, 4.3 years at the H.O.A., and 5.8 at the S.R.S. Less than a year was calculated as half a year on average.

the boarders stayed under the care of the nuns throughout their childhood, while others stayed but a few days or months. Eric and his sister Arlene were transitory boarders. Eric came to the Dolan Home on May 3, 1890. Five days later, his sister was placed. On May 24, their mother took them back.

Mollie and Wilbur, eight-year-old twins, were committed to the Dolan Home by Judge Columbus Hobbs because they were "suffering through neglect and bad habits of their mother." They were later released to different foster families and did not have further contact, so far as the records show, with their mother. Another child committed to the home by Judge Sumner (sometimes spelled Samner), and described in the records in the same manner as the twins, returned to his mother five years later by her request and the consent of the executive committee of the board.[21]

Seven boys, including three pairs of brothers, and one girl coming from five families were full orphans. The Key brothers at seven and ten years of age were committed to the home through a court because "father and mother being dead [they] had no one to care for them." The boys had a married sister, who three years later took the older one home, but soon afterwards her husband placed him in another orphanage.

It seems that in the Dolan Home the legal status of a child was not the most important factor in the decision to admit, the length of stay, or the release; family circumstances and the ability of surviving relatives to take care of the children were more important. Boarders, however, were distinct from committed children in not needing the approval of the board of trustees for their release.

The laconic descriptions in the Dolan Home Record Book suggest that many of the children voluntarily admitted came from poor families suffering a catastrophe, such as illness or death. A surviving parent might not be able to maintain the household, or might have to take a job that required living out. The Dolan Home Record Book reports, for example: "this child's father being obliged to take up housekeeping," or "Jody's mother having to live out could not care for him." Twenty half-orphan children (45 percent of the Dolan Home population) from seventeen families entered the home because their remaining parent was either sick or poor. The vast majority were fatherless (seventeen of the twenty children, or 85 percent). Children whose parents paid for their board stayed in the home as boarders (twelve children, or 60 percent of the half orphans).[22] Other parents, who obviously experienced a similar fate, were unable to pay the fee and had to put their children in the orphanage through a district court decision (five children, or 25 percent). The records describe the child as being committed on "account of suffering through neglect and indigence of her mother," or "committed by M. A. Canton, justice of peace, on account of the poverty of his mother," or "this child's mother, being destitute of support, had him committed by Squire Sumner, Eastern District Station." The language used in the records suggests that mothers manipulated the system in order to obtain proper care for their children and were not necessarily abusive toward their children.[23]

Four children (9 percent of the population) from three families entered the Dolan Home because their parents were separated. Two of the four (brother and sister) were boarders, and two more, a boy and a girl, were committed by their parents through the court.[24] These children reflected the growing divorce rate in the Progressive Era.[25]

Of the eight full orphans with no relatives able or willing to take care of them, the only girl had no recorded relatives in Baltimore. Her parents had died, and she was put in the home only after her guardian passed away. The only full-orphan boy without siblings in the institution was placed in the home by an older sister as a boarder for one year "since he was difficult to manage." The three pairs of fully orphaned brothers had relatives outside the institution who probably were unable to take them but maintained ties with them and assumed some responsibilities for them when they became older.[26]

Children in the third category—those committed by the courts without parental consent—were in the worst circumstances. Jeremy, age five, was abandoned by both his parents and committed by Judge Cashmyre. The twins (Mollie and Wilbur) were taken from their mother and committed by an agent of the Society for Prevention of Cruelty to Children. These three had no other recorded relatives. Other children, committed under similar circumstances, maintained family ties and in some cases eventually returned to their parents. Leni, age eleven, was committed through the Society for Prevention of Cruelty to Children on account of "suffering through neglect of his father, G. Guy—not restrained from habitually begging." A year later Leni was returned to his parents, "though being in a poor health," according to the record book. Three months later he died in his parents' home. The Dion sisters, "suffering through the neglect and bad habits of [their] mother," were committed by the court but four years later were returned to their parents. The nuns thought their bad conduct might influence other children; they "could not keep the Dion girls from the boys in the neighborhood."

The children's family background was not an obstacle to admission to the Dolan Home, but poor conduct was. This point requires some qualification: only certain aspects of what was considered bad conduct mattered, as the case of Christopher shows. At the age of ten Christopher was received by the Dolan Home upon recommendation of the board of trustees, in response to an application from Father Gaitley. "His father," the record book reads, "abandoned his second wife and left Christopher to Mr. Leinbach in Broadway, [Christopher] was accused of stealing [from] this gentleman." Christopher was the only child of the forty-four children examined who had a criminal record. Stealing was evidently not considered an impediment to admission, but other forms of "bad conduct" were. On October 6, 1889, the board of trustees, according to their minute book, directed Sister Chlotilda (the superintendent) "to refuse admittance into the asylum of a child mentioned by Dr. Chatard [president of the Dolan Home] and all other children having immoral habits." "Immoral habits"—probably some sort of sexual behavior—were considered a harmful influence on the other orphans. Children who showed such improper behavior were either sent away or refused admission.

Aside from the dismissed Dion girls, apparently no other children were turned down. Children came to the home in poor physical condition, abused, and even mentally ill or feeble minded. Linda entered the home in December 1886 at the age of eight. Eight years later, when she was sixteen, the board made application for her and an eleven-year-old girl for admission to the Bay View Asylum. Dr. Chatard, who was in charge of carrying out the trustees' request, had failed to find the girls a place in either Mount Hope Hospital or the Home for Feeble-Minded Children. Linda was returned to her mother a year later. It is reasonable to assume that the nuns, unable to find a suitable institution for her, kept her in the Dolan Home and hoped for a solution. Either her mother's ability to take care of her or the sisters' inability to find a better solution was probably the reason for her release.

In 1890, the home had under the same roof children from different family backgrounds and circumstances, in different states of health, and at different levels of education. Their only commonalities were their poor, Irish-Catholic backgrounds.

The Children of the H.O.A.

The forty-five children—twenty-four boys and twenty-one girls—who entered the Hebrew Orphan Asylum from 1888 to 1890 were the offspring of nineteen families, thirteen of which had from two to five children in the orphanage.[27] Their ages varied from three to fourteen years. In terms of today's school age they form three groups: preschool, ages three to five (twelve children); elementary school, six to ten years (twenty-six children); middle school, eleven to fourteen years (seven children). The majority were born in the United States to new immigrant families.[28] The H.O.A. records shed light on the histories of fifteen of the nineteen families, which tend to be similar. The families emigrated from Poland, Russia, or Germany. Some came to the United States after a short stay in England. Some settled first in cities like New York and Boston before coming to Baltimore. The occupations of eight of the nineteen fathers can be established— cigarmaker, cutter, presser, peddler, farmer, clerk, shopkeeper, and teacher (see Table 5).[29] The manual workers were all Russian immigrants while the shopkeeper, the clerk, and the teacher were of German origin. The mothers that were listed in the Baltimore City directories in the 1880s usually did not have a profession, but one was listed as a dressmaker and two as shopkeepers. One opened a store only after her young children entered the H.O.A., and one had a store until she became mentally ill. The families moved almost every year, mainly in the eastern area of Baltimore.[30] These families broke up as a result of death, illness, and desertion. Nine families of the nineteen described here experienced the death of either father (five) or mother (four), and in one case both parents died. In eight families the fathers deserted, and in one the mother left too.[31] In six families in which either death or desertion occurred, the remaining parent was sick enough to be hospitalized. Only one family had both parents at home, and in that case the mother was insane. It seems almost needless to add that in nearly all cases the H.O.A.'s book records that the family suffers from "insufficiency of means" or is "in needy circumstances" (see Table 2).

Three family stories seem to be slightly different from the rest. The Nadlers from Worcester County, Maryland, were the only farm family to seek admission to the H.O.A. They moved to Baltimore temporarily while the father was in the hospital. The mother worked as a dressmaker, and the oldest son, fifteen-year-old Ben, was employed. In April 1888, the mother died while the father was still in the hospital. The four children, ages three to twelve, stayed temporarily in the asylum, not, according to the records, because the family was poor but because the father was ill. Two days after her admission, the oldest among the four, Sara, was taken back to the farm by an older brother, and within the next three months, the rest of the children returned home one by one.

The Ulenberg children were the only ones who entered the H.O.A.

TABLE 5   Occupation of Parents

Occupation	Dolan	H.O.A.	S.R.S.	Total	% of Total
Fathers					
Occupation unknown	32	11	2	45	54.9
Manual work	2	5	15	22	26.8
Skilled or semiskilled work	—	3	12	15	18.3
No occupation	—	—	—	—	—
Total	34	19	29	82	100.0
Mothers					
Occupation unknown	31	17	8	56	68.3
Manual work	3	—	11	14	17.1
Skilled or semiskilled work	—	2	4	6	7.3
No occupation	—	—	6	6	7.3
Total	34	19	29	82	100.0

as full orphans. Their parents were natives of Baltimore, and the father, a clerk, belonged to one of the B'nai Brith lodges. After his death, the mother placed her eight-year-old boy in the asylum, keeping a teenage son, a five-year-old girl, a toddler boy, and a baby girl at home. Half a year later, she died and her five-year-old daughter entered the H.O.A. The youngest boy joined his brother and sister a year later, when he was three. The teenage boy and the baby girl stayed with their uncle.[32]

In the Miller family, the father, a teacher, was of German origin and the mother was a native of Baltimore. When the mother became insane, five of the family's seven children entered the H.O.A. The Miller children were the only nonorphaned, nondeserted children at the asylum. Their father's poverty and mother's inability to take care of them led to their admission.

Although the reasons for admission were similar for the majority of children entering the H.O.A., the length of time they stayed varied greatly, depending mainly on family circumstances. For the purpose of this study the children are divided into two groups, according to length of stay: from one day to two years (seventeen children), and from three to fifteen years (twenty-eight children). (See Table 4.)

Children were released from the H.O.A. for one of four reasons: (1) a parent or a guardian requested the release, (2) other institutional care was provided, (3) the child was expelled for "bad conduct," or (4) the child reached the age stipulated for release. Most who stayed relatively short periods were released because their family circumstances changed. An ailing parent recovered, a deserting father reappeared, or a parent remarried and was able to take care of the children.[33] Eleven of the seventeen children who stayed a short period and seven of the twenty-eight who stayed a long period were discharged for these reasons.

The Solomon and Gdanski families illustrate how family circumstances could change. In 1886, Cornelia Solomon, the New York–born wife of Pinhas Solomon, died, leaving her husband with one daughter and five sons. Pinhas was from Germany. At forty-one years of age, he had been living in Baltimore for six or seven years and working as a cigar maker. Before that, the family had lived in Pennsylvania, where five of the six children were born. When his wife died, Pinhas was not able to take care of six children and work a full day. He put the two school-age children in the Hebrew Orphan Asylum and divided the teenagers and the five-year-old boy among his relatives. Two years later, the young boy joined his brothers in the orphanage. In May 1888, when her Russian immigrant husband died, Clarisse Gdanski, a forty-year-old woman who had immigrated from France in 1867, was left with three children: two boys, aged eight and six, and a two-year-old girl. Although Clarisse knew English, she did not have an occupation. In June, she placed her two boys in the H.O.A. Clarisse Gdanski lived with her little girl on Low Street and was probably supported by one of the Jewish charitable organizations. On June 10, 1889, Pinhas Solomon married Clarisse Gdanski, and in 1891 a girl was born to the couple. A year later they had another. In 1891, Leon Gdanski, the eldest son of Clarisse Gdanski (now Mrs. Solomon) was sent home to the Solomons, labeled "incorrigible." Nine months later, the new family pulled all of its children out of the orphanage. Herbert Gdanski, who was almost eleven, and Saul Solomon, who was about the same age, had been in the H.O.A. for four years. The new family included Mr. Solomon's six children from his first marriage, Mrs. Solomon's three children from her first marriage, and Mr. and Mrs. Solomon's two children. Family circumstances had completely changed. Now Mrs. Solomon was able to attend to the needs of her large family because there were several breadwinners: in addition to her husband, six of their eleven children were teenagers or young adults able to earn wages.

The story of the Solomon and Gdanski families illustrates how changing circumstances could lead to children's release. What was necessary was sufficient income to support the released child or children, as well as other family members, someone, an adult or older child, capable of taking care of the younger children.

Eight children from the H.O.A. were provided with alternative institutional care. Six stayed only a short period in the orphanage before being transferred. One child was transferred to an institution for the feeble minded. A family from Savannah, Georgia, moved to Baltimore with the aid of a B'nai Brith lodge in Savannah. The lodge secured a home for the mother and her infant child and paid for the keep of her five school-age children in the H.O.A. When a Jewish orphanage opened in Savannah ten months later, the entire family returned there. Two boys who stayed several years in the H.O.A. were sent to other institutions for further studies. One, a bright, fifteen-year-old student went to the Hebrew Union College in Cincinnati "under the auspices of the institution." Another, a fourteen-year-old boy, went to the National Farm School, an industrial school for dependent and wayward children in Pennsylvania.[34] These two boys spent seven and ten years, respectively, in the H.O.A.

Four boys were labeled "incorrigible" and returned to their parents. The youngest, eleven-year-old Leon Gdanski, stayed three years in the orphanage. The other three were released to their parents at the ages of thirteen, fourteen, and sixteen; they had stayed at the H.O.A. six, eight, and four years, respectively.

The stipulated age of release differed for boys and girls.[35] Boys were sent out to learn a trade some time between the ages of thirteen and sixteen and were usually placed with their parents, relatives, or guardians at that time.[36] Girls were released in the same manner some time between ages fifteen and eighteen (see Tables 6 and 7).

Forty-three of the forty-five children at the H.O.A. were registered as committed by either their parents, their guardians, or the Benevolent Society. Involuntary admission via court decisions was of small

TABLE 6   Age of Children upon Release

Age	Dolan	H.O.A.	S.R.S.	Total	% of Total
3	—	3	—	3	2.3
4	—	—	—	—	—
5	—	3	—	3	2.3
6	2	2	1	5	3.9
7	1	1	1	3	2.3
8	3	2	3	8	6.2
9	3	3	—	6	4.7
10	6	1	—	7	5.4
11	12	5	1	18	14.0
12	2	3	1	6	4.7
13	8	5	—	13	10.0
14	1	3	—	4	3.1
15	1	8	1	10	7.8
16	—	2	6	8	6.2
17	2	—	7	9	7.0
18	—	4	15	19	14.7
19	—	—	3	3	2.3
20	—	—	1	1	0.8
?	3	—	—	3	2.3
Total	44	45	40	129	100.0

Note: 27.1% of the children were released between the ages of 3 and 10, 28.7% were released between the ages of 11 and 13, and 41.9% were released between the ages of 14 and 20. (Although the Dolan Home's policy did not allow children above 12 years old to remain in the institution, there were quite a few exceptions to the rule.)

significance at the asylum, and children could be released upon their parents' or guardians' request. The H.O.A. also tried to locate the families of abandoned children committed to the orphanage through the Benevolent Society. Three infants were brought from the Children's Hospital and Nursery in 1888. Two were three-year-old twins whose father was recorded as "unknown." The mother, in needy circumstances, had them indentured to the hospital. She relocated, and the children were returned in response to her application six months later. An inquiry on behalf of a three-year-old girl who came to the orphanage from the same hospital and whose parents were unknown led to the discovery of an aunt living in New York. The

TABLE 7   Age of Girls and Boys upon Release

Age	Dolan		H.O.A.		Total Girls	Total Boys
	Girls	Boys	Girls	Boys		
3	—	—	1	2	1	2
4	—	—	—	—	—	—
5	—	—	3	—	3	—
6	1	1	1	1	2	2
7	1	—	1	—	2	—
8	2	1	2	—	4	1
9	2	1	1	2	3	3
10	—	6	—	1	—	7
11	1	11	2	3	3	14
12	—	2	1	2	1	4
13	2	6	—	5	2	11
14	1	—	1	2	2	2
15	1	—	4	4	5	4
16	—	—	1	1	1	1
17	2	—	—	—	2	—
18	—	—	4	—	4	—
?	2	1	—	—	2	1
Total	15	29	22	23	37	52

Note: Between the ages of 3 and 10, 15 girls and 15 boys were released from the two orphanages; between the ages of 11 and 13, 6 girls and 29 boys were released; and between the ages of 14 and 18, 14 girls and 7 boys were released. (See Table 6 for figures for the S.R.S., an all-girl orphanage.)

child was sent to her aunt two years after her admission. Two children were registered as "temporary" residents. One, a half-orphaned, deserted, and feeble-minded girl, was transferred to another institution. The other, a three-year-old girl, was put in the H.O.A. when both her mother and her sister were hospitalized. Fifteen years later, after graduating from Western Female High School and the State Normal School, the girl rejoined her mother, who had moved to New York. This "temporary" boarder was the orphanage's longest resident.

The children who entered the H.O.A. in the late 1880s were a homogeneous group. Most came from a poor, immigrant family and a single-parent household. Many had infant or teen-age siblings, or both, at home. Infants were taken care of either by their mother or in relatives' homes, and adolescents stayed with the remaining parent to assist at home, learn a trade, or work for a living.[37] Most children placed in the H.O.A. were of primary school age, and their average age at entry was 7.3 years (see Tables 3 and 4). They were in good health, and those who were more than six years old at entry had already attended public school, with the exception of two recent immigrants. There was no special time for admission or release; children entered and left the asylum all year round. For the majority of the children, the family circumstances that led to their admission remained the same for a long time. The average length of stay in the H.O.A. was 4.3 years (see Table 4). The Hebrew Orphan Asylum served mainly school-age, Jewish immigrant children from large, single-parent households.

The Children of the Samuel Ready School

When the Samuel Ready School opened in November 1887, seven girls entered. Thirty-five more were accepted in 1887 and 1888, although not all stayed. A six-year-old girl left one day after arrival; her father changed his mind and could not part with her. Four more girls were "dismissed for cause"—meaning unacceptable behavior—during the year. The sample discussed here consists of forty of the forty-two girls admitted between November 1887 and September 1888 (two girls' files are missing). The majority (thirty-two) were half orphans from families in which the father died. A few lost their mother (four), and a few were full orphans (four). (See Table 2.) They came from all parts of Maryland—from Frederick, Anne Arundel, Cumberland, Baltimore, Kent, and Howard counties and from Baltimore City. Two came from Virginia, one from Pennsylvania; two sisters came from Chile. The vast majority were American-born children of American-born parents. The families, judging from the fathers' occupations, must have enjoyed some economic security, even a certain degree of comfort, while the breadwinners lived. The fathers were merchants (four), clerks (three), a railroad agent, a manufacturer, a civil engineer, a bookkeeper, and a school teacher. Some were manual laborers: farmers (three), drivers (three), laborers (three), painters (two), a blacksmith, a coach trimmer, an undertaker, and a small boat owner (see Table 5).[38] The mothers in most cases did not do work for wages until they were widowed. They were seamstresses (four), dressmakers (two), a laborer in a straw-hat factory, a dairy worker, a domestic, a day worker, a farmer, a music teacher, and a clerk. One took in boarders, and one was a superintendent of an orphanage for "colored" girls. Six more mothers were listed as not having an occupation, and eight mothers' occupations are unknown (see Table 5). The girls came from large families, and half of them had siblings in the school (see Table 8).[39] Their age at entry varied from five to fourteen years, and those more than six years old attended school prior to admission (see Tables 3 and 4). Most also attended Sunday schools, and all belonged to one of the Protestant churches.[40]

On November 9, 1887, nine days after the official opening of the Samuel Ready School, three girls of the Durant family, twelve, eight, and six years old, entered the school. They were born in Baltimore to a father who was a manufacturer of plain and ornamental ironwork and a mother who kept house for the large family, which included seven children. When the father died, the eldest child was fifteen years old and the youngest a baby. The father died insolvent. The

TABLE 8   Size of Children's Families

Number of Children in Family	Dolan	H.O.A.	S.R.S.
1	21	5	3
2	10	2	3
3	2	3	6
4	1	1	7
5	—	1	4
6	—	6	3
7	—	1	1
8	—	—	1
9	—	—	1
Total number of families	34	19	29

Note: The average number of children per family was 1.5 in the Dolan Home, 3.7 in the H.O.A., and 4.0 in the S.R.S. (Where no data on siblings were available for the Dolan Home, families were assumed to have one child.)

mother had no occupation. Frederick Durant, an uncle of the girls and an architect with a large family of his own, took the teenage girl and boy (fourteen and fifteen) into his house. Another uncle took the youngest girl. The three remaining girls were sent to a man in Kent County. The relation between the man and the family is not clear, but the girls stayed with him until two weeks before they entered Samuel Ready. The mother kept the baby boy. The three girls admitted were in good health, according to the doctor's certificate as well as the school doctor's examination. The eight- and twelve-year-old girls had attended primary school in Baltimore and their performances at the Ready School were good. The twelve-year-old, Eveline, stayed six years in the school, her eight-year-old sister, Juliet, stayed ten years, and six-year-old Laura spent twelve years there. Each left at eighteen.

The Durant family story represents, with a few variations, other girls' stories. In other families the number of children was larger or smaller, the mother was either without an occupation or was employed as a seamstress, domestic or even music teacher, but the results were the same (see Tables 5 and 8). The father died, and the family slipped into poverty and dependency. The older children and the very young moved in with relatives; the school-age children applied at the orphanage.

The mother's struggle is captured in Abigail Blair's family story. The father had a small boat in which he "conveyed produce from place to place." In 1883 he died of measles and pneumonia and left his wife with no means and a seven-year-old boy, a five-year-old girl, and a one-year-old boy. The family from South River, Anne Arundel County, was probably helped by relatives, friends, or a charity organization. In 1888, five years after the father's death, an aunt applied to the Samuel Ready for then ten-year-old Abigail Blair's admission. The mother was employed as a domestic by a widower who had a three-year-old girl and who allowed the woman to bring her four-year-old son with her to his house. The mother also had an agreement with her employer that her other children could visit her whenever their guardians allowed. It seemed the best solution for a widow with a little boy, although Mrs. Blair lamented that she hardly made enough money to clothe herself and the child. Several years later she tried to run a store in Annapolis, where her sister lived. For a while she had a house of her own where the children stayed during summer vacations. The enterprise, however, was short-lived since Mrs. Blair did not make enough to cover expenses. Abigail Blair returned to her family in South River after graduating from the Samuel Ready at eighteen, having spent eight years in the school.

The story of Mrs. Blair reveals certain features common to widows with young children. A community of relatives, neighbors, teachers, a minister, and a doctor who knew the family was crucial for survival. The widow turned to those people when she needed a job or shelter for her children. Placing a child in the Samuel Ready School required letters of recommendation from the family doctor, the minister, the father's employer, a neighbor who knew the family well, and the principal or a teacher from the school where the child studied. In many of the children's files there were three, four, sometimes five letters testifying that the family "is worthy," "a deserving one," meaning that the parents were industrious church-goers and their children well cared for and well behaved. Applicants also had to pass a test adapted to their age level and a health examination. Accepting one girl from a family did not mean that her sisters would be admitted as well. The school had many siblings, but many more applied and were not accepted.

The board of trustees decided to admit girls between the ages of five and thirteen, but among the first forty girls who entered in 1887–88 were three aged fourteen. All three had younger siblings in the school. The only five-year-old was Susan Vault, who entered the Samuel Ready in September 1888. She was placed in the school by her grandmother, after her father deserted the family and her mother died of pneumonia. There were no other deserted children among the forty girls.

Two children seem to be exceptional in regard to admission policy. Seven-year-old Marylin Chase, according to her application, was born in Baltimore County to a farmer and a seamstress. The father died, leaving the mother with two girls. She was recommended by a doctor's wife and a neighbor who claimed he had known the family for twenty-five years. Marilyn Chase was a good student, judging from her report card, but in the middle of the school year she was caught in a theft of five dollars from a teacher. The event was reported to the trustees. In March 1889, a letter from an agent of the Charity Organization Society explained that the child's mother had turned to that organization for help and that she had not only two girls but also a boy. The agent, who investigated the Chases' home, hinted heavily that Mrs. Chase was immoral and lacked respectability. Marilyn was dismissed at the end of the school year on account of her behavior, but her mother's reputation might have contributed to the decision. No other children at the Samuel Ready had a similar family background.

Another exception is Melissa Taller, who was twelve years old and had finished only the third grade at entry. Three years after admission, she was dismissed and returned to her guardian. In the letter of dismissal, Miss Rowe explained that the child was never satisfactory, was mentally slow in a class with much younger children, never passed her examinations, and was careless and filthy in her personal habits. The question is how such a child entered the Ready School in the first place and managed to stay three years. To qualify for admission, applicants needed at least an average academic standing. Some were above that level and a few excelled, but no other child who failed her examinations at the end of the year was allowed to stay in the school such a long time. The girls at the Samuel Ready had to win reappointment every year by demonstrating scholastic achievement and acceptable conduct.

Melissa Taller's case seems to indicate that admission to the school was not free from partiality or pressure. Melissa was a protegée of the school's doctor, whose mother had raised the girl from the age of four. The girl's father was a laborer and her mother a day worker. There must have been other cases in which strings were pulled and connections played a role, but this one was obvious. It is even more striking if we take into consideration that the number of applications far exceeded the number of admissions and that from the very beginning the school had a long waiting list of qualified girls.

The process of admission to the Samuel Ready was sometimes long and there were girls who entered a year after they applied. The official entrance was on the fifth of September of every year, but vacancies occurring during the year were filled from the waiting list. The Samuel Ready was not a shelter into which a family in crisis could immediately place its children. The children were committed legally to the school but were returned home upon request. The reason for withdrawal was usually an improvement in the family economic situation. There were no boarders in the Samuel Ready, and no money was paid by relatives toward the children's keep. But if a family's economic conditions improved dramatically, the child was returned to her parent. An example is the case of Emellina Guss, whose father died in an accident. The same year the girl entered the Ready School, a judge granted the family $8,000 in compensation. The girl was not reappointed for the following year.

Most of the children stayed a long time in the Ready School. The formal age of release was sixteen, but the girls were allowed to apply for two more years of scholarship, which, if granted, enabled them to learn a vocation. The majority of girls who were not dismissed by the school or withdrawn by their parents left the school between the ages of seventeen and nineteen (see Table 6). The average age of all forty girls at entry was 10.3 years, and the average time they stayed at the school was 5.8 years (see Tables 3 and 4).

For parents, the decision to place a child in an orphanage was not easy, as both the files of the Samuel Ready School and testimonies from H.O.A. graduates demonstrate. Hyman Warsaw's mother died when he was six years old. His father, a tailor, was left with three young boys. For three years, the widower struggled to keep the children at home before he placed them at the H.O.A. Hyman Warsaw's father volunteered to mend the clothes of the children in the asylum so that he could be close to his boys.[41] Michael Aaronsohn's mother placed her children six months after her husband's death.[42] Leon Gdanski's father died on May 14, 1888. Eight-year-old Leon entered the H.O.A. a month later, and his younger brother, six-year-old Herbert, joined him after half a year. The five children of the Semlin family came to the orphanage half a year after their father's death.

The emotions involved in parting with children are recorded in some of the Samuel Ready children's files. One mother wrote Miss Rowe, the superintendent, that although she applied for her daughter's admission, she was still uncertain she would be able to part with the child. Finally, she placed her in the orphanage, explaining that she was doing it for the girl's education.[43] Providing secondary and vocational education for children sometimes required sacrifices that poor, single mothers could not bear. Some decided at the last moment not to leave their children at the school, a decision that was also difficult because it might be irreversible. Once a girl lost her place in the school, it would be filled from the waiting list and she was not assured of readmission.

Some parents rushed to retrieve their children from the orphanage as soon as family circumstances allowed them to do so. Others, under the same circumstances, had to be urged to take their children back. Still other parents fought to keep children in the institutions until their education was completed. These differences were not simple matters of family relationships. For some parents, discharge meant sacrificing their children's vocational education. For others, leaving their children in the institution for further studies meant giving up an additional income that could relieve some of the household's economic burden. As reasons for placing children varied so did motives for asking for their release; complex emotions were involved in both decisions.

At the turn of the century, single parents, mostly women without professions and means, used orphanages as temporary shelters, or as boarding schools for their children.

CHAPTER THREE

Physical Conditions

THE COMMON image of the nineteenth-century orphanage is of a jail-like institution where children dressed in rags suffered from malnutrition and were frail, small in stature, and often sick. Charles Dickens in his melodramatic stories of early nineteenth-century England and Progressive Era muckrakers created such bleak images of orphanages that the positive experiences many had in these institutions were not generally recognized.

Standards of care for children in the Progressive Era, although constantly changing in response to new discoveries, were dictated by a middle-class, professional elite of doctors, social workers, and educators. Physicians had the most influence on physical accommodations. In an era before contagious diseases like measles, mumps, and whooping cough were controlled by vaccination and antibiotics, doctors emphasized the role of the environment in preventing and curing diseases. Their advice in regard to proper nourishment, hygiene, and health care was carefully followed. For example, doctors recommended fresh air during the summer months. At the end of the summer of 1909, Dr. Freudenthal, H.O.A. superintendent, reported the health of the children of the asylum as excellent and attributed this to outdoor living. Castor oil was considered the standard preventive and cure for stomach ailments and was used extensively, as the graduates of the Samuel Ready School recalled: "The pear trees were . . . irresistible . . . and during green pear season a number of names adorned the work list and the castor oil supply was reduced by an equal number of doses. The 'monkey nut pickle' party is a famous one in Ready annals as was its cure—the same bottle of castor oil."[1] Sanitation, meticulous personal hygiene, and isolation of the sick were believed to control contagious diseases.[2]

Psychologists and social workers also rose to professional prominence in this era. They emphasized the importance of a pleasant environment for children, encouraging adults to allow play, to create an imitation of the family unit in children's institutions, and to respect the child's need for privacy.[3] The new ideology had its effect on the architecture of child care institutions. The preferred structure for dependent children was a small cottage in the country, surrounded by grass and trees, with access to a playroom and a playground.[4] Communities often competed with each other in building modern and sometimes extravagant facilities. They exhausted their budgets and drew criticism of the cost of child care institutions.[5]

Children raised in orphanages were taught middle-class values and manners and as a result developed high expectations that could not always be met by the orphanage or by their families when they returned home. Families rarely rose high in economic status, and physical accommodations in orphanages did not meet middle-class standards of living in all respects. As comparatively good conditions in orphanages attracted more children, institutional budgets became strained. This was the main reason for the downfall of the orphanage.

BOTH THE Hebrew Orphan Asylum and the Dolan Home began to operate in the early 1870s. The Dolan Home opened in a house that had previously belonged to its benefactor, Father Dolan. The three-story row house at 1709 Gough Street adjacent to the yard of St. Patrick's Church in East Baltimore sheltered thirteen children. By the 1890s, however, needs dictated that thirty to thirty-five children live in the house. All the buildings in the block belonged to the church, including another row house Father Dolan willed to the church for St. Patrick's Orphanage and two buildings that served as schools. In 1946, a social worker, Miss Mary Keeley, described the Dolan Home as located in a congested neighborhood and having no front or back lawn. It is not known if the Dolan Home ever had a lawn, but East Baltimore was considered congested at the turn of the century. Although no description of the interior of the house in the 1890s survives, its rooms were probably crowded with beds.[6]

THE FIRST Hebrew Orphan Asylum building was the fifty-year-old Baltimore almshouse.[7] Though renovated in 1872, it burned down, and in 1876 a new building was erected on the same site at Calverton Heights and Rayner Avenue on the outskirts of Baltimore City and with a view of green pasture and trees.[8] The building was designed to meet children's needs and to house 150 children.[9] It was never filled to capacity. During its first forty years, the number of children accommodated varied from 30 in the early 1870s to 80 during the first decade of the century. After 1910 the number of children staying in the orphanage at one time rose to 120.

The basement had playrooms for boys and girls and, after 1907, classrooms for manual training. On the first floor were the office, the superintendent's apartment, the dining room, and two attached wings, one a kitchen and the other a laundry room. The second floor had school rooms and a chapel. The third floor had sleeping rooms and bathrooms. In 1894, a local newspaper described the orphanage as having forty-four rooms.[10] The youngest children slept in sexually segregated dormitories, and older children had bedrooms designed for eight boys or girls each, according to interviewees.

At the end of the nineteenth century reformers debated what architecture was appropriate for child care institutions. Although available resources limited the possibilities, the reformers attempted to follow the latest ideas regarding children's welfare. Both the community and the institution gave a great deal of attention to the children's principal surroundings.[11]

The H.O.A. building has many windows, for example, reflecting the modern belief that a well-ventilated building offers a healthier environment, particularly in a hot, humid climate. Fear of fire dictated employing a sentinel to make sure the children were safe during the night. In the 1910s, when the building was renovated, fire escapes were installed as well as new shower baths and a new stove.[12] According to the company that insured the building, it was well heated in the winter (70 degrees).[13] The building was surrounded by a playground with a baseball diamond, a miniature farm with cows, horses, and chickens, and a garden, which by 1910 included small plots planted by the children: "There were forty-eight gardens each 3.5 by 10 feet for the larger children and thirty gardens, each 3.5 by 5 feet for the smaller children. In the gardens were planted lettuce, beets, beans, turnips, carrots, peas, corn, radishes and a few flowers (portulaca, poppies, sweet alyssum, marigolds, etc.)"[14]

Early twentieth-century reformers preferred housing dependent children according to the cottage system rather than in congregation-type facilities. Cottages, which were more homelike, encouraged individualism, intimacy, and close relations between the resident adults and their small charges. More expensive than the congregational system because it required more space for buildings and more staff, the cottage system offered more possibility for growth to keep up with the demand for shelter.[15] In 1915, a donation for the construction of new buildings stipulated that H.O.A. must adopt the cottage system. Some nine years elapsed before the orphanage could amass the funds needed to change the system so radically. Ironically, when the cottage system was introduced—at a new site near the Hebrew Hospital—the ideology for caring for dependent children changed and institutional care was deemed outmoded. A few years later the H.O.A. closed, and the Jewish community of Baltimore turned to foster care as the favored method of dealing with dependent children (see Chapter Six).

THE TRUSTEES of the Samuel Ready School, which opened in 1887, confronted similar dilemmas. Having decided that Ready's house on North Avenue was unsuitable for an orphanage, they petitioned the state legislature for permission to disregard the will and buy another lot on the same street, known as the "Belmont," which stretched over sixteen acres and had better drainage. The trustees renovated the big mansion on the site, eliminating other buildings, and built a separate structure for the kitchen, a gardener's house (the gardener was in charge of maintenance), and a greenhouse. The school accommodated only forty-five students in its first years, but a building added in 1892 allowed an incrase to sixty students. A wing added to the main building in 1908 increased capacity further to seventy-five students. A library and an auditorium were funded through a contribution from a Ready School trustee.[16] From its beginning, the Ready School used small bedrooms in which eight girls of the same age group slept together. The classrooms were two large rooms, separated by a wooden partition that could be opened to form one room. There were several playrooms, and in 1892 sewing, typewriting, and music rooms were added.[17] Like the H.O.A. superintendent, who had a separate apartment two floors away from the children's bedrooms, the Ready School superintendent and teachers had separate living quarters from the students. Although they supervised and monitored the children twenty-four hours a day, the adults who ran both the Ready School and the H.O.A. felt they needed privacy and distance in order to maintain discipline and respect.

The Ready School, like the H.O.A,, was surrounded by pleasant pastureland, gardens, trees, and flower beds. "What good times the Ready Tramp Club had! Armed with baskets we tramped off to fields and woods for a joyous afternoon to return laden with wild flowers." Testimonies show that the children appreciated their environment. M. J. Craig entered the Ready School in 1897 at the age of eight and left at eighteen to go to a training school for teachers. Seven years later she described the town in which she lived to Rowe, emphasizing that it had nothing as beautiful as the grounds at the Ready School.[18] Ilene B. and Mr. Benjamin were at the H.O.A. in different periods. In separate interviews, they said that they thought the Hebrew Orphan Asylum was a mansion built for one of Maryland's gentry families. When Ilene B.'s father remarried and took his children home to his farm, Ilene could not adjust to her living quarters—a crowded room over the chicken coop. It was dirty, smelly, noisy, and without privacy. She longed for the orphanage but remarked that in those days parents did not ask children their preferences. Michael Aaronsohn also contrasted the neighborhood where his mother lived with the orphanage:

> Can it be that I am to call this neighborhood my home? . . . This is terrible . . . a row of three-story brick buildings with broken shutters and unsightly curtains, a large church with the aspect of shattered glory, whose stained glass windows were demolished, whose roof was caved in as though it had been bombed from an airplane. . . . Such was the picture which confronted eyes that for ten years had looked upon a wide sweep of landscape, expansive fields and woods, where birds sang and twittered, where children played and cattle grazed.[19]

The orphans appreciated their accommodations. A woman wrote Rowe that her young relative, who had just entered the Ready School, could not stop telling the neighbors that she had a bed of her own. Sharing beds with siblings was a common practice in poor American homes, especially in those of immigrants.[20] Isabelle Pine's mother, who had remarried and withdrawn her eleven-year-old child, asked Rowe to accept her daughter back because she could not provide for the girl even half as well as the institution had. Isabelle could not adjust to her mother's home, although it was probably not very poor; her stepfather was a merchant.

Jewish houses in East Baltimore were considered among the most crowded in Baltimore.[21] Family activity was usually centered in the kitchen because the stove was the primary source of heat. Few bedrooms were heated because coal was expensive and central heating nonexistent. Nathan Cooper, who grew up in East Baltimore, described in an interview the way he helped his widowed mother to heat the house:

> I remember one thing that I used to do to keep the house warm in the winter time. You know, in those days we had the stove in the kitchen, a big stove and we used coal. . . . We lived near the railroad tracks. . . . I used to go over there and I would take part of an orange crate or carton. . . . I'd put stones in there and when the trains would go through with the coal—they had these cars of coal that were being shipped out to the midwest and wherever—and I would throw stones at the fella, not only I would, but several boys, and we would throw stones at the fella sitting on the top of the coals. We didn't want to hit him, but we would throw stones at him, and he used to throw coal back at us and I would collect the coal. And that was one of the ways we could help heat our stove in the wintertime. We had to think up a lot of different schemes.

According to Samuel Ready's family, he decided to donate his money to found an orphanage for girls because he was moved by the sight of "poor waifs who resorted to the lumberyard to collect such refuse wood as would afford them warmth and comfort."[22]

Many houses had outdoor toilets and many also served as workshops where members of the family brought in piecework. Boarders, a source of additional income for many families, contributed to crowding of poor households. Alleys and busy, often smelly, streets (a sewage system was built in Baltimore only in 1916) were the playgrounds for children of immigrants and other poor Americans at the close of the century. The orphanages, by contrast, were healthy, safe, and spacious.

Sixty years after he left the H.O.A., Michael Aaronsohn was proud to be one of the first children in Baltimore to experience the

American technological revolution firsthand. Central heating, electricity, and household appliances such as washing machines, dishwashers, and vacuum cleaners, were part of the orphans' homes long before Americans at large used them.[23]

Food

The food in child care institutions seems to have been nutritionally adequate; whether it was abundant or appealing is hard to say. Autobiographies of people who spent their childhood in institutions frequently criticize the quantity, quality, and taste of the food, although some graduates of orphanages realize that different dietary standards prevailed in their childhood.[24] Michael Aaronsohn claims that he did not have enough food as a child in the H.O.A., though the food was more plentiful when he was a teenager. One of the privileges of being a high school student in the orphanage, he noted, was to have two eggs at breakfast.[25] When I asked Aaronsohn's classmate at City College, who had lived with his parents, about breakfast, he could not recall the meals but said that two eggs seemed to him to be a rich person's breakfast. In 1912, a graduate of the Samuel Ready School, in an evening of nostalgia on the twenty-fifth anniversary of the school, remembered the time when she and her friends returned from field trips: "Our mouths have watered for some of that good hot brown bread and butter . . . which was a favorite Ready supper." If for Aaronsohn a supper of bread, butter, and milk was meager, for Ilene B. it was torture. Ilene, who entered the H.O.A. in the 1910s, had to drink milk everyday although she could not tolerate it. She remembered that one evening a mouse fell into the chocolate milk jar, and besides the commotion and fun it aroused, she was spared having to drink milk for once. Reformers believed that milk was essential for a child's development, even after infancy, and orphanages required children to drink a glass of milk every day. Indeed, a number of organizations distributed milk among poor people in the big cities in the first decade of the century.

Eileen Simpson, in her account of life as an orphan in New York, declared that she could not remember being hungry, but added that she was sick and might not have had a normal child's appetite. Other autobiographical accounts by orphans such as Michael Sharlitt and Art Buchwald describe meager meals.[26] Sharlitt explained that the food was insufficient and unsavory by comparison with what was served in later years in orphanages.[27] The food should be judged not according to the dietary standards of a later time but according to those that were prevalent among poor people at that time. Moreover, a child's feeling about food is often more related to the person who prepares and serves it than to the food itself. A monotonous potato dish prepared by a loved parent might be remembered with longing, while the same dish served in an institution might be recalled as poor and dull.

Poor people at the turn of the century generally ate one-pot dishes and were frequently hungry: "Even the more prosperous knew a markedly monotonous diet." The main food expenditure of a poor family was for meat, milk, bread, butter, potatoes, and tea. A social worker who registered the food expenditures of two hundred poor families in New York at the turn of the century wrote about their menus: "Potatoes are used freely, often a quart for a meal in large families. The vegetables are mostly canned corn or tomatoes, turnips, carrots and cabbage. . . . The poorer families live on bread, tea, soup or stew and oatmeal." Summing up the consequences of poor families' diets, historian Ruth Schwartz Cowan writes:

> In the neighborhoods in which such diets were commonplace, evidence of malnutrition was everywhere to be found, from children bent with rickets to adults lacking teeth. For babies, the diet of the poor was particularly threatening, since anything that they imbibed (other than mothers' milk) was likely to be either contaminated or difficult to digest. . . . For this reason (as well as others) infant mortality was horrifyingly high among the poor; scarcely a child grew to adulthood without witnessing the death of a little brother or sister.[28]

The evidence, however, does not indicate that malnutrition was a major problem among the families that sent children to Baltimore's orphanages. In 1911, research was conducted in some Baltimore public schools to find out whether Jewish children were underfed. The results showed that malnutrition was rare.[29] John Spargo, in his muckraking book, *The Bitter Cry of the Children*, praised New York Jews because, though they lived in crowded tenements, they fed their children properly.[30]

But no doubt food was not in abundance among poor Jews. The

Hebrew Benevolent Society admitted in 1911 that "it finds itself unable to meet the food demand in any reasonable way." The Federated Jewish Charities in the same year raised the question of food supply. Should the community be involved in actual food giving, besides medical and financial aid? Many doctors, the writer noted, prescribe three meals a day for sick people when referring them to various charity organizations. The problem was not limited to Jewish or other groups of immigrants and was not confined to city dwellers; it was known among Marylanders of all backgrounds and in the rural areas as well as the city. The little girl from the Samuel Ready who was enthusiastic about having a bed of her own was equally excited to know that she would have a glass of milk every day.

The Hebrew Orphan Asylum served four meals a day, according to the *Baltimore American* of May 20, 1894. Breakfast, lunch, and dinner were eaten in the dining room at routine times and based on a standardized menu. The children knew, according to Simon Z., what menu to expect each day of the week. They ate meat, vegetables, and wheat and dairy products every day.[31] The quantity of food increased when children became teenagers. Both Aaronsohn and Simon Z. recalled fondly the H.O.A.'s cook, Mary, who served in the first two decades of the century and indulged her "helpers" with "goodies." In contrast to Aaronsohn, who complained to his mother as a seven-year-old that he did not have enough food,[32] Simon Z. said some children were always hungry no matter how much they ate, and some were not hungry at all. He did not remember being hungry.

In one of his reports to the trustees, Dr. Freudenthal expressed a concern that changing the lunch time in the H.O.A.—because the public school voted to end the lunch break—would badly affect children with poor appetites, indicating at least a sensitivity to the matter of providing enough food. There is also evidence that food was not so monotonous in the H.O.A. after all. Among contributions from members of the community every month were meat, fruit, cakes, and ice cream. Money was sometimes designated for a special meal or treat. The most frequent donations were turkey meals, peaches, cinnamon cakes, candy, and ice cream. On Sabbath and during holidays, different menus and treats broke the routine. Ice cream appeared during holidays and during the summer, and turkey meals were contributed during the holidays.[33]

Children who were raised in the orphanage did not know that in their homes meals were not always rich and diversified and were not always on a punctual schedule. Aaronsohn recalls that when he returned home at age sixteen, he found that dinner was not ready at six o'clock in the evening because his mother was busy washing clothes. He had difficulty adjusting to the fact that his hardworking mother did not prepare meals on a routine schedule. It is also doubtful that she had time to prepare a variety of dishes. Most likely, she resorted to one-pot cooking. Had he and his siblings been raised at home, it is questionable whether his mother, who worked ten to twelve hours a day finishing pants, could have cooked three regular meals, washed, cleaned, and attended to the other needs of three children. When Aaronsohn returned home, his mother was remarried and his sister was still in the H.O.A. But even with an improved financial situation, his mother was not able to attend to the family's needs on the regular schedule of the H.O.A.[34]

On visiting days mothers and relatives brought treats of food to children at the H.O.A. Although the superintendent forbade certain foods for reasons of health and hygiene, parents very often brought partially eaten food that threatened to introduce diseases to the institution. An example was partially eaten fruit. Since fruit was expensive, bringing it was an act of affection but nonetheless a health hazard. The parents often tried to smuggle in forbidden items.[35]

The Samuel Ready School confronted many of the same problems. Rowe understood the value for the children's morale of food brought by relatives. But when time and again "the habit of the relatives and friends of the pupils of the Ready School in bringing and sending sweetmeats and other eatables . . . had an injurious effect upon their health, causing in some cases serious sickness," she asked the board of trustees to ban all gifts of food. The board accepted her recommendation because the girls suffered stomach ills after each visiting day. On special occasions the Samuel Ready School, like the H.O.A., broke the routine. The *Ready Record* from July 1, 1910, describes a cooking exhibition the girls prepared: "Harlequin jelly, snow pudding, cup custards and other delicious desserts had a prominent place. The rolls, bread and Maryland biscuits were beautiful and would have filled the heart of a baker with envy." An account of a day when the girls convinced Rowe to allow them to prepare taffy and another of a trip to the garden to pick fresh tomatoes indicate that Rowe understood the need for varying the diet. There were presents from the outside, in spite of the trustees' ban. When one trustee brought a basket of cherries, the news spread fast and the cherries disappeared quickly.

The Ready School served nutritious meals every day. The teachers and the superintendent ate with the children, although at a separate table, and the way the food was prepared and served was part of the teaching process.[36] The Ready School had a constant flow of visitors, who often stayed for dinner and ate with the children. In the H.O.A. the superintendents ate with their families in their own apartments, although the institution's cook prepared their food as well as the children's.[37] In both institutions the meals were at a specified time and followed certain rules. The children entered the dining room in orderly fashion, and they sat according to age group. Speaking loudly while eating was not permitted. In the Ready School a "silent table" was reserved for those who talked loudly during meals.[38] The school tried to impress table manners upon the girls. In the H.O.A. manners were less emphasized, although the upper-middle-class German Jewish gentlemen and ladies who ran the institution were held up as role models for the children.

In the mid-1910s, Dr. Reizenstein, the "Reformer," as he was nicknamed, suggested changing the way meals were served. Instead of having a two-dish meal—soup and then meat, vegetables, and potatoes together—he sought to serve each item separately and to cultivate the children's table manners by teaching them how to serve food properly and further to improve its appearance and taste. The change required not only buying china, but also more work for those who served and cleaned up after dinner. As a result, these chores were shared by boys and girls, whereas previously they were girls' chores only. In short, the H.O.A. adopted in the 1910s the philosophy Rowe had formed in the late 1880s, that the education of orphan children should pay attention to every detail of everyday life.

Food expenditures per child varied among the three institutions. The Dolan Home spent the smallest amount of money and most likely had the poorest diet for its children. The budgets for food in the H.O.A. and the Ready School were much the same, although the H.O.A. had frequent food donations not calculated in the budget.[39] But there was a great difference between the two institutions in regard to preparing and serving food. At the Ready School the students were involved in preparing and serving meals, while at the H.O.A. the meals were prepared by paid workers. Moreover, at the Ready School, the superintendent and teachers ate with the students, while at the H.O.A. the superintendent and his family ate in their own quarters. In both institutions the food was nutritious and according to physicians' recommendations. But, in the memory of the Samuel Ready School graduates, food was also tasty and sufficient, probably because they helped to prepare meals and shared them with the adults in charge.

For Nathan Cooper, a half orphan who lived with his widowed mother, five siblings, and grandparents in East Baltimore, the meals served at the H.O.A. or Samuel Ready were rich people's meals. On one Jewish holiday, his mother put on the table for the family of nine "a loaf of bread . . . and a quarter peck of apples." Cooper's mother ran a store and his grandparents shared both the store and the household work with her. From a historian's perspective the Coopers were not the poorest among Baltimore's poor.

Clothing

At the end of the nineteenth century poor families wore mostly homemade clothes and the children generally wore their siblings' hand-me-downs.[40] The Samuel Ready School kept a record of the clothing belonging to each child upon entry and departure. Since the children were either from declining middle-class or working-class American-born families, the clothing lists serve as indications of what children in humbler neighborhoods wore. Most girls had two dresses, two skirts, one or two aprons, and three to four blouses, one coat, one to two pairs of shoes, a few pieces of underwear, a handkerchief, and sometimes a towel. Since the girls spent part of all seasons at school, the lists probably included all the clothes they owned. Some girls had three and four dresses, but the differences among them were not great. In cases where there were more clothes, there were also remarks like, "One in good condition," or "two old." By today's standards, the girls would be considered very poor, but they were not poor compared to boarders at the Dolan Home, whose parents paid four dollars a month for their keep, which included everything. With this sum of money it is doubtful that much could be acquired. When Freudenthal bought spring clothes for the three Morris children (temporary boarders in the H.O.A.), the bill was $23.50, or about eight dollars per child. Winter clothes such as coats and boots must have been yet more expensive.

Even though the budgets for all three institutions include allocations for clothes, it is impossible to calculate accurately the amounts of money actually spent. The budgets reflected mostly the sum spent on raw materials, on cloth. At Samuel Ready, the H.O.A., and most likely the Dolan Home, clothes were made in the institution. In the Dolan Home in July 1890, expenditures on shoes and clothes were $54 for three months for thirty-five children. If that amount represented a typical quarterly expenditure, we can calculate that the home spent about $220 yearly or $6 per child. It is highly probable that the nuns received contributions of clothes from St. Patrick's parish.

In the Samuel Ready the clothing budget in 1891 was $618 for forty-five children, about $13 per child. In the eleventh annual report of the H.O.A for 1883, clothing, bedding, dry goods, hosiery, shoes, neckwear and notions amount to $884. That year the asylum housed fifty-one children and spent about $17 per child on these items, but contributions from stores and firms were also available. The children at the Dolan Home wore uniforms. In the Samuel Ready and the H.O.A. there was no uniformity in clothes. The children were measured, and clothes were prepared for each one individually. In the Samuel Ready the girls were allowed to choose the colors they thought would be becoming to them, and then the seamstress, with the sewing teacher and girls from the advanced sewing classes, prepared the new clothes.[41] In the H.O.A. the clothes for the youngest girls and boys were made by the Ladies Orphan Aid Society, a volunteer group. Once a week, the ladies came to the orphanage and worked in the sewing room. The older girls prepared their own clothes, under the seamstress's supervision. The Ladies Orphan Aid Society also made linen and towels. Pictures from the Samuel Ready show well-dressed girls. Even allowing that they wore their best clothes for photographs, there is no way to tell that these children were poor orphans.

In an interview, Simon Z. could not recall the procedure by which he received his clothes in the H.O.A. or their quality. He assumed that they were secondhand, but a picture of him and two girls shows well-dressed teenagers. Simon Z. thought he was wearing the clothes he received upon leaving the institution, but the picture was taken more than a year before his departure. Aaronsohn complained about, and even felt humiliated by, the coarse materials from which his clothes were made.[42] Simon Z., on the other hand, stated that the children of the H.O.A. were not different in appearance from others in the public schools. As previously mentioned, Wilfred S., Aaronsohn's classmate at Baltimore City College, was surprised to discover that Aaronsohn was raised in the H.O.A. and came to school from the orphanage every morning. Aaronsohn's clothes did not set him apart from other students at City College. Stores and firms contributed clothes to the H.O.A., most likely from unwanted stock such as clothes from the previous season, but they were not used.[43]

Each child in the Samuel Ready and the H.O.A. had his or her own clothes and had enough of them, since in both institutions the children were required to be neat and clean and their daily appearance was observed. Upon leaving these orphanages, children received new clothes and shoes. At the H.O.A., the Ladies Orphan Aid Society assumed responsibility for providing wedding dresses for girls who married soon after leaving the asylum.

Hygiene

A sewage system was not completed in Baltimore City until 1916. Sanitation did not keep pace with the rapid expansion of the city during the late nineteenth century. Baltimore's topography aggravated its sanitary problems. It stood on low ground and "was bordered on three sides by marshes, through which flowed streams subject to overflow." The work of grading and paving was difficult and slow. Storm water and household water—toilet and kitchen waste—were disposed in the Patapsco River traversing the city. The river very often overfilled and flooded the low sections of the city, bringing filth, bad odors, and offensive gases.[44]

At the end of the nineteenth century, those areas of Baltimore were populated mainly by Italians, Russian Jews, and blacks. Being poor meant living in houses crowded with either family members or boarders who contributed to the family's finances. Being poor also meant no indoor toilet facilities. The woman of the house was burdened with laundry and cleaning, sewing and mending—not to mention cooking, shopping, and attending to the small children. As a result, cleaning was put off; often these homes were dirty, and clothes were worn until they were heavily soiled.[45] Bathing was infrequent because it involved boiling water and pouring it into a tub, most likely in the kitchen. Because the kitchen was the center of household life, bathing could take place only when the stove was not being used to heat an iron or to cook. "The only warm place in the home is the kitchen and there's a door which also warm the dining room. Everything else is cold. So in the winter you're on the third floor sleeping you grab your clothes you run down to the kitchen to go the bathroom, it's an outhouse out there, snow on the ground, cold we didn't have no hot water."[46]

The three institutions discussed present different pictures of hygiene. All three hired workers to clean the institutions and the children's clothes, and they had laundry machinery and employed laundresses.[47] Cleanliness and neatness were not solely the staff's responsibility; the children were required to straighten and clean their rooms, and their personal cleanliness was carefully observed. They had to bathe, comb their hair and brush their teeth and were given personal towels, combs, and toothbrushes. Although many children did not come to the institutions with good habits of personal hygiene, they nevertheless adjusted. In a letter of dismissal, Rowe stressed that the teachers could not impress "proper habits" on the girl. The clothing lists upon entry at the Ready School often reveal the standards of hygiene in the families' homes. Many girls did not have a towel, a toothbrush, or a comb. When one of the girls graduated and found employment as a teacher in another orphanage, she was disappointed by the level of hygiene in that institution; the girls were not as clean, as neat and careful about their personal appearance, as those at the Samuel Ready.

Aaronsohn experienced the difference between the clean environment in which he was raised for ten years and the neighborhood to which he returned when he was released from the H.O.A. He marveled that his mother kept a very clean house in such a filthy neighborhood. His description of the synagogue, located on the floor below his mother's apartment, conveys his dismay. "How different it is from the chapel at the Asylum," he wrote. "Here the floor was uncarpeted. The windows were draped with unsightly curtains. The benches were of rough hewn wood. Cuspidors were scattered about in every part of the room."[48] In a time of prevalent tuberculosis and other lung diseases, cuspidors presented a health hazard.

Cleanliness marked the division between those who could afford a clean environment and personal appearance and those who could not. It also marked a division between those at high risk medically and those who could avoid health hazards. The orphanages could isolate the sick. That was not possible in a tenement. Moreover, a disease requiring quarantine could spell economic disaster in poor families if the breadwinners were not allowed to go to work. Poor people very often tried to conceal contagious disease in their families. Baltimore's laws from 1898 on required informing the authorities about any dangerous infectious disease, including from 1904, tuberculosis and other pulmonary diseases. Poor people found it difficult to obey other laws as well, such as the requirement to disinfect the house after a contagious disease, not to lease out any part of it, and to arrange for burial of the dead by sanitary authorities.[49]

Orphanages carefully observed sanitation laws, and disinfectants were a constant expenditure. They also tried to contain the spread of diseases through isolation. Although in some cases they succeeded, as the records of the H.O.A. show, isolation rooms could not solve all the problems of contagious diseases.[50] Some diseases had a period of incubation in which a child could be contagious but the illness was not yet apparent. By the time the malady was discovered, other children were already infected.

Besides the dangerous contagious diseases such as smallpox, chicken pox, measles, and diphtheria, there were minor ailments such as lice and ringworm. While the serious diseases were treated by medical personnel, the minor ones were handled by the barber. "On Monday afternoon the barber made his appearance, and the little girls had their hair cut," the Ready Record declared on September 23, 1892. "We think they look much nicer with short hair, and it seems as though we should call them little boys' names for some of them do not look much like little girls." This description by one of the older girls in the Samuel Ready whose hair was not cut does not register the feelings of the little girls. Such measures were not taken only in the Ready School. Aaronsohn recalled that his curls were shorn in the first month after he entered the H.O.A.[51] The reason for cutting the children's hair was not to humiliate them or to save time in combing. Repeated treatment for ringworm or lice, which was done either by medicine or by washing the hair with chemicals, was not healthy. Short hair was easier to keep clean and free of bugs. Older children were more capable of caring for their hair and did not need the barber's services. Frances Garate describes the rules that prevailed in a Catholic orphanage in the 1920s. Every Saturday the older girls checked the younger ones' clean hair. Any bugs found were recorded. A girl whose hair yielded more than twenty bugs during the winter was shaven in the summer.[52] Rowe tried at first to send the girls home for treatment, but this policy was impossible to pursue when more than a few girls had bugs.

Anti-institutional reformers often used pictures of orphans with short hair to move their readers to protest the inhuman conditions in orphanages. R. Reeder in his guidebook, *How Two Hundred Children Live and Learn*, pointed to the importance of explaining to children why they should keep clean rather than simply imposing hygienic laws on them.[53] Parents in the early 1980s who experienced the lice plague that was rampant in schools across the United States found themselves in the same position as orphanage superintendents in the first decade of the century. Many of them cut their children's hair short after medical treatment failed.

Medicine

Emellina Guss was twelve years old when she entered the Ready School in 1889. Her father had died in an accident two years earlier, and her mother was left with four girls to raise. Emellina was the eldest. The others were eight, six, and three years old. In December of the same year the youngest sister died. Emellina was not present at her beloved sister's funeral. Both her mother and her aunt wrote Rowe asking her not to allow the girl to return home. The death occurred on the ninth, and on Christmas Emellina's aunt took the girl to her house for a short visit. Not before summer would Emellina visit her family.

The story reveals part of the reality of the American household at the turn of the century. Not all children lived to adulthood. And, especially when the mother was the sole provider for the family, the oldest girl probably raised the younger siblings and was likely to feel a strong attachment to them. Spargo called these girls "little mothers."[54] Fear both of the psychological effect of her sister's death and of contamination dictated the decision to prevent Emellina Guss from seeing her beloved sister for the last time.

In the annual report of 1912 to the governor of Maryland, the Samuel Ready School's trustees emphasized that no serious case of illness had occurred and "no fatal case since the foundation of the institution." Their explanation of the phenomenally good record over the past twenty-five years was that "a high location, ample grounds (16 acres) good food, plenty of it, and above all, the motherly care and oversight of a corps of teachers, pulling together and having the same interest at heart, all contributed to the agreeable result."

On July 2, 1902, Rowe wrote Mr. Perine, secretary of the board of trustees, that Clara Ray "seems to be better this morning. Her temperature is lower and she has less pain." Clara had been very sick for several days, and there was fear for her life. Upon being notified, her mother rushed to the school and asked Rowe's permission to take the girl home. Her request was turned down. As cruel as the refusal seems, especially in what might have been the girl's last days, Rowe's decision was medically correct. The Samuel Ready School had an excellent doctor, a twenty-four-hour trained nurse when circumstances dictated, and a comfortable sickroom. Moving the girl, in her condition, could have further imperiled her life. The child's mother later thanked Rowe for her decision, recognizing that she could not have provided her daughter with equally good medical care. Poor people could not ordinarily consult the best doctors in Baltimore or hire a trained nurse, and they did not have adequate space to care for seriously ill children.

The case of Clara Ray raises the question of who was responsible for the health of children in orphanages and to what extent parents were involved in decisions regarding their children's health. The Samuel Ready School had legal authority over the children for the entire year but did not ordinarily hold them against their parents' wishes. In this case, Rowe resisted the mother's plea, but she seems to have weighed each alternative. When one of the Been girls suffered from asthma and bronchitis, Rowe sent the girl home, with her sister as an assistant. The fresh air in the country was believed to cure lung diseases fast. In another case, she declined an invitation for a seventeen-year-old student to sleep over in a teacher's home because the girl's health was delicate and could be damaged by a chilly evening. The girls must have viewed Rowe as a truly concerned guardian. In letters years after they left, they continued to report their health as well as to consult her about medical problems.[55] The school informed parents about their children's health, and sometimes parents instructed or requested Rowe to restrict their children's activities on account of delicate health.

It could be claimed that the Ready School's record of good health was the result of careful selection of children. Applications included a physician's recommendation, and Samuel Ready's doctor made his own evaluation of the child's health.[56] The Samuel Ready doctor's reports, found in most of the children's files, show that the school sometimes admitted children who were not healthy. Examination revealed that Dolores Sanderson was poorly developed and had tuberculization in both lungs, but the doctor's recommendation to reject her was not accepted. She entered the school along with her sister Myra Sanderson. Another sister entered a year later. The young women kept Rowe informed about their lives long after they left the school. For years, their letters showed great concern for Dolores's health, but it was Myra, who entered the Ready School healthy, who died young, leaving her husband, a minister, with six young children. Life was precarious at the end of the century, and even careful selection of students, though necessary, did not guarantee their survival. Even children who entered the institution healthy could die if a cold turned into pneumonia or if a severe case of a common childhood disease like whooping cough, measles, or chicken pox was contracted.

Samuel Ready's trustees could justly credit the teachers and physical conditions in the school as responsible for the institution's health record. But it should also be pointed out that girls who were constantly ill and unable physically to handle the amount of work the program required were dropped. In June 1913, when the trustees considered renewal of scholarships, Rowe suggested dropping two from the program who were "unable to keep up with the work of the school, though everything had been done for their health and happiness." One was aged fifteen and had been in the school nearly two years, and one was sixteen and had spent seven years at Samuel Ready. They were dropped not because their health imperiled the other girls but because they were unable to achieve academically. It was thought that other girls should be permitted to benefit from the opportunities the Samuel Ready School offered.[57] Colonel Allan advised Rowe and the trustees, before the school opened, against aiming at two different kinds of children's populations, such as healthy and sick, in order to avoid having a school and a hospital under the same roof. The Samuel Ready was, first and most of all, a school, and children with physical disabilities that affected their studies could not be admitted or allowed to remain.

The H.O.A. had an admission policy similar to the Samuel Ready's. The H.O.A.'s doctor evaluated the candidate's physical condition and made a recommendation to the Committee on Admissions and Discharges. As at the Ready School, some of the children were not healthy but were admitted nonetheless, although admission of unhealthy children had a different basis. The effect of illness on academic performance was not important. The main considerations in deciding whether or not to admit an unhealthy child were whether the disease was contagious and whether the child's care would require a special allocation of resources, especially of staff members' time.[58]

A very sick child requiring extensive medical care was transferred to the Hebrew Hospital and returned only with the H.O.A. physician's approval. The hospital was used frequently because it had all the specialists the orphanage needed. The superintendent took care of bruises and minor cuts occurring during play, but when a child had high fever and other symptoms, a doctor was called. The superintendent hired an extra nurse when a child needed constant care and transferred the child to the hospital upon the doctor's recommendation.[59] All operations, simple or complex, were done at the Hebrew Hospital.

When the Federated Jewish Charities was established and the H.O.A. became part of it, published reports revealed for the first time the extensive medical care the orphans enjoyed. A list of doctors concerned with the children's health included some famous Jewish doctors in Baltimore. There was a male physician for the boys and a female physician for the girls. Three doctors' telephone numbers were listed for emergency cases. Twelve specialists from different departments in the Hebrew Hospital took care of special needs. A dentist kept the orphans' teeth healthy.[60]

Like the Samuel Ready, the H.O.A had a remarkably good record.

No deaths were recorded until 1916, perhaps because seriously ill children were transferred to the hospital. When a hospitalized child died, the asylum reported the death and its cause and the children attended the funeral. Between 1893 and 1916 four such deaths were registered. One girl died from pernicious anemia (a form of leukemia), another from blood poisoning, one boy from meningitis, and one boy from a serious heart condition of several years' duration.

In 1916 Reizenstein reported the first sudden death of a child in the H.O.A. The boy died two days after he first complained of pains from unknown sources. An autopsy did not reveal the cause of death. The detailed monthly medical report of the superintendent, given at the beginning of every meeting, testifies to the doctors' watchfulness on health matters. When parents requested a child's release, they were required to sign an agreement to consult a doctor should the child become ill. Such care was not common among poor Russian Jews. One member of the board, Harry Friedenwald, was an eye specialist whose father and brother were also prominent physicians. The Friedenwalds provided free medical care to the poor in Baltimore.[61]

The superintendents' reports do not show any pattern or cycles of maladies in the institution. There were periods without sickness, and there were periods when diseases like whooping cough, measles, and chicken pox occurred. Diphtheria was rare, and few cases of pneumonia were reported. Recurring colds usually resulted in a tonsillitis operation.

The Dolan Home medical record is not very different from the records of the other two orphanages. No cases of death in the institution are revealed. A child who was seriously ill when he entered the home returned to his parents after a year. The nuns did not succeed in improving his health, and he died at home three months later. This child was exceptional because he had been committed by the court on account of neglect. He had been living and begging in the street, where his health had perhaps been undermined. The records describe no other child as sick. There is no description or other information about how the children's health was maintained. The budget does not include physician's fees or other medical bills, but neither does the H.O.A.'s expenditures report. In the H.O.A. doctors' services were given gratis and the cost of hospitalization was picked up by the hospital, which was itself supported by many of the same contributors who supported the H.O.A. From 1908 the Federated Jewish

Charities maintained both the hospital and the orphanage and charged the medical expenses of the H.O.A. to the hospital. Dr. Ferdinand E. Chatard, a well-known physician in Baltimore, had served as president of the Dolan Home from 1885 to 1900 and as a member of the board of trustees since 1877 (see Chapter One). It is possible that he himself provided medical care for the children. It is also possible that St. Patrick's Church, which supported another orphanage, provided medical care and paid the bills in the same way it provided schooling for the Dolan Home children. In one instance, when the board convened during an epidemic outbreak (March 7, 1892), Sister Chlotilda reported "four children sick with 'grippe.' Both Sisters have been down but are up today." The absence of detailed medical information implies no disregard of the children's health. Because the board convened every three months, it might have seemed unnecessary to record information on day-to-day operations.

At the turn of the century, tuberculosis was the most dreadful disease and the number one killer of infants, adults, and children above eleven. The best defenses against the disease, according to Progressive Era experts, were good living conditions, large ventilated rooms, good food, good hygiene (both public and personal), and exercise. Philanthropists and social workers estimated that a high percentage of the parents of children in orphanages had died of tuberculosis.[62]

Many changes in orphanages between the 1880s and 1920s were a result of a new concern for children's physical conditions, with an emphasis on the health effects of the environment. Efforts to find high, well-drained ground for the Samuel Ready, the design of the H.O.A. to include many windows and a gymnasium, reduced study hours in order to give children more time to play outside, exercises for the girls and plenty of plain food in the Ready School, meat and milk everyday in the H.O.A., and a strong emphasis on personal hygiene in both institutions were all responses to prevailing ideas about public health of the time and indicate that the material conditions of life may well have been better inside the asylum than outside.

CHAPTER FOUR

The Children's Education

THE THREE orphanages strove to provide an academically sound education as well as ethical and religious instruction and an appreciation of culture. Their success is evident from comparisons of the achievements of children in their care with those of their peers who didn't live in institutions. Recall that in the 1890s there was no nationally accepted standard for years of school attendance much less curriculum. School was not even mandatory at any age, and a child's educational opportunity was determined largely by family choice. Although all Americans had access to free and readily available education, parents who were economically stressed were often forced to remove their children from school and send them to work.[1] In rural areas where the one-room school still operated, farmers' children worked in the fields in spring and summer and attended school only in the three winter months. Teenagers in poor families were likely to work whether they lived in the country or the city.[2] Middle-class children were able to use both the public school and the private school systems more extensively. An exception to this class generalization was Jewish immigrants, who eagerly used the public school system to foster opportunity in urban America. Coming from Eastern Europe, where educational opportunities were restricted, they considered the United States the "Golden Medina," because education was free and available.[3] According to Stephen Steinberg, Jews attended high school and college in disproportionately high numbers at a time in America when an "individual who graduated from high school was the exception not the rule. Those who completed high school came mostly from the more affluent strata of society."[4] Though most children of Jewish immigrants in the early 1900s did not attend high school, they were more likely to do so than other ethnic groups.

School attendance was not obligatory in Baltimore in the late nineteenth century. Although child labor laws began to limit children's work, many children still did not go to school and school attendance was irregular. In the 1890s and early 1900s public school officials in Baltimore lamented low enrollment, poor attendance, and a tendency of parents to take their children out of school before the fifth or sixth grade in order to send them to work. In the 1890 and 1900 annual reports, the superintendent of school commissioners stressed the need for good education in English and arithmetic, especially in the early grades. The report for 1890 said, "Of the entire number of pupils attending the schools, about sixty-four per cent are in the three lowest grades which constitute the primary school. . . . The number in the five grammar grades make about thirty-two per cent of the enrollment, while only four per cent are found in high schools." Only a little more than 1 percent reached the fourth year of high school. In 1900 the number of students who continued beyond the primary grades reached about 50 per cent.

The superintendent's statistics represent only children who were enrolled in the schools. They did not include the many children who did not attend school at all. Some children attended school intermittantly, when the economic situation in their homes permitted. Baltimore's public schools had already adopted the grade system so that a child of ten who left school in the third or fourth grade might return to school two years later and be placed in the fourth or fifth grade with younger children.[5] Some children were embarrassed to be ranked with younger students and quit school.

The public schools in Baltimore were considered very good, and in the 1890s and early 1900s children from wealthy families were well represented among their graduates.[6] Still, only 7 per cent of all Baltimore children attended high schools in 1889–1900, and only about 10 percent of those who entered graduated at the end of the fourth year. About five of every two hundred children entering first grade completed high school. Between 1890 and 1920, however, great changes in attitudes toward child labor and children's education occurred across the nation. Reformers emphasized the special needs of children, the ability of education to uplift the next generation, and the importance of the children of immigrants as carriers of "Americanism"; they encouraged prolonged schooling and ultimately achieved compulsory attendance laws.[7]

As the urban industrial revolution intensified during the final decades of the nineteenth century, more and more voices called for
adaptation of the educational system to modern society's needs. The
public school system was attacked for failing to train students in the
skills required by the contemporary labor market. The proportion of
boys dropping out of public schools between grades six and eight
reached 90 percent in 1889. Critics charged that boys did not consider the intellectual academic course relevant to their future.[8] The
remedy in the 1880s was to introduce manual training into the public
school curriculum. The benefit of giving boys courses in drawing,
carving, and carpentry would be immense. They would take greater
interest in school, stay there longer, acquire skills helpful in their
vocations, learn important values such as diligence, accuracy, self-
control and neatness, and acquire self-reliance and self-respect.[9] As
for girls, educators believed that the knowledge and skills of running
a household were no longer handed down by mothers to daughters.
In poor neighborhoods, mothers themselves lacked that know-how.
New scientific discoveries related to hygiene, sanitation, and technology made proper care of family members and households more complicated. Domestic skills such as cooking and sewing should be introduced into the school curriculum so that the American household
might be properly managed. The manual training crusade of the
1870s and 1880s, which culminated in the introduction of these subjects in the public school cirriculum, paved the way for vocational
education. Its supporters argued that manual training did not prove
to be helpful for youngsters in the new industrial world of the 1890s
because artisanship and manual work was giving way to mechaniza-
tion. Vocational education, which prepared youngsters for skilled
and semiskilled jobs in industry, bore greater relevance to the changing reality.[10]

In fact, the new trend was not so new. Child care institutions, and
especially reformatories and institutions for wayward and dependent
children, had long put heavy emphasis on manual training and vocational education. The novelty was the belief that the majority of children should receive vocational education as an integral part of the
public school curriculum.

The new trend was also controversial. It was opposed by educators who saw an antidemocratic division of students into those des-
tined for the professions and those headed for the labor force. Oppo-

nents also argued that vocational education, with its limited aims, did not contribute toward the goal of the public school curriculum to raise the general level of culture in the population.[11]

The inclusion of industrial and vocational education into the public school system, whether at the elementary or the secondary school level, was designed to help children compete in the job market and to give them an opportunity to move up the social ladder. Two recent studies of late nineteenth-century Pittsburgh have concluded that working-class youngsters successfully used vocational education in clerking and teaching to rise in status.[12] Especially interesting is the finding that children of widows tended to stay in business schools and graduate, while children whose fathers held white-collar jobs often did not finish their courses. Apparently children from white-collar families could use their fathers' connections to find clerical or teaching jobs and had less need of a diploma than poor children without good networks. The public school commissioners of Baltimore City recognized the risks of such favoritism. In their report of 1890, they lamented that too many teaching jobs had gone to unsuitable persons because they had connections. They hoped that opening a normal school would enable the public schools to recruit teachers upon merit. Just as middle-class children had an advantage in acquiring an education in the first place, they had an advantage in finding jobs even when they had less preparation than poorer young people.

Being poor and lacking connections were not the only impediments to finding a suitable position. Girls had limited opportunities to advance themselves; only teaching, clerking, and nursing were within reach and considered respectable professions for young women. Once working, women had a more difficult struggle to become self-supporting because of wage discrimination both in conventional women's work and even when they worked in the same positions as men. Ethnicity, religious affiliation, and foreign birth might be significant obstacles to opportunity. Jews in Baltimore, for example, knew that they would not be hired by some of the big companies in the city if they were recognized as Jews.[13] Irish Catholics, and Italians faced similar barriers. And having been raised in an orphanage increased the risk of discrimination because these institutions had a negative image in the public mind.

With a vivid awareness of the difficulties in store, the administrators of Baltimore's orphanages tried to prepare their children for the struggle to succeed in the outside world.

Elementary Education

The principal of the McDonogh School envisioned the Samuel Ready as a school for poor orphan girls; as Colonel Allan saw it, the Ready School would serve the same group the McDonogh School had served since its opening in 1872. It would be "a first-class home school for girls of good character and sound body and mind, and of fair capacity."[14]

The model school, according to Allan's suggestion, should provide an equivalent to a strong public school education along with an industrial one that would enable the graduates to support themselves. The adopted public school curriculum would put strong emphasis on English because "power of expression, or a good serviceable command of our language in reading, writing and talking, is of the very essence of education." Arithmetic and geography, as well as history and literature, would be taught in the general course of study of the public school curriculum. Drawing, vocal music, hygiene, physiology, and science were to be incorporated into the industrial program. By way of illustration, Allan explained that in a subject like chemistry "the theory of bread-making should be more necessary than that of the reduction of iron ores; in physics it would be more important to have taught heating and ventilation than solar physics." The curriculum had to be practical and suit the needs of young women in that period. The ideology behind the curriculum was to educate girls to be mothers and nurses but also self-supporting women in case they did not marry or became widows.

Allan's twenty-two-page letter of suggestions (published by the Samuel Ready trustees in 1883) was adopted as a statement of principle by the Samuel Ready School in 1887 without any change. Allan had advocated flexibility regarding the program and experimentation with the curriculum until the most suitable one was found. Students at the Samuel Ready School received a thorough training in English, with heavy emphasis on reading and writing as well as speaking correctly. Those who made grammatical mistakes wore a "Grammar Key" around their necks, a symbolic reminder to improve their lan-

guage.[15] Reading was an important evening activity. From the outset
the school had a library, and the girls were encouraged to read. Every
school event included a recitation of poetry or literature organized by
the girls. They studied the lives of the great writers and had to write
a composition every two weeks. They also wrote letters to their relatives every two weeks. And they were encouraged to write to Rowe
about their summer vacation experiences. Rowe sometimes corrected
spelling and grammatical mistakes in the letters she received. Perhaps
she used them as a teaching device. In September 1892, an article in
the *Baltimore Sun* demonstrated the new vertical script that was introduced in the United States by the Samuel Ready School. Rowe,
who brought the script to the Samuel Ready students after consulting
with Dr. Lewis H. Steiner from the Enoch Pratt Free Library and
ordering teaching material from London, praised the method because
of its legibility, neatness, and grace and its supposed hygienic benefits. The school, reported the newspaper, would have an exhibition at
the world's fair of maps, wallpaper and oilcloth designs, lettering,
sewing, and composition books using the vertical script.[16]

The achievement of high-level language skills was evident in the
bimonthly *Ready Record* which the girls began publishing in 1892.
Besides describing everyday life and social events at the school, it
included fiction and historical and geographical riddles. The girls
wrote and produced the *Ready Record* and circulated it among their
friends and the alumnae.

The school had eleven grades, starting with kindergarten through
four years of preparatory school, three years of middle school and
three years of high school (grades D, C, B). At that time children in
kindergarten were between five and seven years old. Most children
started first grade at the age of seven. Although high school had four
grades, the good students at the Samuel Ready were expected to
complete the program in three years. The teachers were two of
Rowe's colleagues when she was a principal in the Frederick Female
High School; they were supplemented by special teachers for some of
the industrial subjects. A high level of instruction, a selective curriculum, and an emphasis on scholastic achievement made the Samuel
Ready an outstanding school that was noticed by the U.S. Department of Education and by educators at large.[17]

Rowe cultivated an atmosphere of competition, a pride in being a

"Ready girl," and a drive for prizes and honors that was reflected in the girls' writing. Sentences like "now you can call me a Ready girl," or "I am sure she will be a source of comfort and pride to you" often appeared in the correspondence between Rowe and the girls or the girls' relatives. Every success of a girl, whether in a concert at the Peabody Institute or an exhibition of art at the Maryland Institute, a scholarship, or an honorary mention in a normal school examination was a source of excitement and pride shared by the whole school. There was a monthly exhibition of the children's schoolwork (maps, drawings, and so forth) on visiting day, and the honor roll hung every week on the school's information board.[18] The yearly reappointment of students to the school was based on scholastic achievement and conduct. At commencement, annual prizes and awards were given in the presence of friends, alumnae, and guests. All this created an atmosphere of competition, achievement, and excellence.

EXCEPT FOR a kindergarten class, the Hebrew Orphan Asylum had no school on its premises. The children attended public school number 65 (later renamed the Alexander Hamilton School). Those who excelled were sent to the preparatory school, a special school that prepared talented students for high school, and then to high school. The curriculum of School 65 was no different from that of other public schools in Baltimore. It included English, arithmetic (in the seventh and eighth grades algebra and geometry), science, history, physiology, music, and drawing. Manual training for boys and sewing for girls were added during the 1890s. The school was two blocks away from the orphanage and had approximately three hundred students in eight grades. During the 1890s and early 1900s, the H.O.A.'s sixty to eighty children made a significant contribution to the school's student body. Their presence was especially notable because they attended school regularly. In 1900, for example, the enrollment at School 65 varied: 366 children over the entire year, 302 in December, and 277 each day on average. The average attendance, however, was 197 (71 percent), of which the average of seventy students from the H.O.A. were a third.

H.O.A. children must have accounted for an even higher percentage of students in the upper grades. In 1900 School 65 had about 40 students in each grade from first to fourth. The fifth and sixth grades had 33 and 24 students respectively, but the seventh grade had only 8 students and the eighth grade only 3.[19] Since all H.O.A. children under fourteen attended school, it is reasonable to conclude that they were highly represented in the upper grades of the school.

The H.O.A. not only ensured that the children attended school but also that they prepared their lessons. Every day after dinner, all children were required to go to study rooms and do their homework under the supervision and coaching of monitors. Encouragement to excel in school came in Saturday's preaching, in the superintendent's monitoring of their education by consulting with their teachers, and through a system of prizes and honors. The annual examinations of the Hebrew School, an afternoon school at the H.O.A. in which Judaism, German, and Hebrew were taught, were conducted in the presence of a large audience of relatives. At the end, the H.O.A. gave prizes to the best scholars. Michael Aaronsohn describes the H.O.A. as a place where competition and drive for excellence thrived.[20]

In 1911, the new superintendent, Dr. Reizenstein, added a summer program in which students who had not been promoted and those who missed school on account of illness studied with a special teacher in order to make up deficiencies. Classes were also offered for excellent students who wished to skip a grade. The teachers of School 65 cooperated by providing the superintendent with detailed reports on each child's weaknesses and strengths, as well as by supplying books for the summer program.

Like the Samuel Ready, the H.O.A. had its own library. Superintendent Freudenthal placed high priority on enlarging it and stimulating the children to read. His attitude is evident in his reports, which cite the titles and authors of contributed books, and his use of half of a donation for a special meal for the children for books for the library. The H.O.A. library was divided into religious, fictional, and reference books, as was the Samuel Ready School library. The superintendent, not one to encourage indiscriminate reading, banned dime novels; such books found their way to the orphanage and were circulated clandestinely.[21]

Little is known about the education of children at the Dolan Home. They attended the Catholic school adjacent to the orphanage that was run by the Sisters of the Holy Cross. But since most of them were placed out by the age of twelve, they could not have completed more than five or six years.

Manual and Vocational Education

In 1886, the year before the Samuel Ready School opened, Superintendent Helen J. Rowe inspected child care institutions and public school
curricula she had carefully selected from reports in the Educational Bureau in Washington. In two tours of schools and orphanages in Pennsylvania, New York, Massachusetts, Ohio, and Michigan, Rowe was
especially interested in manual and vocational training. Her letters and
reports to the trustees show that every institution she visited had a different policy with respect to such training. Following a visit to the
McDonogh School, Rowe and the trustees decided to adopt Colonel
Allan's plan, which integrated manual training with a thorough general
education. Vocational and professional education was reserved for the
last two years of high school for those who wished and were qualified
to apply for it. The subjects the Ready School offered were chosen after
scrutiny and analysis of the job market for young women at the time.
The purpose of the acquired vocation was to enable the young graduate
to be completely self-supporting, and the training had to be tailored to
each student's abilities and talents.

Drawing, cooking, sewing, and gardening were at the core of the
manual training education. Drawing seemed to be the basis for hand
training and had "great utility as a mode of expression in so many
departments of work," wrote Allan. It was used in the study of history and geography, where girls had to draw maps of the parts of the
world and in the study of science, when the human body or plants
were discussed. It was also the basis of sewing, which required patterns of clothes to be drawn. Once a month on Sunday (visiting day),
the girls exhibited their best drawings. Those who showed talent
took art classes at the Maryland Institute.

Sewing was also taken seriously. The girls received thorough training in both hand and machine sewing, as well as in model cutting
and in theoretical subjects such as the history of garments, the fabric
and texture of clothing, and the treatment of different fabrics.[22] Each
girl learned how to wash and iron during her stay at the Ready
School.[23] The aim was to ascertain that every girl would be able to
sew at least for her own needs or those of her future family. Some
girls were later trained as teachers of dressmaking.

Cooking also formed a serious part of manual training, and examinations were difficult, according to the children's testimony. In

1892, for example, six girls attended the cooking class. Three cooked on Wednesday and three on Saturday. The kitchen was outside the building, and the girls had to bring wood for the stove the preceding night. They also had to clean the kitchen afterwards. The results were a source of pride to both the girls and their relatives. A girl's mother thanked Rowe in a letter after receiving the first loaf of bread her fourteen-year-old daughter had baked. Other girls received compliments for their cooking from their friends in the *Ready Record*. Cooking was also part of the final year's training, when some girls studied scientific cooking, including food chemistry, food hygiene, nutrition, and special diets. Graduates of this course received certificates enabling them to teach cooking in public schools.[24]

Gardening was studied outdoors, whereas botany was taught in the classroom. Every resident of the Ready School had a flower bed which she tended year round. The girls gave flowers to relatives on visiting days.

The main aim of the Samuel Ready School curriculum was to educate its students to be self-supporting women. The children were trained to become teachers in public schools, and in such subjects as dressmaking, cookery, art, and music, as well as office work such as bookkeeping, stenography, and typing.[25]

The decision about a child's vocation was based on her performance at school and was made by the superintendent after consulting with various teachers, the child, and her relatives.[26] In some cases students studied at the school with a teacher who came twice a week to instruct them. In other cases, students went to other institutions for lessons; advanced music students studied at the Peabody, and art students at the Maryland Institute. Typewriting and stenography were taught in the school, but the final course in business was taken at Eaton and Barnett, one of the Baltimore business schools. Those who prepared for teaching positions studied at the normal school, and students of scientific cookery took a special course in New York for three months. An exceptionally talented girl who was selected to go to college was sent to Girls' Latin, a highly rated private day school, for her high school studies. In a few cases, the school's responsibility for a girl's professional education did not end when the girl turned eighteen or nineteen. Girls who excelled either in their general studies or in music and who received a scholarship from the Peabody Institute or the Women's College of Baltimore (later

Goucher College) were offered board at the Ready School in exchange for tutoring or light teaching while they continued their education The first forty girls who entered Samuel Ready School in 1887–88 exemplify the school's vocational education policy: twenty-nine stayed until they finished their vocational training, eleven were expelled or were withdrawn by their relatives; nine studied sewing and dressmaking; seven took business courses, which included typewriting, stenography, and bookkeeping; seven finished a teaching course with a certificate from the state normal school; three specialized in scientific cookery; and three studied music. The list of vocations of the twenty-nine girls does not reveal the full extent to which the Samuel Ready School carefully encouraged each girl's talents. Cathy Sullivan, for example, was talented in music and studied at the Peabody Institute, but during her last year at the Samuel Ready School she also studied scientific cookery.

Since the school had children from different social backgrounds and decisions about children's vocations were made by the school in consultation with relatives, intriguing questions arise concerning the weight of outside influence on vocational decisions and possible prejudice against children of humble origin or less educated parents. The stories of the Donaldsons, Elizabeth Darling, Seraphina Cook, and Carol Fleet are instructive. Beth Donaldson, aged twelve upon entry, was "honorably dismissed" (she completed the full program successfully) on July 3, 1893, at the age of eighteen. Her vocation was teaching. She graduated from the school after completing grade B and within two years graduated with honors from the state normal school, fourth in her class of fifty-four with a grade average of 93. Her sister Heidi, aged ten at entry, was exceptionally gifted. She played the piano, served as editor of the *Ready Record,* and at the age of seventeen graduated with honors from the Girls Latin School and obtained a teaching certificate from the normal school. Heidi Donaldson received a scholarship to the Women's College, where she excelled and became an instructor. Little sister Iris Donaldson, aged seven upon entry, had different talents. At the age of eighteen, after eleven years at the Samuel Ready, she graduated (completed grade B) with training in dressmaking, curtaining, and drapery, a partial course in cooking, and training as a nurse. The three girls, whose father was a clerk and a railroad agent, received different vocational educations, each according to her talents.

Were daughters of clerks and teachers pushed toward the professions while those of manual workers were directed toward manual
vocations? An examination of the vocations of daughters in relation
to those of their parents shows no correlation. Elizabeth Darling,
whose father had been a house painter and whose mother had had
no occupation, was a full orphan when she entered the Ready School
at the age of eleven. Seven years later, Elizabeth graduated from the
normal school; she had won a scholarship at entrance and finished as
one of the best students in the class. Seraphina Cook, whose father
was an undertaker and whose mother's occupation was listed as
"dairy," entered at the same age as Elizabeth and left as a typist and
stenographer when she was seventeen, after graduating from a three-
month course in business at Eaton and Barnett. Seraphina's brothers
became a candy maker and a laborer. Seraphina was probably the
only child in the family to graduate from high school. Carol Fleet,
whose father was a temporary car driver, graduated as a teacher,
while Melinda Gates, whose father was a clerk, was trained in dressmaking.

Aid to students who won outside scholarships and needed the
Ready School as a temporary home while using them exemplifies the
extent to which decisions were free from class partiality. Extending a
student's stay beyond school training meant denying entrance to another candidate. The school did not accept a single child above its
capacity. In 1892, Idaline Delphy asked the trustees of Samuel Ready
School to let her stay at the school while she studied at the Peabody
on a scholarship. Idaline Delphy and her sister Florence were twelve
and fourteen, respectively, at entry. Their father, a merchant, had
died and left them with their mother, a music teacher. Idaline graduated from the Ready School at the age of seventeen, after finishing
high school and the third year of piano at the Peabody. The school
bought her the musical instruments she needed but refused to let her
stay. The reason given was that Idaline was able to earn her own
living and the school needed to cede her place to another student.
From the letter that Rowe sent to Idaline's mother, it is clear that the
trustees were under pressure from friends of the Delphys to retain the
girl. When Monica Kimmel, a full orphan, arrived at the age of eighteen and received a scholarship from the Peabody, the trustees
granted her the extra years, probably because she had no family to
support her. The economic circumstances of the two girls dictated

different decisions, and the two cases lend support to the conclusion that the school responded to each girl on the basis of her merit and need.

THE REPORT from H.O.A. Superintendent Freudenthal to the board of directors on June 12, 1893, discloses his policy with respect to education of the orphans in his charge. The Hebrew Orphan Asylum sheltered and educated children until their parents were able to take care of them or they could support themselves. Children who remained under the institution's auspices fell into two categories. Those beyond fourteen or fifteen who showed talent and determination to study were promoted, helped, and pushed toward their goals.[27] Those who did not show any enthusiasm for studying or interest in a vocation were sent to the city to learn a trade. In this case, the child returned to his or her parent, and the H.O.A. secured a position for the child in the city.[28] Though the child lived at home, he or she was legally still under the institution's care; therefore, if the child did not make enough money to pay for board, the H.O.A. paid the mother for board. Even when parents requested their children back, the asylum still attempted to find the children jobs or to bind them to learn a trade. Binding a child to learn a trade did not mean giving the employer legal authority over the child. The agreement was usually that in exchange for a small amount of money, the teenager would help in the business and the owner would teach the child the trade. When there were no relatives to live with, the teenager might board with the employer, but in most such cases, the teenager would board with a family and the H.O.A. would cover any gap between salary and expenses.

When parents became able to provide fully for a child, the H.O.A. just returned the child to them.[29] In many cases the H.O.A. initiated the return by urging parents whose family circumstances had changed to take their children back. As soon as the superintendent learned that a parent had remarried, a mother had recovered her health, or a deserting father had returned home, he would inform the board of directors and recommend that the child be sent home. The board would meet with the parents, and the subsequent record would read: "withdrew by their parents" or "return to their parents upon their request."[30]

Fully orphaned girls often stayed in the H.O.A. until they reached eighteen. Then the Hebrew Ladies Orphan Aid Society would find a home for them and send them to learn a trade. The same society would provide vocational education for the girls who were half orphans and did not continue their studies after age fifteen or sixteen. The full-orphan girls who stayed in the orphanage past the age of sixteen and did not go to high school received lessons in sewing and helped the seamstress. Since the number of full orphan children was usually very small, the number of girls just boarding in the H.O.A. was also small (between three and four, at most).[31]

Most of the teenagers in the Hebrew Orphan Asylum were in pursuit of a vocation. Freudenthal knew each child's abilities and inclinations very well. He was constantly in touch with the public school teachers. The chosen vocation was not Freudenthal's exclusive decision but was discussed and planned with the child.[32] Since there was no industrial school in the H.O.A., children with inclinations toward manual and artistic vocations were sent to industrial schools in New York and New Jersey. Boys went either to the National Farm in Doylestown or the Baron de Hirsch Industrial School in New York. Girls went to the Clara de Hirsch Industrial School in New York. A *Jewish Comment* article from November 9, 1900, on the Clara de Hirsch Home, describes one such girl as "having her voice cultivated," and another as having "won a scholarship at the Teacher's College and . . . now taking a course in domestic science." In a later period some of the girls studied dressmaking at the Girl's Home in Baltimore.

The procedure by which a child's vocation was chosen and planned is exemplified in the cases of Alfred Samueloff and Levy Sofer. In August of 1898, Freudenthal brought before the board of directors the question of the two boys' vocations. These children had graduated from the grammar school and were "recommended to City College." Alfred Samueloff showed "talents for drawing and desires to become an architect." Freudenthal brought examples of the boy's drawings to the meeting and recommended that the child be sent to Maryland Institute "or to any other school where he will have an opportunity to develop his talent." Levy Sofer had weak eyes that might interfere with his studies. Freudenthal asked the board to act quickly because the children had to be enrolled in August for the year that started in September. On September 1, the superintendent reported that the two boys were at the Baltimore Polytechnic Institute, a public high school specializing in engineering, mathematics, and physics. In June 1899, a year later, the question of these boys' education was raised again, although there is no explanation as to why they did not graduate from the Polytechnic Institute. After corresponding with the principal of the National Farm School, where, Freudenthal reported, the boys were willing to go, the superintendent pointed out that "it is very hard to find positions or bind them out to learn a trade" and also that a former ward of the H.O.A. finished a two-year course at the farm school and "obtained a position which secures him a livelihood." In August, having no reply from the farm school, the superintendent applied to the Baron de Hirsch Woodbine Colony in New Jersey. Finally the farm school rejected the boys' applications, but the Baron de Hirsch School admitted them. This story shows that decision making at the H.O.A. first considered the child's wishes and ability but depended as well on the job market and the vocational schools' admission policies.[33]

The board of directors was very much involved in deciding each child's vocation. Recommendations came from the superintendent, but the board did not act as a rubber stamp and had suggestions and solutions of its own. The decision-making process regarding the children's vocations resembles the one at the Samuel Ready School with the exception that the Ready School superintendent had greater influence because most of the education, vocational and academic, was given at the school. Sending a child to another institution required financial and legal decisions that could not rest solely in the superintendent's hands.

Children in the H.O.A. who were academically talented and diligent were first directed toward secondary education. Boys commuted to City College or the Baltimore Polytechnic Institute and girls to Western Female High School.[34] Once graduated, the girls were sent to the normal school to become teachers, to business school to learn stenography, bookkeeping, and typewriting, or to nursing schools; all of these institutions were in Baltimore. Boys were sent to Baltimore schools to become bookkeepers, engineers, doctors, and teachers; a few were sent away to study for the rabbinate because Baltimore had no rabbinical schools. For education beyond the high school level, the board found a patron who would lend the student the money required for living expenses and tuition.[35] Simon Z. reported that in some cases the teenager would live in the institution, studying in the morning and paying his keep by monitoring the young children in their afternoon activities. The policy of helping the promising children to develop their talents and enter the professions was firm, and the methods used resembled those the Samuel Ready School used for the same purpose.

Freudenthal frequently reported on students for the rabbinate. A rabbi himself, perhaps he had a preference for this vocation, though another reason for his attention might be that these studies required nine years, four spent pursuing a liberal arts college degree and five more dedicated to Judaic studies.[36]

Examination of the sample of forty-five children who entered the H.O.A. between 1888 and 1889 shows that of the group that stayed a long period in the H.O.A., only seven were not returned to parents or other relatives in order to learn a trade when they were between fourteen and sixteen years old. The seven children came from three families: the Millers, five of whose seven children were at the orphanage; the Semlins, who had six children at the orphanage (only four entered in 1888–89); and the Luries, who had two girls there (only one in the sample). All three mothers were sick. The Semlins and the Luries were half orphans at entry, but the Semlins became full orphans during their stay in the H.O.A. Both Miller parents were living, but the mother was permanently ill in the hospital and the father was unable to take care of the children. In short, the children of these families did not have a home to return to, and they could not expect a reconstruction of their household. Their education was entirely in the hands of the H.O.A.

Joanna and Chaya Miller stayed in the orphanage until each reached eighteen, and then Joanna was secured a position and boarded in a family. Chaya studied dressmaking at Hutzler Brothers, a Baltimore department store. Enoch Miller passed the eighth grade with a grade average of 90, entered City College, and at the same time studied twice a week with a rabbi and professor of Biblical history at Johns Hopkins University. Two years later he was sent to Cincinnati to study for the rabbinate. He was advanced enough to enter the second year of college, and he graduated in seven years instead of nine. Aaron Miller was sent to the Baron de Hirsch Industrial School at Woodbine; two years later he graduated and found a position. Little Lizzie Miller was released from the H.O.A. at age fifteen upon her father's request and went to live in New York with a married sister; she had completed a year at Western High School. The Semlins showed a similar pattern. Mendel Semlin was released at fifteen to study a trade and live with his mother. His brother Louis, who was labeled incorrigible, was sent to live with him three years later. In between the two brothers' discharges, their mother died, and the two little girls living at home with her were admitted to the H.O.A. Louis Semlin went to the National Farm School to study farming. When she reached eighteen, Eta Semlin was employed by the H.O.A. as a seamstress. The younger girls, who entered the orphanage many years after the others, remained in the asylum until their elder siblings were well established and asked for them. Henrietta Lurie was an excellent student who graduated from the Western Female School and was then sent to the normal school to become a teacher. Henrietta's sister, who entered the H.O.A. after 1889, also graduated from high school and was sent to the business course at Sadler's Bryant and Stratton Business College.

The fact that the two students singled out as especially talented in this sample were of German origin raises the question of bias and discrimination in an institution built and run by German Jews but in whose population German Jews were a minority. But the fact is that the four siblings of Enoch Miller did not receive the same education he got. Children of German origin do not seem to have had advantages as a result of familiarity with the institution's customs or of special treatment. The system apparently worked upon merit and estimates of individual talent.

In the late 1880s "German children" were still represented in the H.O.A.'s population. The big waves of immigration after the pogroms in Russia in 1882 and 1903 increased the number of Russian Jewish children who were either half orphans or orphans or who for other reasons could not be cared for by their parents.[37] In 1902, Russian Jews opened an orphanage, the Hebrew Sheltering Aid Society or the Betsy Levi Home, which accepted both orphans and children whose parents were sick and needed a temporary shelter. The H.O.A. then ceased to be a temporary shelter and received only children who required long-term shelter.[38] The number of children in the H.O.A., however, grew steadily from about 70 in the early 1900s to 120 in the 1910s.[39] The proportion of older children to younger ones increased during these years because of a new wave of immigrants and the greater emphasis on completing secondary school. In 1900 only 10 percent of the students completed high school.

New notions and debates regarding institutional care and the needs of children in general contributed to changes that were introduced at the H.O.A. In the beginning, the public school system provided elementary, manual, physical, and secondary education, and the H.O.A. provided religion, Hebrew, and German. In 1902, the superintendent asked the board of directors to drop the study of German, as other Jewish institutions in the country were doing. Philanthropy added new facilities—a gymnasium and a teacher—so that the children had lessons in physical education and dancing (in 1904). A manual training school and lessons in drawing, designing, woodcarving, and sewing were added in 1907. In 1910, when Freudenthal died and Reizenstein took over, the industrial education program expanded into the summer vacation and intensified. Boys received more lessons in cabinet work and light sewing. Girls were instructed in sewing and cooking, in addition to carving. All children worked in the garden and studied farming. During the school year, the manual training lessons continued two afternoons a week. Industrial education was intended as an enrichment that would help the children in their future home life rather than as preparation for a vocation. An academic course of studies leading to the professions was still emphasized and was what the children were encouraged to choose. Oddly enough, in most of the Freudenthal era, the H.O.A. offered no manual training or industrial education, though a child sent to industrial school was expected to return with a vocation.[40] The only child to enter an industrial school under Reizenstein's superintendency was a problematic boy whom the H.O.A. sent to St. Mary's Industrial School to be reformed.[41] In this respect, the H.O.A. reflected the general trend in the Jewish community to prefer the professions over the industrial vocations and also the general trend in the United States to view industrial schools as reform schools.[42]

WITH FEW exceptions children in the Dolan Home did not stay beyond the age of thirteen. Children who were boarders or had one parent returned to their parents. The Dolan Home decided the future of children committed by the court because they had been neglected or abused, and those who were full orphans. Some of the full orphans and neglected children were placed out in families, and some were sent to St. Mary's Industrial School.

In the records of the Dolan Home, placing out was called "adoption." In the nineteenth century an adopted child lived in a house with a family until the age of twenty-one for boys and eighteen for girls.[43] The adopting family signed a contract with the institution in which it essentially promised to treat the child as one of the family and to provide fifty dollars when the child turned eighteen. The child was expected to contribute to the household, although the precise obligations were not spelled out or written down. In return, the institution expected the adopting family to provide the child not only with a home but also "with occupation or business in life."

The process of adoption started with a form on which the applicant stated the age and sex of the child wanted. The applicant could be a man or a woman, not necessarily a couple; some of the records show widows among the applicants. The Dolan Home then mailed the applicant a contract with notes explaining its demands. The applicant had to answer questions and have two witnesses countersign the form. The names and addresses of three references and a pastor's endorsement were also needed. If the applicant met the board's standards, a child was selected and sent to the applicant.

The Dolan Home Minute Book shows that some applicants were refused: "Mrs. Zenlin having applied for Julius Pratt for adoption, she to give him only two months schooling per annum, on motion of Mr. Donnely (trustee) the application was rejected unless Mrs. Zenlin comply with all the usual conditions including at least three months schooling per annum." The applicants were either farmers who wanted a helper or housekeepers who wished to have girls to help with the housework. Applications came from farmers in various Maryland counties (Kent, Prince George, St. Mary's, Charles, Anne Arundel) for children between the ages of five and eleven. The children sent, however, were between eight and eleven.

The success of these arrangements varied. Some children returned to the institution after a few days or ran away from their adoptive families and found other families to take them in. Others stayed with the adoptive family until their eighteenth birthday or beyond. Of the children who entered the Dolan Home in 1890, nine children were placed out (eight boys and one girl). Six of the nine were pairs of siblings from three families: one set of twins (a boy and a girl) and two pairs of brothers. Oddly enough, the Dolan Home, which was established in order to keep siblings together, separated them when it placed them out. Most children were ten or eleven years old when they were placed (four were eleven, three ten, one nine, and one girl was eight.) Since they were either abandoned, neglected or full orphans, a successful "adoption" meant a long separation from their siblings or what was left of their family of origin. Little eight-year-old Mollie O'Mallie was committed to the Dolan Home with her twin brother, Wilbur, on account of suffering "through neglect and bad habits of her mother," on April 20, 1890. Six months later, on November 8, 1890, she was placed in Mrs. Link's house. Her twin brother remained in the Dolan Home. Mollie O'Mallie stayed with Mrs. Link for ten years. In January 1901, the Dolan Home minute book reveals that Mrs. Link had not yet paid the fifty dollars she owed the girl when she reached her eighteenth birthday, although the girl had turned eighteen the preceding April. Mr. Link promised the executive committee of the Dolan Home that he would send a check for Mollie to the Dolan Home. There was no further discussion of the problem in the minute book; perhaps Mollie was paid. In 1892, the Dolan Home sent ten-year-old Wilbur O'Mallie to Mr. Hunt of New Port, Charles County. In 1898 the Dolan Home asked a committee to find Wilbur O'Mallie a new home; Mr. Hunt had reported that the boy was difficult to manage and ran away. The committee sent a visitor to inquire about Wilbur and the other boys who had been "adopted" in the same area. The visitor reported that the eight boys other than Wilbur were satisfied with their homes. The committee eventually approved for sixteen-year-old Wilbur a farmer that he had found for himself. Because the O'Mallie children lived at some distance from each other, it is reasonable to assume that the twins seldom, and perhaps never, saw each other during those eight or ten years.

Placing out orphans and neglected children in farms was a common policy among children's aid societies and other child care institutions in the second half of the nineteenth century. The fresh air of the country and the simple life on the farm were thought to be healthier for children than crowded urban centers with their dangerous temptations. Farms were especially recommended for poor and orphan children, who were more likely than others to live in crowded houses on meager diets and to spend time unsupervised in the streets. Farmers, for their part, were eager to have these children because many of their own offspring left the farms.[44] Theoretically such matches might have been perfect: the farmers needed help, and the children needed a home and a vocation. The results in the case of the Dolan Home were mixed. Jack Watts and Gary McGregor both had experiences similar to Wilbur O'Mallie's. Gary McGregor, adopted when he was eleven years old by a farmer in New Port, Charles County, left and moved to another home. At nineteen, he left the second family. His change of home was discovered only when the second family informed the Dolan Home of his departure. Later, the home tried to recover fifty dollars due to the boy from his first adopting family. It seems likely that the boy left the first family at the age of eighteen when he realized that he would not be paid the sum due him.

Such stories appeared frequently in the minute book of the Dolan Home because they required the trustees' intervention. They point to two weak aspects of the adoption program: supervision was inadequate, and the home had no power to enforce the adoption contracts. Children were sent only to Catholic families in Maryland, which, according to the contract, had to send the children to Mass and Sunday school. Had pastors in the various places kept an eye on the children, as they were expected to do, that might have been sufficient supervision. But pastors did not always report problems promptly, nor were they eager to be on a boy's side when a dispute with a farmer occurred.[45] Children placed on the farms were minors and outsiders, while the adopting families were part of the community from which the church derived its worshipers and supporters. The local clergymen were not the right choice to guard the interests of these children.

In 1892 the Dolan Home employed a visitor who traveled to the various farms, talked with the children, and checked on their welfare. The home tried to enforce the contract the families signed. The families were required twice a year to write a report about the children. Some wrote regularly, but some failed to do so and had to be reminded. The number of complaints from children who were not paid when they reached eighteen compelled the trustees to write a new contract that was more binding and enabled them to bring to court families who failed to fulfill their duties toward the children.

Not all adoptions ended in dispute and running away. Jeremy

Deane, abandoned by both his parents at the age of five, stayed six years in the Dolan Home and was adopted by Mr. Gopher from Chaptico, St. Mary's County. Two years previously, another boy, Cory McDonald, had been adopted by the same gentleman. Cory and Jeremy enjoyed their farm life and were satisfied with their new family, according to the reports of the visitor. The farmer wrote the board of trustees regularly and expressed his satisfaction with the boys as well. Later, the same family applied for another boy, and he also adjusted to the farm. The third boy stayed on after reaching eighteen.

Of the nine children from the sample who were placed out, five stayed on the farms and one girl stayed in a house in Baltimore until they turned eighteen. Three either changed families or returned to the Dolan Home in Baltimore. Wilbur O'Mallie changed families, and Jack Watts, who ran away from a woman in Hartford County, was adopted by his older brother. After a year Chuck Anderson was returned by a woman from Hartford County because he had problems with his eyes. The Dolan Home sent him to a doctor and then entered him at St. Mary's Industrial School.

Although St. Mary's Industrial School for boys accepted delinquents or unruly children, it was not a reformatory. It had been built as an industrial school for Catholic orphans, replacing the former system of binding children out to learn a trade, a system in which many children were overworked, underpaid, and placed in the most difficult unskilled jobs.[46] St. Mary's sought to teach children skills that would enable them to become self-supporting. After two or three years of training, the children were transferred to St. James Home. This institution housed them and found work for them while providing meals, medical aid, an enrichment program in the evening, and Sunday school. Although the children paid toward their keep, the St. James's Home sustained them in periods of unemployment and sickness.[47] The opening of St. Mary's Industrial School to children committed by the court and labeled "delinquent" or "wayward" gave the school financial support from the city. Children whose parents thought they would profit from the program were also accepted. The school required full legal authority over the children, however, and therefore most of the students were committed through the courts.[48]

Seven children of the sample of forty left the Dolan Home to continue their studies at St. Mary's Industrial School. Jay Cole and John Bline came from unremarkable situations. Charles Bower, however, was five years old when Brother Dominic, the principal of St. Mary's, placed him in the Dolan Home. Six years later Brother Dominic sent two six-year-old children to the Dolan Home and asked to take back two of his protégées in exchange, Charles Bower and another boy he had placed in the Dolan Home at about the same time. Ronald Hall's mother had died, and his father, who was sick and unable to take care of him, placed the ten-year-old in the Dolan Home. Two years later, Ronald's father had him committed to St. Mary's Industrial School. Clearly these children were not delinquent. As Barbara Brenzel has already shown, parents who had concerns about their children's future vocation (and sometimes also about their behavior) committed them to industrial schools through magistrates, even when the children were not guilty of any crime. It was enough to declare that the child was difficult to manage to secure the court's permission to enter him into an industrial school.[49] Christopher Gavin, however, may well have been a wayward child. His father abandoned his second wife and left the ten-year-old with a gentleman who accused him of stealing and placed him in the Dolan Home. A year later, Christopher was sent to St. Mary's.

At the Dolan Home, children who reached thirteen were returned to relatives who could provide homes for them, and some of the children who were either full orphans or neglected and abused were placed in Maryland county farms. The Dolan Home did not provide industrial education for its children: the orphanage housed children between ages six and twelve, who were too young for such training. The Dolan Home also sent some children to St. Mary's Industrial School to learn a trade. From the sample of forty children: eight boys were placed in farms and one girl in a household in the city, six boys were sent to St. Mary's Industrial School, and twenty-five children were given to relatives.

Religious Education

At the end of the nineteenth century in Baltimore, religious education seemed to be part of every child's life, though with different emphases and degrees.[50] The charters and bylaws and other records of the three Baltimore institutions in this study give the impression that these orphanages were open in principle to people of all faiths and creeds.[51] In practice, each served a specific religious clientele.

The Samuel Ready School, a self-proclaimed nondenominational school, was open to all children regardless of faith, but recruited its students among Protestant groups, chiefly the Methodist Episcopal church. Other denominations such as Lutherans and Baptists as well as a few Roman Catholics and a few Jewish girls attended,[52] but the religious education provided in the school was Protestant. The policy was to send the young children to the Methodist church across the street from the orphanage on Sundays and holidays and to let the older girls attend churches of their own denominations, provided that teachers were able to accompany them. The stipulation was prompted by concern for the girls' safety, but it evoked anger and protest from at least one of the girls' relatives.

Ten-year-old Agnes Devine was the daughter of a "poor people's doctor" who died insolvent and the granddaughter of a prominent minister, who objected to her attending the Methodist church and demanded that she be allowed to go to the church of her denomination. The child's mother, fearing that the child would be expelled, asked Rowe to ignore the grandfather's demands. Expulsion eventually came, and although a letter attributed it to failure in studies and bad conduct, the documents make clear that the grandfather's attempted intervention was seen as threatening to provoke a flood of similar demands. In a letter to a friend at the Ready School, the child defended her grandfather's position, explaining that he could not understand why Catholic girls were allowed to attend their own church while she could not go to hers. That the letter is in the child's file means that it might never have reached Agnes Devine's friend and that everything related to this delicate and problematic matter was considered important.

The Samuel Ready School was not dependent economically on any religious community, but the people who ran the school were sensitive to religious differences. The constant flow of visitors from various churches, especially ministers, shows that the school tried to cultivate good relations with many denominations beyond the Sunday visits of the girls to churches.

Sunday School classes were conducted by Rowe and the teachers. The children learned to recite long passages from the Bible. Sunday was strictly observed. The children went to church and read only religious books. In inclement weather, services were held in the Samuel Ready chapel. There was an organ, and the girls formed their own choir. Every day the Ready School opened with services organized by the teachers and students and ended with prayers. Indeed the girls at the Ready School were deeply attached to the church, as their letters often express. While on summer vacations they often wrote Rowe about their everyday life. These letters are filled with descriptions of their visits to church and of church picnics and camps.

THE HEBREW ORPHAN ASYLUM declared itself open to any child regardless of religious affiliation but also stated its intention to give Jewish education to Jewish children.[53] As in the case of the Samuel Ready, the H.O.A. was confronted with the problem of imparting religious education to children whose families' religious affiliations and Judaic practices varied. The H.O.A. was founded by Conservative and Reform Jews, but many Russian immigrants it housed during the 1890s came from Orthodox homes.[54] Its origins as an institution founded and conducted by German Jews presented a further problem of language. Services in the 1870s and 1880s in the H.O.A. were at least partly in German. Freudenthal, a German immigrant himself, was a rabbi in a Pennsylvania Jewish congregation for ten years before becoming superintendent of the H.O.A. in 1886. The rabbi spoke and preached to the children in English, but he taught them German as well.[55]

Religious education in the H.O.A. during Freudenthal's regime was taken very seriously. The children studied at public school from nine to three-thirty and at the home from four to six. The H.O.A. curriculum included German, Hebrew, and Judaism. Friday afternoons were dedicated to memorizing and reciting passages of scripture the rabbi required the children to know on Saturday.[56]

The service on Saturday was conducted by Freudenthal and, as Michael Aaronsohn recalls in his memoirs, the rabbi was a convincing preacher who tried to show the children through Biblical stories that their future lay entirely in their hands and depended on hard work and good behavior.[57] Once a year at the end of May or the beginning of June the board of directors, the children's relatives, the Jewish community at large, the mayor, and other important city officials, were invited to final examinations at the home. The event was

advertised in the newspapers and special electric steer-cars of the rail-
way line were allocated to bring the visitors to the hall where the
examinations were held. In the early 1900s, when the H.O.A. had an
auditorium of its own in the gymnasium building, the examinations
were held there. Singing and other performances accompanied the
oral examinations. The school choir was coached by the religious
music teacher, who came once a week during the school year.

When a student excelled in both public and religious education
and wished to pursue a career in religion, the superintendent directed
him to rabbinical studies, as already mentioned. Daniel Lowe and
Enoch Miller, who were sent away for rabbinical studies during the
1890s, went to different schools. While Enoch Miller, who was of
German origin, went to a Reform theological school in Cincinnati,
Daniel Lowe, who was of mixed Russian-German parentage, went to
the Conservative theological school in New York. Both young men
spent their summer vacations at the H.O.A., and Daniel Lowe, being
older and more advanced in his studies in the 1890s, was honored by
the superintendent in being permitted to conduct and preach at some
of the Saturday services to which the board was invited. No doubt
the superintendent attempted to make examples of these theological
students for the other children. Besides the superintendent and the
sacred music teacher, another rabbi came to the institution regularly
in order to prepare the boys for their bar mitzvah. A celebration took
place each time a boy arrived at the age of thirteen, and an announ-
cement in the Jewish newspaper invited the community.

Because they were orphans, the children recited a special prayer
(kaddish) for those who had died. People who either did not have
children to recite the prayer after their death or who wanted their
relatives to be remembered donated money to the orphanage, asking
in return that the children recite that prayer yearly on the date that
they or their relatives died. The children held special services in the
evenings to remember these persons.[58] In 1911 and again in 1916,
Reizenstein asked the board to put an end to special services during
the week because they interfered with other activities, such as gym
classes and manual training. His requests were denied, probably because they represented a deviation from Jewish law.

Reizenstein's superintendency, however, marked a change in religious education. The H.O.A. became more a Reform Jewish school;
it used Reform prayer books, introduced confirmation classes besides

the individual bar mitzvah preparations, and established social connections with the children of Sinai's Reform temple. Classes in religion and Hebrew, which in Freudenthal's era met every day, were held only twice a week, and annual examinations were taken in the presence of the board of directors only. Children who wished to continue their religious studies and proceed to the rabbinate continued to be sent to Cincinnati, however. While Freudenthal was a rabbi who perceived religious education as crucial in shaping the children's world view and morals, Reizenstein paid less attention to this aspect of the children's education.[59]

THEORETICALLY THE Dolan Home was also a self-proclaimed non-denominational orphanage, open to all children of Irish ancestry. But in practice, the Dolan Home was committed to providing Catholic education. Run by the nuns of the Holy Cross Order, the Dolan Home maintained a Catholic religious atmosphere and sent its children only to Catholic schools. An episode recorded in the minute book illustrates the importance of religious education at the home. A married women applied for custody of her brother, a full orphan at the home. The Board was uneasy about giving her the boy because she had married a Protestant. The case was brought before Cardinal Gibbons, the archbishop of Baltimore. Cardinal Gibbons ruled that a family home was more important for the child than Catholic education provided in an institution. The nuns allowed the woman to take her brother home, but they made her promise to provide for his Catholic education.

Although there is no evidence about daily religious life in the Dolan Home, autobiographies of people who grew up in other Catholic orphanages describe a routine filled with religious ceremonies and prayers, strict observance of Catholic holidays, Mass on Sundays, Sunday school, and important ceremonies like the first communion.[60]

The three institutions provided religious education for their children, although each in a different way. The Samuel Ready had a Sunday school, the H.O.A. had a daily religious school (at least until 1911), and the Dolan Home sent its students to a Catholic school. All three orphanages had good connections with the religious establishment (see Chapter Five), and all were run by religious people. A rabbi ran the Jewish and a nun the Catholic institutions, while the

Samuel Ready had a laywoman at its head. The Ready School girls and the Dolan Home children lived in almost complete isolation from religious groups other than their own, but the H.O.A. children, though virtually all of them were Jewish, were exposed to Christian workers and teachers, both in the orphanage and in the public school. The neighborhood where the H.O.A. was located was not Jewish, and the public school children with whom the orphans mingled were non-Jewish as well.[61] The H.O.A. children, who were for the most part from Orthodox Jewish homes, were educated in a Reform orphanage and in public schools with children of other faiths and ethnicity and were therefore exposed to the rest of American society more than their peers in the Samuel Ready School and the Dolan Home were.

Schedule and Extra-Curricular Activities

The Samuel Ready School, the H.O.A., and the Dolan Home kept their children on very busy schedules, partly because at the end of the nineteenth century educators believed that children should be busy. The idea that a child should not be idle was not new. The Puritans perceived idleness as sin, part of the child's corrupt nature. In the first decades of the nineteenth century, reformers found connection between idleness and juvenile delinquency. The Massachusetts General Court, for example, enacted a law in 1826 that allowed confinement of "children who live an idle or desolate life" to a house of reformation. At the end of the nineteenth century the "new psychology"—a response to the idea of evolution—viewed children as "more or less morally blind." G. Stanley Hall, the paramount authority on child psychology, noted that crime increased markedly at the ages of twelve to fourteen and that "adolescence is preeminently the criminal age when most first commitments occur and most vicious careers begin."[62] The solution was to keep children occupied. "The problem of the parent and the teacher," wrote Dr. Rudolph Reeder, the child care reformer, in 1909, "is to bring about such a proper adjustment of the three factors of the above formula—play, work and school—as will leave no room for waste time."[63]

In child care institutions, a planned schedule was not a choice but a necessity. The schedule had to accommodate the different needs and timetables of children of different ages and the adults who took care of them. Typing and shorthand classes, for example, were held at the Samuel Ready School in the evenings to accommodate the teacher's schedule and not interfere with regular school hours. Because some students in these classes might also take music lessons, the music lessons had to be offered on different days. As another example of institutional scheduling, meals at the H.O.A. had to accommodate public school hours, and when School 65 decided to change from two short sessions a day to one long one, the H.O.A. had to rearrange its schedule.

The children's day stretched from six or seven in the morning to between seven and nine in the evening, according to the age group. The mornings included dressing, washing, straightening up rooms, praying, and eating breakfast. Then came school hours. The children of both the H.O.A. and the Dolan Home walked two blocks to school. The children of the H.O.A. spent the morning from nine to twelve, with a fifteen-minute recess, at the school and then returned to the H.O.A. for lunch. At one-thirty, they resumed their studies until three-thirty, with another fifteen-minute recess, and at four started studying again at the H.O.A. school.[64] Evening prayers were said before supper, which was served at six o'clock. Immediately after supper, the children went to study rooms to prepare their homework and read. Manual training and gym classes, vocal music, and drawing lessons took place in the evenings. This tight schedule allowed little space for the chores each child had to do during the day.

Chores were divided among the children according to age and sex. The girls were responsible for cleaning the rooms as well as setting the tables for meals, serving, and cleaning up the dining room. Boys were occupied with working on the little farm, helping the janitor, cleaning the barn, and shoveling coal. Ouside the regular schedule were special events requiring special preparations, which were held almost every month. On Hanukkah and Purim, for example, the children prepared theatrical performances, and Passover required a thorough cleaning of the asylum. Children who worked more than they were required to earned extra money, which was saved for them in a bank account.

With such a schedule, was there any time for play? While the Puritans viewed playing as a sinful waste of time, early twentieth-century Progressives thought it as important as school and work.[65] Playing, they claimed, strengthened the body and contributed to happiness by lifting the spirit. It also taught children how to relate to other children, to cooperate and share. Children who imbibed these values would become good citizens in a democracy, the Progressives believed.[66] Play, for reformers, also meant venting youthful energy away from the streets, where children were lured by vice and crime. But Reformers did not leave play time in the hands of children, for they believed that it should be organized, structured, and supervised by adults.[67] Several institutions providing facilities, equipment, and leadership for children's play time emerged in the era: the kindergarten, the settlement house, the Boy Scouts, and the playground movement. The understanding behind these developments of what play time meant was rather broad; and the word "play" was often used interchangeably with "recreation" to include everything that a child did besides work and school. It could mean athletic competition and playground play but also dancing, music, and manual training.[68] Recreation was also classified by age group and gender.[69]

Russian Jewish immigrant children had limited play time because they were required to earn money at an early age. Young children (as young as nine years old) ran errands, sold newspapers, or peddled in the streets after school.[70] Some children, especially those from Orthodox families, had Hebrew school in the afternoons five days a week. But there was a tendency to drop Hebrew school when children reached thirteen in favor of an afternoon job.[71] Children who did not study in the afternoon and were not otherwise employed roamed the streets in small groups called "gangs" that were involved in fistfighting and petty shoplifting. Those caught persistently breaking the law ended up in reformatories.[72] The constantly growing number of juvenile delinquents worried the leaders of the Jewish community. Between 1910 and 1915 the Hebrew Benevolent Society handled 965 cases of juvenile delinquency (of which 504 persons accused were under sixteen years of age). Dr. Flora Pollack, an H.O.A. physician, described the nights of these youngsters: "I go to Highland town three times a week and late at night on my return I see tiny youngsters swarming in the streets . . . where dope fiends, pickpockets, murderers and white slavers congregate. . . . The value of an 'untouched virgin' [is] from $250 to $1,000."[73] A few children like these were placed in the H.O.A. but did not stay long because the superintendent feared their influence on other children. The Jewish community's response to juvenile delinquency was to embrace the

Reform movement's innovations with regard to children's free time. Jewish reformers organized a kindergarten movement, opened playgrounds in Jewish neighborhood schools, and built a settlement house—the Jewish Educational Alliance.[74]

As Michael Aaronsohn complained with some bitterness, play time in the H.O.A. was limited because the superintendent preferred for the children to read rather than play outside. Although Freudenthal's explanations to the children for not letting them play outside were usually bad weather and concern for their health, they no doubt sensed that he favored intellectual activities over sport. Freudenthal brought many new recreational activities, such as gym classes, manual training, and vocal music, to the H.O.A., but Aaronsohn and his friends did not consider them play. Aaronsohn nevertheless recalled playing war games with swords supplied by the rabbi and baseball and basketball, as well as stealing out of the institution to a nearby swimming pool.[75]

Sundays and the ten weeks of summer were the great play time of the children, when baseball and football teams were formed. The summer also provided a Fourth of July picnic and visits to the amusement park, the zoo, the museum, the theater, and, in later years, the movies. In Reizenstein's era, the H.O.A. school shrank in size and importance, and the children had more time to play in the afternoon. The new superintendent also changed the division of chores by teaching the boys some of the housework traditionally allocated to girls, such as darning socks, making beds, and serving in the dining rooms. He also persuaded the board to buy work-saving devices, like a dishwasher, a vacuum cleaner, and potato peelers, which allowed the girls more leisure time. But Reizenstein also reorganized the summer vacation into full days of study, manual training, domestic science, gardening, and such entertainment as sports, dances, movies, literary clubs, and Boy Scouts. He was attentive to the need for more toys in the playrooms and for children to choose how to occupy their leisure time indoors. Although he believed that children should be systematically supervised by adults and that the children's schedule should be organized all year round, he fought in his own way for more variety in the activities scheduled for the children.

THE GIRLS at the Samuel Ready School did not have much leisure time either. Like the children of the H.O.A., they studied at two schools. The public school curriculum was taught in the morning, and industrial classes in the afternoon. The school emphasized music, vocal and instrumental, and the girls had to practice sometime during the day. Chores had to be done carefully in order to earn precious points that determined the length of each girl's summer vacation. As at the H.O.A., children who worked more than they were required to earned money for their services.[76] Chores included all housework women of the period did. Chores were regarded as part of the girls' education for their future roles as wives and mothers, and performance in them was graded and commented on like performance in any other part of the curriculum. Saturday mornings were dedicated to a thorough cleaning of the premises. The girls could earn extra money by volunteering for chores beyond those assigned.

Routine was broken by special events. Besides holidays, there were occasional field trips to pick flowers, visits to an art gallery, and concerts or lectures at the Peabody. The institution was within walking distance of these cultural sites. The Samuel Ready School not only put an emphasis on refining the girls' cultural tastes but also tried to acquaint them with important social and political events of their time. (At the H.O.A., Freudenthal tried to do the same). Encouraging political and social awareness in young girls in the 1890s seems innovative, considering that politics were not considered part of "women's sphere" at that period.

Summer was divided into two parts; July was spent at the school and August with relatives. The length of time a girl stayed with her relatives depended on the number of points accumulated through work or lost through bad conduct. Summer vacation could vary in length from year to year and child to child. July, however, was spent at the school, though the schedule of activities was less strict than during the school year. An excursion on the bay, nature trips, music, reading, gardening, and housework were the order of the day.

CHILDREN IN the three orphanages received a better education and richer range of activities than they could have expected in their homes. The orphanages monitored their progress in school and encouraged them to improve and excel. The orphanages also attended to their moral, ethical, and cultural well-being by providing them extensive extracurricular enrichment. The multivocational education at the Samuel Ready, the academic pressure at the H.O.A., the vocational education the Dolan Home children enjoyed at St. Mary's Industrial School and St. James's Home are examples of efforts the orphanages made to give their children an edge in life through education. Chapters Five and Six will show that the orphanages also tried to give the children the advantage of connections.

CHAPTER FIVE

Social Life in the Orphanages

THIS CHAPTER examines relationships within the three orphanages studied—relationships among the children, between the children and the staff, and between the children and their families. It also examines ways in which the orphanages related to the world outside—to the children's families, the community, and other institutions concerned with the children's welfare.

The Samuel Ready School operated like a public school with a grade system. Because the school was very small, there were few girls in each grade. Social life was organized along the same lines: children in the same grade at school, and usually in the same age group, shared a room, ate at the same table, and played together.[1] Friendship in this small and intimate world was crucial for survival. Friends were the glue that cemented these girls to the place and helped them overcome homesickness, family troubles, and childhood crises. Attachment to friends is apparent in letters the girls wrote during summer vacations or after they left the institution.

Six-year-old Eva Heinrich cried during her first days at the school. She was a full orphan, the youngest of eight children raised by two aunts. Some weeks after leaving Eva at the Samuel Ready School, her older sister was relieved to know that she had found friends and adjusted to the new environment. In a previous letter, the girl's aunt had expressed concern that Eva tended to be introverted.

Friendships, though they grew from living together for sometimes eight, ten, and twelve years, were not free of difficulty. There was a spirit of competition in the Ready School, and the best students—those who followed the rules and were docile—were favorites among the staff and privileged in other ways. The merit and demerit system of the school, described earlier, affected relations among the children.

The girls received marks each week for conduct and performance of chores and school work. Girls who did not accumulate a ninety-point average were put on the work list, and those with ninety or more points received credits. Credits determined the length of each girl's summer vacation, but they also had money value and could be traded.[2] In this system, cheating on an exam could result in a lower average for the other girls, which meant reduced credits and extra work during the week. The system encouraged honesty, but it also encouraged tattling. Ethel Ellis asked to talk to Rowe personally because she felt she had been discriminated against. One of the girls told Ethel's teacher, Cathy Sullivan (a former student), that Ethel had not done her history homework, which Ethel, of course, denied. Ethel was instructed to complete the homework during math class. Her school average dropped from 85 to 80.4, which not only shortened her summer vacation and forced her to do extra work (because her name was put on the work list) but also jeopardized her position in the school: Girls who did not achieve satisfactory marks and repeatedly appeared on the work list could not be recommended for reappointment the following year. Good, well-behaved students earned long vacations and extra money for candy and small gifts. There was also pressure from staff and sometimes family to associate with the "good girls." In a letter Rowe received from a student who was later expelled, the girl promised to befriend only Gertrude, described as a good girl who would show her the right way. Yet another girl, Andrea Beller, complained to Rowe that her aunt pressed her to follow the example of Monica Kimmel in her choice of double vocation, though Andrea did not feel capable of that. The "good girls" were talented, ambitious, and most likely to be chosen by the teachers or the girls themselves to act in plays, recite poems in a holiday celebration, or organize other social activities.[3]

Tensions between girls sometimes broke out into quarrels involving parents, too. Mellinda Gates, age twelve, on November 24, 1887, was one of the first children to enter the school. Her father was listed as a clerk, but he was also a partner in a business that had financial difficulties. Two years later, in July 1889, Mellinda had an argument with Cathy Sullivan, who implied that Mellinda was socially inferior because her father operated a laundry. Cleaning other people's clothes was considered, at the turn of the century, poor immigrant work, and there was an apologetic tone in the letter Mellinda's father wrote Rowe informing her that he could no longer take laundry from the girls because he was not ready to take the laundry of the offending girl. His daughter, protested the father, was in no way Cathy Sullivan's inferior. Cathy Sullivan's deceased father had been a clerk and her mother a seamstress; these weren't occupations that would bestow superior status on the Sullivan children. But Cathy was a musically gifted, bright, socially active girl. Mellinda Gates did not excel in school and graduated at the age of eighteen without completing even the first year of high school. She was handy with a needle and became a dressmaker.

Attempts to create an elite based on parental occupation or social standing are rare in the records, however. There was a girl from a well-known Maryland family, and there were daughters of ministers, doctors, and high school principals. But these girls were not necessarily excellent students, artistically gifted, or endowed with social skills. These are the qualities that seem to have characterized the leadership of the Samuel Ready society.[4]

The Ready School girls were also divided into older and younger girls and into families. The "large" girls were the seniors, the teenagers (aged approximately fourteen to eighteen years), and the small girls were divided into the juniors (middle-school girls) and the little ones. Little children were those who still played with dolls in the playroom, pretending to be housekeepers or superintendents of a boarding school (aged approximately six to ten years). The juniors were in-between; they went to the library in "playtime" but were not yet allowed to go to the church they belonged to, or wished to attend, rather than the Methodist church across the street.

Seniors had privileges such as sleeping late, taking classes outside the institution, sleeping over when invited by a teacher from an outside institution, and shopping for the whole school for Christmas. The older girls had more responsibilities than the younger ones. From the beginning, Rowe organized an "adoption" system in which every teenage girl was responsible for a little one. The older girl took care of the younger one on museum visits, or field trips and sometimes read her stories at bedtime. Family ties among siblings at the school reinforced such bonds between older and younger girls.

An interesting relationship existed between junior (middle-school) and senior (high-school) students. Every second Friday evening the girls prepared an entertainment. Sometimes the seniors invited the juniors to their party, and sometimes the juniors prepared the evening for the seniors. Criticism of the entertainment appeared in the *Ready Record* and was often harsh. The seniors criticized a singer who did not know the words of a song, grammatical mistakes, or errors in playing the piano and other flaws. Juniors had to live up to the seniors' standards in order to gain respect.

The system of three separate age groups in the Ready School allowed the two younger groups to look up to the girls in the next group as role models. The division into dormitories and classes and the individual allocation of privileges did not create antagonisms among the groups nor were the older girls cruel toward the younger ones. The reasons for the relatively healthy atmosphere of the school might have been the presence of siblings, the school's small size, and the fact that there was not much unsupervised time in which aversive behavior could occur. The encouragement of competition among the girls probably mitigated much of the cruelty exercised by older children toward younger ones in other child care institutions.[5]

It would be a mistake, however, to view relationships in the Samuel Ready School as entirely harmonious. On April 1, 1892, one of the juniors described in the *Ready Record* a make-believe game played by the younger girls in the playroom.

A New Establishment
It is called the Hat and Hopwood boarding school and has now eighteen scholars. . . . Some of the children have pretty clothes, which their mothers bring them from home, for all their dresses are furnished by the parents.

Clothes at the Ready School could be furnished by relatives. As a result some girls left the school with eleven dresses (not counting skirts and shirts), and others left with just two. The enthusiasm and excitement with which new items of clothing were received and reported in the *Ready Record* and in the girls' personal letters underlines their importance. Differences between girls on this subject could create jealousy. In two students' files are copies of letters Rowe wrote to guardians asking them not to send any more clothes. She pointed out that some girls at the school were completely dependent on the school for clothes and suggested that girls with relatives able to provide an abundance of clothes perhaps did not need the school at all. She allowed one dress to be brought to a girl from home but no more because of the effect on other children. Jealousy on account of clothes was clearly a problem, and Rowe tried to mitigate it. Other differences producing similar friction were summer vacations. Some girls enjoyed vacations in the country among relatives and friends with special entertainments such as camps and excursions on boats, while other girls spent vacations at school or in the city. Jealousy of economic advantages probably exists in every children's society, but it was perhaps pronounced in an orphanage, where those advantages carried emotional value. Clothes and summer vacations symbolized relatives' attention and affection.

Rowe, who was probably aware of such differences among the girls and the feelings they created, might have but did not change the program. Uniforms might have eliminated clothing differences, and a standard short summer vacation might have removed the second difference. Rowe, however, put a heavy emphasis on maintaining relations between the children and their families. She scheduled a special hour during the school day for the girls to write home. She herself informed parents of their children's progress. She organized a display of the girls' work on the monthly visiting day. The summer vacation and clothes received from relatives contributed to the bond between children and their families.

But there was most likely another reason why Rowe let her girls have long summer vacations. For Rowe the Samuel Ready School was not so much an orphanage as a boarding school. On that score she was following the model of Colonel Allan, the principal of the McDonogh School. As early as 1883 Allan urged McDonogh's trustees to open the school to day students. By having outside students, McDonogh could become another Eton, the famous English school that started as an institution for poor children.[6] Poor students could benefit from mingling with well-to-do students with connections who could help them find work when they graduated. The only difference between the day students and the poor orphans would be the summer vacation—day students would have vacations at Christmas and during two months in the summer. Although, Colonel Allan's idea was not endorsed by McDonogh's trustees, it left its mark on Helen J. Rowe. She kept referring to the Ready School as a boarding school and treated students accordingly.[7] The short Christmas vacation and the long summer break were part of her policy of making the students feel that they were boarders in a fine school.

Another possible reason for the school's relatively long summer vacation probably had to do with its location in Baltimore City. The humid, hot, foul-smelling city was a health hazard during the summer. Citizens who could afford to usually moved to the country or traveled north for the season. The girls' files show that many spent the vacation in the country, in the fresh air, with nature excursions, camping, and sport activities.[8]

While some boarding schools had uniforms, Rowe seemed to regard clothes not only as means to develop personal taste but also as an incentive for the girls to learn to make their own garments. Girls at the Samuel Ready School who made one dress well could proceed to make another, if time permitted. In other words, Rowe believed that girls would be better motivated to sew well if they could choose what they would make and wear. In assessing free choice of clothing and vacation venue, the benefits to the girls' health, family ties, self-perception, and individuality outweighed the disadvantages of jealousy among schoolmates.

AT THE Hebrew Orphan Asylum, children were divided into age groups, with a special status for seniors. There were a spirit of competition and a heavy emphasis on excellence, and many children had siblings at the institution. Unlike the Samuel Ready School, the H.O.A. had both boys and girls. Girls studied and played in their own playroom and did not mingle with the boys. Boys and girls met on the playground, while doing chores, in the dining room, in the public school, in the Hebrew school, and in the library. They saw each other all day, yet they formed two separate societies. Siblings, however, even of different sexes, met more frequently and shared deep emotional bonds.[9]

Any suggestion of intimacy between the sexes was considered improper, and offenders were sometimes removed from the H.O.A.[10] This code of behavior was imposed on the children of the Dolan Home and the Samuel Ready as well, and offenders were liable to the same severity of punishment. When a Samuel Ready girl exchanged a few words with a boy in church, giggled, and turned her head to look at him during prayers, Rowe wrote a sharp letter to her mother, adding that an investigation revealed that the girl was behaving in the same manner at her home. The girl denied the allegation and, after promising to mend her ways, was allowed to stay at the school. Three sisters at the Dolan Home were sent home because the two older ones "could not be kept away from the boys in the neighborhood." The behavior of a newcomer to the H.O.A. enraged the superintendent so much that when the board placed her in a foster home, his language had to be modified for the records to protect her reputation. Separation of the sexes, especially for teenagers, was the norm at the turn of the century, but it seems to have been strictly enforced in the orphanages both to protect the institutions' reputation and to prevent undesirable behavior from spreading among the orphans.[11] Boys and girls frequently met in the literary clubs formed at the H.O.A. during the 1910s and at entertainment and social activities, especially during the summer vacation, holidays, and weekends, but adults supervised these gatherings closely.[12]

Mischief occurred nontheless. Aaronsohn described social life at the H.O.A.:

On the surface, the children seemed to be decorously docile and virtuous. . . . Not withstanding within the ranks of the meticulously regulated lives of these wards, there emerged all the mischievous vices so repugnant to the enlightened and ethical man: lying, cheating, toadying, bribery, bullying, torture, self-abuse, treachery, billingsgate and in some instances, sex deviation.[13]

In other words, with all the supervision and regulation, this society of children was in some respects like any other. The H.O.A. transformed the children from "waifs to wards" but not into angels.

Supervisors of the children's activities at the H.O.A. were called monitors. The system of monitoring was introduced by Freudenthal and was probably modeled after English boarding schools in which older boys supervised and coached younger ones during study hours. In the H.O.A. monitors were sometimes students who had graduated from high school and were staying in the asylum while completing further study. Having been adolescents at the institution themselves, they knew children's vices well and acted upon them harshly.[14] As a teenager, Aaronsohn despised the monitors' intrusion into the children's lives and rebelled against it shortly after Freudenthal died. But he and three friends found themselves in the minority, and for days the other children and the monitors battled against them. Rabbi Miller (a former graduate and Freudenthal's substitute) finally offered a compromise in which the four rebels were dismissed from the monitors' authority. Later the H.O.A. employed only young adults as monitors.[15] At the Samuel Ready School, Rowe also employed former students as supervisors with responsibilities similar to those of the H.O.A.'s monitors, but Rowe called her supervisors teachers' assistants.

In 1916, influenced by new trends in child care institutions, Dr. Reizenstein introduced a "children's republic." In other words, he established a mechanism of self-government at the H.O.A. Children who broke the rules were judged and punished by a court of their peers.[16] As LeRoy Ashby has pointed out, the sentences of the children's courts were harsher than the superintendent's punishments.[17] Self-government also involved fund-raising. The children ran their own candy shop and financed their own parties. Later they published a monthly named "The Monitor." But as former H.O.A. ward Hyman Warsaw pointed out, the children's republic was merely a clever device of Reizenstein's for controlling the children.

An examination of the McDonogh School, where social life was largely uncontrolled, sheds light on the needs and dilemmas of the H.O.A. Dr. Rudolph Reeder of the New York Orphan Asylum, who in 1914 was invited to critique McDonogh, sharply criticized the school's "free" system. Reeder recommended that the school separate the young boys from the teenagers or stop admitting young boys altogether. There was a tradition of "torment" at McDonogh by which the older boys controlled the young ones. The boys ranged in age only from ten to seventeen, but they were carefully selected and could always be sent home if there was any serious breach in discipline.[18] The children of the H.O.A. were not selected, and some came to the institution with a rich street-life experience. Aaronsohn emphasized the difference between his life in the H.O.A. and his early childhood in East Baltimore. As a child he "knew nothing of parental solicitude or supervision." His father had been too preoccupied with his daily toil and his frequent illnesses to keep track of the boy's wild roamings through the streets and along the wharves near their tenement flat.[19] While Aaronsohn came to the H.O.A. when he was only seven years old, others entered at ten or eleven and brought street language and behavior with them. Although Aaronsohn complained about the harshness of the monitors (as did several other graduates who were interviewed), their supervision to some degree prevented a tyranny of bullies. It seems that giving boys freedom to create their own society and giving seniors or young graduates responsibilities over the young were both problematic.

A child could gain prominence among his peers in studies or in sports. The gym and the baseball diamond were centers of competition for social status. Seniors, who studied in high schools in the city, were revered and envied not only for their academic achievements but also for being able to tell the youngsters about sports activities outside the orphanage.[20] During the summer, the boys played team sports and competed fiercely for positions on the H.O.A. teams, which played against teams representing other institutions. The principal rivals of the H.O.A. were the boys of the "Russian" orphanage, and intense preparation and anticipation preceded the annual athletic matches between the two institutions.

Girls at the H.O.A. were more peaceful, although as with any group of children some girls were at the center of activities and others were at the edges. Some H.O.A. children were slightly retarded or dull, Ilene B. recalled. Esther D., for example, could hardly talk but could crochet beautifully. The girls never took advantage of these children but accepted them as they were. In one of his reports, Reizenstein asked the directors to find a suitable way of handling retarded children, whose number reached 30 (out of 130) in 1912. The directors provided a special teacher, and these children stopped attending public school but studied from that time on at the H.O.A. Other children with special needs (like little Libby, who was born deaf) were sent to special schools but lived at the H.O.A. among their siblings and fellow orphans, according to Mr. Benjamin.

Ilene B. recalled two little girls who arrived at the H.O.A. dressed in fur coats. She had never seen children dressed so grandly, and the event was engraved in her mind. But other children from wealthy or middle-class families were occasionally sheltered at the H.O.A. In November 1895, Freudenthal reported that his brother paid for his children to be kept there. Although the records do not specify why Freudenthal's nephews were admitted, it is likely that they needed a temporary home. From time to time the H.O.A. had temporary boarders who stayed until their parents recovered from illness or until another home could be found for them. Such temporary residents included twelve full orphans rescued from the pogroms in Russia and brought to the United States by the Baltimore Jewish community. The orphans had no relatives in the United States and they stayed at the H.O.A. until adopting families in the city were found. Within a few days of their arrival, these children became fully integrated in the children's social structure, recalled Aaronsohn.[21]

A custom that passed through "generations" of H.O.A. children was name-calling, which usually pointed to children's weaknesses and physical features. Although superintendents fought against name-calling, which probably hurt some children's feelings, the practice remained part of the orphanage tradition.[22] Nicknaming was another popular custom. When Ilene B. was asked what her nickname was, she explained that being a shy and quiet girl she had not been given one. Nicknames were apparently reserved for those at the center of institutional life. In 1968, when Bernice S. wrote a letter to graduates of the H.O.A. about an upcoming reunion, she reminded them who she was by using her nickname. She was not sure anybody would recognize her real name.

THERE IS not much evidence about the social life of the Dolan Home, but some characteristics can be assumed. The separation of boys and girls was strictly observed. The Dolan Home had only young children aged six to twelve, and most of them were boys. Although its boys shared a playground with the St. Patrick's Orphanage, there is no evidence that they played together. Since the Dolan Home had between thirty and forty children at most, it was probably impossible to divide them into separate age groups; the groups would have been exceedingly small and the choice of friends very limited. Catholic schools at that time put a high premium on good conduct and religious observance, and it is reasonable to assume that the sisters highly esteemed the obedient and devout child.[23] It is not known whether these were the qualities that the children valued most.

The H.O.A. and the Samuel Ready School had different kinds of populations. The Samuel Ready had a more homogeneous body of residents. The H.O.A. was more diversified in terms of gender, family background, and children's intellectual capabilities. Yet the problems children at the two institutions faced were remarkably similar: adjustment to strict discipline, tight schedules with little unstructured leisure time, and limited private space. Homesickness, peer pressure, and competitiveness no doubt contributed to tense relationships—

tensions that were at times ameliorated and at time exacerbated by the supervision exercised by older orphans over their juniors. Such a dynamic, one might argue, would characterize any institutional community of children, whether at an orphanage or an elite boarding school. Still, life in orphanages had unique characteristics. Orphans' pain and suffering created a sense of comraderie that was manifested in the mature and gentle way the H.O.A. children treated special children in their society and the long-lasting bonds formed among the Samuel Ready girls. The phrase so often used by orphans—"we were in the same boat"—pointed to feelings of equality in suffering, before the law (or the institutions' rules and regulations), and in opportunity to rise from the bottom.

The Children and the Superintendent

"The superintendent and his wife, the matron, the legally constituted officials of the Asylum, were conscientious in their devotion to duty. Their relationship toward its ward was that of foster parents. They were not guardians."[24] This description of Dr. Freudenthal and his wife by one of his former "foster children" reveals part of the special relationship that developed between the superintendent and the children.

Most of the children of the H.O.A. had at least one biological parent living and sometimes other relatives who were interested in their well-being.[25] Yet the superintendent and his wife were their legal custodians, in charge of their education and health and determining, to a great measure, their future.[26] But Freudenthal and his wife were not just administrators who provided shelter and education for these children; they and their families lived in the H.O.A. and were awakened at night when a child was sick. It was they who called a doctor and accompanied the child to the hospital, if necessary. When problems arose in school, the superintendent talked to the teachers and the principal. He knew each child's tendency, talents, and weaknesses and was there to encourage and develop the talents or correct the mistakes. Although Freudenthal was a busy administrator, he was involved in the details of the children's everyday lives.

The children of the H.O.A. were not accustomed to such parenting. Their mothers and fathers had toiled all day and could not supervise their activities. Freudenthal was their teacher and rabbi, as well as a foster parent. His preaching on Saturdays was engraved in their minds many years after they left the orphanage. He used the portion of the Bible read each Saturday to speak to the children's problems. When a child broke the rules, it was not the punishment that hurt most, but the lecture the rabbi gave before or after the punishment. Freudenthal's moralistic tone reduced the culprit to a "criminal" among the children.[27] The lesson would not be quickly forgotten. Freudenthal also clearly cared for the children: his faith in them gave the confidence that they needed to believe in their own abilities.[28]

But Freudenthal was not an informal person. He was a German Jewish aristocrat, a learned man who commanded awe and respect. The children knew his kindness and warmth but also his discipline; he expected them to behave like well-mannered, upper-middle-class children, regardless of their background.[29]

An incident described in one of Aaronsohn's books exemplifies Freudenthal's attitude toward the children. Freudenthal enters the playroom and finds the hero reading a forbidden "dime novel." He summons the boy to his office, where "the master brought out his whip."

> He placed the lad in front of him while he sat in his swivel chair. "Put out your hand," the Rabbi commanded. . . . Slash, Slash! The whip descended. The voice of the rabbi rose above the whimpers of the youth. "A fine Bar Mitzva you are! What kind of a rabbi will you turn out to be? You know I want to send you to Cincinnati to be trained as a rabbi. Haven't I told you not to read 'dime novels'? Let this be a lesson to you."[30]

The crime and punishment reveal some of Freudenthal's pedagogical traits. Upper-middle-class parents in that era censored and monitored their children's reading. While Aaronsohn did not understand the great sin of reading dime novels, educators at that time considered the genre inappropriate for children.[31] The punishment also reveals the Jewish side of the rabbi's educational philosophy. Jewish laws forbid beating an orphan for any reason except one related to education and specify that only a rabbi or a teacher may administer such a punishment.[32] The rabbi used the punishment to remind the child that he was already "a man," according to Jewish law, but also that

he should become a leader in the Jewish community and should behave accordingly. Aaronsohn, in retrospect, attributed Freudenthal's
strictness in this matter to his German background.[33] German Jews
and Germans generally were often strict disciplinarians as parents,
demanding obedience, diligence, punctuality, neatness, and politeness
from their children, according to Jacob Beser. To be sure, Russian
Jews did not tolerate disobedience or impudence, but they were often
more lenient in regard to manners and discipline, according to Wilfred S. and Harry S.

The question of corporal punishment of children was much debated in Baltimore at this time. In 1906, when a child at McDonogh
complained about whipping to the Society for Preventing Cruelty to
Children, a committee was formed whose final report stated: "Although city schools are better taught without corporal punishment
[which had been officially abolished] McDonogh represents the
Home and the school in one and to deprive it of the power to punish
even in extreme cases a breach of discipline might easily result in
harm to the school as well as to the indifferent pupil."[34] In a report,
Freudenthal explained that the board of directors and he were opposed to corporal punishment, yet he obviously used whipping from
time to time.

Girls had fewer discipline problems than boys. Undeterred by the
superintendent's punishments, boys found their way to athletic com-
petitions outside the H.O.A., picked fruit from neighbors' trees, and
committed other mischievous deeds in spite of warnings and preach-
ings.[35] Girls in the H.O.A. were more obedient and, according to a
Baltimore American report from May 20, 1894, were particularly
attached to Freudenthal. "On several occasions discharged girls have
so bitterly wept for Father Freudenthal, as the children like to call
him, that those who volunteered to give them homes have been
obliged to send for the superintendent."[36] In May 1910, on Exercise
Day, which officially ended the academic year at the H.O.A., before
an audience of parents, relatives, children, trustees, and official
guests, Dr. Freudenthal suffered a fatal stroke. For weeks the children could not be consoled. "We both lost a father," said Freudenthal's daughter to Aaronsohn's crying sister in an effort to console
her.[37] Many came to pay last respects to the man who had dedicated
twenty-four years of his life to raising the community's orphans.

In August 1917, seven years after Freudenthal's death, the girls at the H.O.A. gave a birthday party for Mrs. Freudenthal. In his monthly report Reizenstein described the event: "On Sunday, August 26, the two girls' groups of the Children's Republic presented an enjoyable play entitled 'Women Who Did,' in honor of Mrs. Freudenthal's birthday. The girls planned and made their costumes practically unaided and produced the play very creditably with very little assistance. The relatives and friends of the children were invited to be present." Since not many children stayed eight years or more in the H.O.A., it is not likely that many girls knew Mrs. Freudenthal as a matron. It is more reasonable to assume that the girls honored Mrs. Freudenthal because she and her children maintained close ties with the institution after Dr. Freudenthal's death. Evidences of these connections are the donations of candy and other goods noted in the superintendent's reports during the 1910s.

One of Freudenthal's former foster children volunteered to serve as acting superintendent until a candidate for the post could be found.[38] The young alumnus, a rabbi in Philadelphia, had served only two months when a new superintendent was chosen. The board wanted to pay him for his service. The Rabbi refused, writing the president of the board: "I would now beg of you and through you, of the Board that you permit me to have this happiness throughout life. As I put it before, an exceptional opportunity had come to me of doing a special service for a parent of mine. Can a child think of receiving anything for doing some service for a parent?" Closing his letter, the young alumnus asked the board not to mention his letter: "The less publicity this is given the deeper is my pleasure." The young rabbi and his four siblings had been raised by Freudenthal.

The new superintendent of the H.O.A., Dr. Reizenstein, was not welcomed by the children. Although he was an experienced social worker and a man of progressive ideas who tried to bring the H.O.A. the latest innovations in child care, he did not gain the children's sympathy and affection.[39] A few weeks after Reizenstein initiated his reforms the children rebelled and openly mocked him, according to Simon Z. Aaronsohn, who sided with the "Reformer" (Reizenstein's nickname in the H.O.A.) because he was the "underdog," explained the rebellion as the inability of the children to adjust to freedom and informality.[40] But the children did not rebel against the informal behavior of the young rabbi who served in the interim period and who was not an authoritarian figure.[41] It seems that Reizenstein lacked affection and kindness toward children. He knew what professionals considered best for them but did not know how to reach them personally.

Reizenstein introduced a disciplinarian regime and stayed aloof from the children. They feared the man even though he did not use corporal punishment. His wife, the matron, was the one who administered those punishments, spanking the culprits with an open hand. Dislike for the superintendent, however, stemmed from the man's strictness on the one hand and his lack of warmth on the other.[42] His own children fared no better. Reizenstein's eldest son, Dr. Milton Reizenstein, described his father as a scholar who was especially interested in psychology and a man who sternly drove both his own children and the children of the H.O.A. to academic achievement.[43]

One might find in the contrast between Freudenthal and Reizenstein the difference between amateur and professional, between someone who views work with children as a vocation and a professional social worker who brings rules and regulations to the work but not always his heart. But this explanation, which would be supported by Roy Lubove's analysis of career social workers in *The Professional Altruist*, fails when the next superintendent of the H.O.A. is considered.[44] Michael Sharlitt, a teacher, social worker, and graduate of a Jewish orphanage in New York, maintained discipline and also won the love and affection of the children.[45] He came to the H.O.A. in 1918 and left two years later to become superintendent of the Cleveland Jewish Orphanage, one of the largest and most modern child-care institutions in this era.[46] Jacob Kepecs, who was the next superintendent and, also a professional social worker, again commanded the children's obedience and respect. He wrote on questions of children's social welfare and advocated foster care instead of institutions.[47] Of the four superintendents of the H.O.A. from the 1880s to the late 1920s, when the system changed completely to foster care, three had close relations with the children. Two of the three were professionals.[48]

One cloud in the memory of our happy childhood at the Ready was the time when our dear Miss Rowe lay ill for weeks with typhoid fever, and we never knew what morning we might wake to find she had gone from us. I don't believe she has ever really known how anxious her girls young as they were felt about her and now with what joy we received the message that she would get well. How could we have spared her? To us the Ready is Miss Rowe, not as the principal of whom we stood in awe, but just the biggest and best girls of us.[49]

Rowe's relationships with her girls were in many ways similar to Freudenthal's relations with his children. She was a stern, demanding woman with upper-middle-class aspirations for her girls. But she also established warm relations with them. When the Ready School was small, the relationships were close. Rowe was the girls' Sunday school teacher; she read them stories and the news every day and followed each girl's progress closely. Every week they waited for her to tell them how many points each girl had scored. Like Freudenthal, she was everywhere, watching carefully every detail of the girls' education, discussing their future vocations with them, and encouraging them to excel. She knew when to be soft and kind and when to be tough and strict.

One of the girls recalled how Rowe helped a homesick girl on her first day at the Samuel Ready. Four girls came on the same day, December 6, 1887, three of them from the same family. The little one cried incessantly. "Teachers and pupils tried every persuasion, but nothing availed until Miss Rowe sprang the grand surprise," recalled the girl's older sister:

> None of us had ever heard of the ancient Dutch custom of celebrating St. Nicholas eve, so you may imagine our surprise when we were taken into the library—now the teachers' sitting room—to see St. Nicholas himself, fat and jolly come down out of the fire place. His back was bent beneath the weight of a great bolster case filled with all sorts of goodies—apples, candies, peanuts, cookies—and before one could say Jack Robinson all the children—Johnny included [the little girl's nickname]—were laughing with delight at his jokes and pranks.[50]

The woman who wrote this piece for the twenty-fifth anniversary of the Samuel Ready added that although her sister grew up to become a nurse and had comforted many homesick boys and girls in the hospital, "still she marvels at the kindness and patience with which Miss Rowe treated a homesick child." Another girl recalled "the treat of a trip down town with Miss Rowe who never forgot a girl's sweet-tooth."[51] Rowe, like Freudenthal, also knew the difference between routine "naughtiness" and a serious breach of discipline. Picking green pears from the trees, for example, resulted in being put on the work list and being treated with generous doses of castor oil. At the H.O.A. these "sins" were routinely committed, and the punishment was probably spanking. Reading through the Samuel Ready students' files, one can detect the tough, strict lady who could also be lenient. Her drive to make the orphanage like a boarding school that did credit to its graduates dictated many of her harsh decisions. She believed that the girls at Samuel Ready had a golden opportunity to receive an excellent education free of charge. This view influenced her decision to reject or dismiss girls who did not meet her standards.[52] Freudenthal, of course, could not send underachievers home nor could he dismiss a child until there was a long period of maladjustment.

Because some decisions not to reappoint were made at the end of year when the girls were on vacation, reactions came in summer letters to Rowe. The frankness that marked the girls' questions and Rowe's explanations reveal an openness between the superintendent and her charges. Although reformers urged educators to explain their decisions and motives to children, it was still considered daring for children to inquire about an adult's decision and unusual to receive an explanation about matters that did not directly pertain to them.[53] But the letters between Rowe and the children suggest an uncommon familiarity. In addition to asking direct questions, the children spoke of family members without identifying them. It is clear that Rowe recognized the names of most of the people in the girls' lives.

The girls' relationship with Rowe was far from strictly formal, although it was probably always respectful. Children came to Rowe to complain about injustice or to ask for a special treat like a short trip to a nearby flower field or taffy for dinner. Returning from a vacation in Atlantic City, Rowe brought the girls little china dolls and sat down to tell them her own impression of the place. At other times she surprised them with tickets to a theater show or a concert.

Yet when a girl disappointed her, Rowe could be harsh. To fall from her grace was traumatic and sometimes ended a child's stay at the school. Twelve-year-old Lee Fleet was at Samuel Ready six years. When her older sister graduated, Lee came back to school in September feeling lonely and homesick. She ran away but returned the same day. Among eighty children's files examined, this was the only case of running away. The rules about running away were like the ones at McDonogh: it spelled expulsion, and Rowe in this instance observed the rules strictly. Lee's older sister, the Ready graduate, wrote Rowe apologizing for her sister's disgraceful and hasty act and pleaded with her to forgive the girl. In response, Rowe explained that the act was serious because it set an example for the younger girls and therefore the punishment should be severe. The family tried to enroll the twelve-year-old in a small orphanage that had only twenty girls, hoping she would feel better there. The superintendent of that orphanage asked Rowe for a recommendation, expressing surprise that the girl was expelled for one act of running away. Rowe's reply described the girl as having a long history of behavioral problems. In view of the family's meager circumstances and the fact that the child was already expelled from Ready, the letter has a somewhat vindictive tone.

The correspondence in these sisters' files and others reveals the extent of the girls' dependence on Rowe's relationship with them. Once a girl failed to rise to Rowe's expectations or disappointed her, she lost favor, respect and help.

The girls' relations with Rowe varied in their intensity and duration. Some girls in their letters to Rowe declared themselves to be her little girls, and others were more formal. Relationships with the superintendent tended to become close as the girls entered high school and started vocational training. Girls who stayed that long at the Samuel Ready often maintained contact until Rowe's death; others less attached stopped writing or visiting after a while (see Chapter Six). When the Samuel Ready School celebrated its twenty-fifth anniversary, some alumnae told the students how fortunate they were to have new facilities, improved equipment, and the new opportunities open to girls in the 1910s, but they added that the girls of the 1890s had enjoyed very intimate relations with Rowe and the teachers. The atmosphere of a small, warm, busy family no longer prevailed when the Samuel Ready expanded to include seventy-five students.[54]

Freudenthal and Rowe had much in common in terms of outlook, manners, and blend of kindness and strictness. Both were religious people who believed that through education, discipline, and motivation their orphans could become self-supporting, well-educated, respectable people.[55] In both cases, the discipline was perhaps excessive at times. Freudenthal whipped a child for reading a dime novel, and

Rowe expelled a homesick girl who ran away for part of a day. Their strictness, however, was consistent with the high level of discipline in middle- and upper-middle-class homes at that time and reflected the fact that they not only were foster parents but also ran institutions in which all children had to be treated equally. The fact that the children knew the rules and the consequences of breaking them contributed to the stability of life in the institution and the children's adjustment to it. As several interviews and autobiographies point out, the rules were well defined and there was no discrimination.

The Children and the Staff

The small size of the Samuel Ready School's student population created a family atmosphere in which the teachers took part. Some of the teachers lived at the school and, partly perhaps because most of them were single, regarded the girls as their own family. The children were very attached to their teachers, as numerous references in their letters show.[56]

Three teachers in particular were popular. Clara H. Steiner, who taught general studies (math, literature, history, geography, English) and came to the school at its beginning, gained the children's respect for her expertise. Years later the girls, many of whom followed her in her profession, commented that she had endeared history and literature to her pupils.[57] The importance of literature, in particular, in the girls' lives testifies to the success of Miss Steiner. Every two weeks when they organized a Friday evening performance, poems or a short story was part of the program. And The *Ready Record* frequently carried articles on literary figures and books.[58] Miss Mary S. Yeakle, like Rowe and Clara Steiner, was a graduate of the Frederick Seminary. She taught at the Frederick public school before she accepted Helen Rowe's offer to come to the Samuel Ready School. The general studies department was already occupied by Clara Steiner; Mary Yeakle consented to become sewing teacher as well as school nurse and organist for the Sunday school. Besides the love and affection conveyed in the students' letters, there was also appreciation of her competence. Years after graduation they still consulted her taste regarding clothes and materials and sought her advice for patterns and instruction.

Mrs. Agnes O. Tilghman, the housekeeper who taught cooking

and Sunday school, was the third teacher the girls expressed affection for in their letters.[59]

Other teachers who did not reside at the school left their mark on its life and created warm relations with the students. Miss Cobb, a music teacher, was among them. The *Ready Record* reports that she donated pictures of great composers to the classroom and invited the girls to a "musicale" at her home. One July evening, the girls prepared a recital to surprise the music teacher with when classes resumed in September. They chose the pieces and the performers and practiced in their free time. The success of the music teacher was also apparent in the musical clubs the girls organized for themselves and the number of students who played musical instruments or sang.[60]

The attachment of teachers to the institution was manifested in the length of time they served at the school. Some spent their entire career at the Samuel Ready.[61] The trend of long-term teachers continued well into the 1950s. The school frequently employed its own graduates,[62] some of whom started as teachers' assistants, helpers, or matrons and gradually assumed senior teaching positions. After 1900 in the period studied, the teaching staff consisted solely of Samuel Ready School graduates and the teachers who had been there since the school's beginning. The graduates were an inspiration for the girls and had warm and affectionate relations with them. A girl wrote Rowe that she was impatiently awaiting the visit of two teachers' assistants, both Ready graduates, to her house during the summer vacation. Warm relations between teachers and students did not, however, mean loose discipline or informal behavior on the part of a teacher. Instead, it meant mutual respect. Students consulted their teachers and trusted their advice and were eager to satisfy their demands and win their appreciation and respect in return.[63]

Because H.O.A. children attended public schools, their principal teachers did not reside at the orphanage. Vocational teachers, however, came to the institution in the afternoons. As at Samuel Ready, some of them taught at the H.O.A. for years and left their mark on the institution's life. The manual training teacher, Mr. Steiner, was one. Among former H.O.A. students interviewed were some who still had crafts made in Mr. Steiner's classes in their homes. Three men had stools (one with a beautiful engraved pattern), and a woman had an engraved box and two watercolor pictures that she had painted and the teacher framed as a present for her.

Teachers were not the only persons to whom the H.O.A. children felt close. Everyone, said Ilene B., had an adult whom he or she liked best and who in return indulged the child. Ilene B. was very fond of the watchman and helped him close the gates and lock the doors. A special honor was bestowed on her when he let her use the keys. One night, she recalled, she felt something near her cheek; the watchman had left her a bag of peaches. Simon Z. liked the gym teacher and was given the honor of keeping the gym clean and in order. Simon Z. was also one of the many boys who roamed around the kitchen, chitchatting, helping a little, and receiving special treats from the children's beloved cook. Aaronsohn's idol at the H.O.A. was the janitor, whose work was taking care of the stove and heating system, the plumbing, and the garden. Aaronsohn was the janitor's helper and followed him wherever he worked.[64]

Not all staff members at the H.O.A. gained the children's affection. When Mildred's regime began in the kitchen and the children discovered that she did not meet the standards of cooking Mary had set, "poor Mildred" became an object of the children's teasing, Simon Z. recalled. Being an adult in a well-ordered and disciplined children's institution did not automatically confer authority or respect. Respect and affection had to be earned.

I found no indications in the children's files or the *Ready Record* of what relations were like between the girls and the nonteaching staff at the Samuel Ready School.

The teachers at the Dolan Home lived near the orphanage in the complex of buildings that consisted of the two orphanages and two schools adjacent to St. Patrick's Church. Staff members of the home included a hired laundress and the two sisters who cleaned and cooked. That the children were fond of the sisters is clear from their visits to the home after they were bound out. But relations between the children and the sisters during their stay at the orphanage cannot be established from the scant resources available.

Long years of service, dedication to work, and affection toward the children characterized some staff members in all three orphanages. As a result, children became attached to staff members and looked up to them as role models. The staff contributed to the stability of all three institutions, providing continuity of care and satisfying the children's need for attention and affection.

The three orphanages differed in staff composition and function.

At the Samuel Ready School, three middle-class, educated women filled all teaching and nursing positions and lived on the premises. Their presence added to the fine boarding school atmosphere that the institution wished to create. The Dolan Home had, in addition to the superintendent, two nuns who lived with the children and attended to their needs. They helped to preserve the religious atmosphere of the institution. At the H.O.A., in addition to the superintendent and his wife, who was the matron, other staff members were dayworkers from the nearby village, vocational teachers who came two afternoons a week, and the cook, the seamstress, and the laundry women, who lived in the orphanage. The latter were either H.O.A. graduates or Christian working-class and immigrant women. While the staff at the H.O.A. might not have reinforced the upper-middle-class behavior or Jewish values the superintendent and his wife modeled, the children recalled them as affectionate, sensitive, and friendly persons.

The Children and Their Relatives

Only a small number of children at the H.O.A, the Samuel Ready School, and the Dolan Home had no parents or other relatives— uncles, aunts, grandparents, siblings. Although relations between the children and their families varied, generalizations can be made on the basis of the groups of children studied.

Siblings at the H.O.A. in most cases had close relationships. Simon Z. had very affectionate relations with his older sister and was also close to his two brothers. The four children of the Z. family had a living mother who was hospitalized and whom they never saw after entering the institution. When the first boy left the H.O.A., the superintendent asked the board of directors to try to find him a room with his sister, who was already working as a nurse. Simon Z. remembered that until he married, his sister used to prepare the Sabbath meal to invite all three brothers to it. His wife was his sister's friend, a nurse at the same hospital. Aaronsohn describes meetings and discussions with his sister under the tree in the big yard at the H.O.A.[65] The relations between them were so close that when Aaronsohn lost his sight during World War I, his sister went with him to study in Cincinnati. Until his marriage to another graduate of the H.O.A., she accompanied him on all his trips.

Older siblings sometimes assumed an air of responsibility, feeling that they must fill the vacuum left by the missing parents. Some younger children did not like that kind of patronage. Michael Sharlitt, who followed Reizenstein as superintendent of the H.O.A. and who was raised in a New York orphanage, described relations between his older brother and himself as strained, because the older brother attempted to supervise Michael's behavior. He had a warm relationship with his sister, although he saw her less frequently because gender and age barriers in the orphanage separated their activities.[66] Ilene B. said that in general her family was never close and that relations did not warm up, even though she was placed with one of her brothers in a foster home.

Very often among H.O.A. orphans' families, an older or responsible sibling rebuilt the family nest. When Daniel Lowe graduated from the Theological Seminary in New York, his brother and sister were released from the H.O.A., and with their mother they joined him in New York. Daniel continued his studies toward a Ph.D. from Columbia University, but he was securely employed and could support his younger siblings. Throughout the years of his studies in the seminary, Lowe had visited his siblings at the H.O.A. every summer. When the Semlin brothers found work in Pennsylvania after graduating from the H.O.A., their young sisters were released to be with them. The older brothers were all the family the teenage girls had. That was also the case with the Sadovski family, who could not come to the H.O.A. reunion in 1968 but explained in a letter that they still lived together and worked and helped each other. The brother and the two sisters apparently did not marry.

The Samuel Ready had fewer siblings than the H.O.A. because the school was selective and did not always accept siblings; the H.O.A. resembled a family shelter because of the number of siblings among its wards. Yet there was a good deal in common between the two institutions in terms of sibling relations. Letters to Rowe, report how siblings felt and fared. Visits, trips together, and living and working together are described. The letters also reveal siblings' devotion to each other in time of crisis. When an elder sister died from tuberculosis, a second sister who had signs of the disease was monitored closely by the remaining sisters.

The letters also suggest that family units in many cases were intact. Once the children were released, they returned to live with parents or relatives and became part of the family again.[67] The biweekly letters the children wrote to relatives, the short Christmas and long summer vacations, and the monthly visits of family members probably kept the families informed and in good relations with the girls. The fact that each September, upon returning from vacation, most Samuel Ready girls experienced a period of homesickness testifies to close relations with their families that were maintained throughout long years of separation.

Samuel Ready School letters also show in some cases strained relations between relatives and children. In a few instances there were obvious conflicts. Sometimes the conflict was between the child and his relatives and sometimes between different relatives about the child's welfare. While the latter disagreements usually were expressed in correspondence with Rowe, the children were nevertheless frequently aware of them as well. The tension between a grandfather and a mother about a child's visits to a certain church, recounted in Chapter Four, was known to the child involved. And the Durant sisters were aware of the conflict between their mother and their uncle, who objected to their spending their summer vacation in Boston with their mother.

But the most serious problems for the children were conflicts between their loyalty to their families and their obligations to the Samuel Ready School. Mrs. Jefferson wrote her daughter that she had to come to home for Christmas. The girl had exhausted all her vacation points because the mother kept her at home past the time limit. She furnished doctor's notes and other pretexts, but Rowe, who kept an evenhanded attitude in these matters, explained that she could not give the Jefferson girl more privileges than she gave the others. While the girl understood the rules, her mother had difficulty adjusting to them. After a year, the mother, a government clerk, enjoyed a secure position and wanted the girl to return home. The letter in which the mother asked the girl to come and live with her again is instructive. Promise of a good school, a big house with a room to herself, and lots of privileges were the lures the mother used to entice the child to leave the school. Relying on the parent-child bond, however, was not always enough. Harriet Jefferson returned home, but when Cathy Sullivan's mother, who remarried, asked her daughter to spend two weeks of summer vacation with her, the fifteen-year-old girl refused. For reasons not clear from the records, the trustees decided that she would spend the summer in the Samuel Ready School. Going with her mother, even for a short period of time, meant disobeying the school's rules and losing her place. Cathy Sullivan decided not to jeopardize her future stay in the Samuel Ready School.

The full orphans and the children whose surviving parent was not their guardian were more vulnerable. Some relatives took a summer vacation in the country with their own family but left their orphan nieces in the city under other relatives' supervision. Sometimes girls in these circumstances got no summer vacation because relatives were not able or willing to take them. In one case, an aunt pressed her niece to take on an additional vocation, stressing the need to be self-supporting. The girl, not knowing how to respond to her aunt, turned to Rowe in distress. Some relatives tried to treat their pro-tégées especially well on vacations: Monica Kimmel's uncle asked Rowe to allow him to give the girl a treat by taking her to the country on a weekend. Ethel Fog wrote Rowe that her aunt took her on a visit to a park and to a gramophone concert. The letter also describes homesickness for the school and her friends there.

THE CHILDREN of the H.O.A. had similar problems dealing with relatives other than parents. When Saul Ulenberg, a full orphan, was released to his uncle's home upon the latter's request, the boy probably did not adjust to his uncle's crowded household and soon after was placed in Boys' Home, an orphanage for working boys.[68] One visiting day, a girl who had been released came to Dr. Freudenthal to complain about her aunt's treatment. "Her father wanted her to learn the millinery trade," the superintendent reported. The orphanage secured the girl a position, but her aunt did not keep her promise of assistance. The girl, released to her aunt's home upon the aunt's request, was taken back by the Ladies Hebrew Orphan Asylum, which was instructed by the board of directors to provide her with the vocational education she desired. When Sophia Adler died in 1893, she left a detailed will. The sick woman, whose husband had also passed away, entrusted the education of her young adopted daughter to the H.O.A. and willed the institution a thousand dollars. The eight-year-old girl and the woman's nephews and nieces were provided with the same sum of money. Although Mrs. Adler made her brother-in-law executor of her will, she did not leave the child in his custody. Sophia Adler was not poor. She could have established a trust for the girl to be administered by one of her relatives, but she chose the H.O.A., possibly because she did not trust her relatives or felt that to leave the child in their care was too great a burden to place on them.[69] Sometimes there were good reasons not to place an orphan with relatives, as Eileen Simpson in *Orphans: Real and Imaginary*, recalled. When her mother died, her father placed Eileen and her sister, three and four years old respectively, in an Italian orphanage. Apparently no one in the family could take care of the small girls. When the father died several years later, he left a large sum of money for the girls' education in trust of his brother. When Eileen reached age nine, the uncle took the girls into his house. The man was a very strict disciplinarian who claimed that the girls were dependent on his money. His wife protected her own two daughters and left the orphan girls to the mercy of her strict husband. Only years later Eileen Simpson learned that her father had left enough money for her and her sister's education and that her uncle had stolen from the trust.[70] Nothing so dramatic happened—as far as I know—with orphans from the three institutions reported here, but blood relationships did not always prevent abuse.

Relations between children and parents were different. Parents in most cases did their best to indulge their children on visiting days with what they could afford, sometimes even smuggling items of food that were not allowed. They deposited money in the children's savings accounts when they could. Close relations with parents can be assumed in cases of children who ran away from the H.O.A. for short visits at home. Only boys for the most part ran away, and they usually did not intend to stay at home because they understood their family situation. Running away meant visiting home for a few hours and hoping that the superintendent would not find out, according to Simon Z.[71]

Since Simon Z. did not have a home to run to, he joined the Weinstein brothers for short visits with their mother, returning "home" with some treats in his pockets. Such incidents caused embarrassment to the H.O.A when police intervention was required to find the boys. But most of the time, the children returned the same day and the episode was not reported or recorded.[72] Frequent visits of parents and relatives were considered harmful because they made it difficult for the children to adjust to the institution. Infrequent visits were seen as hurting the children's feelings and harmful to the family's connection with the child. But as Mr. Benjamin pointed out, the

H.O.A. was flexible and lenient in its policy toward relatives' visits. He remembered visits of aunts and cousins besides his father. Breaking the rules, he recalled, sometimes resulted in taking away visitation rights.

There was some correlation between relations of children with their relatives and relations of the same children with their siblings. Children who had warm and close relations with relatives outside tended to have close relations with their siblings inside. And close relations between siblings while they were in the institution tended to endure after they left.[73] Children who had no close family relations outside and no siblings in the institution had long-lasting relations with the superintendent, at least insofar as can be judged from the Samuel Ready School children's files.

It is hard to produce conclusive evidence from fragmentary sources. The letters, the interviews, and other indirect references to relations between children and their families frequently indicate special relations among siblings in the orphanages, which could be explained as compensation for the loss of a parent or parents. Surviving parents, in most cases, tried to be close to their children.

The Institutions and the Outside World

Although located in Calverton, quite a distance from the Jewish district of East Baltimore, the H.O.A. had close relations with the community.[74] The Jewish community at that time was divided into German and Russian groups that had developed parallel institutions.[75] The H.O.A. was linked to both. It derived its financial support from the German Jews and its wards from the Russian Jews.[76] The H.O.A. needed to have a good relationship with the entire Jewish community. The poor wanted to be assured that their children were treated well, and the rich that their money was wisely spent. Contact with the community was made mainly by the superintendent and the board of directors.[77]

Confidence in the orphanage had to be especially worked for in the Russian Jewish community because such institutions were not widely used in nineteenth-century Russia, where the extended family usually provided for orphans. Children were sent to relatives or stayed with their widowed mother and were supported by the community.[78] Suspicion toward the H.O.A. was also the result of differences in religious practice. The H.O.A. was not a "kosher" Jewish institution for Orthodox Russian Jews because it gave a reform education and was run by German Jews.[79] The H.O.A. had to demonstrate to poor Russian Jews that it educated their children properly. The legal document they had to sign relinquishing guardianship over their own offspring probably added to the suspicion parents felt when they met authorities of the H.O.A.[80] Their attitude usually changed once the children were in the institution. They may never have accepted the visitation rules, which did not allow them to bring certain items of food, but they appreciated the care and the education their children received.

Except for Aaronsohn's autobiography and a few letters in which parents thanked the superintendent for what he had done for their children, there is no indication of parents' attitudes toward the H.O.A. Yet the fact that the superintendent on several occasions had to urge parents to take their children back probably indicates that they fully understood the advantages of the institution. It can be argued that such parents faced economic difficulties that prevented them from reclaiming their children or that they simply did not want to take responsibility for their offspring. These possibilities, however, are unlikely. The superintendent had constant contact with parents and knew about changes in family circumstances, including their economic situation, and his suggestions were based on an assessment of both the families' and the children's needs. Children were not released to relatives that the H.O.A. thought could not take proper care of them or would in any way abuse them. The board of directors and the superintendent understood the plight of parents or relatives, but what seemed best for the parent was not necessarily best for the child.

In extreme instances conflicts in these cases ended up in court.[81] But whether the law had to be invoked or not, it is clear that the H.O.A. relentlessly pursued the child's interest. An example is the case of Jacob, one of seven children of a carpenter who faced financial difficulties during the 1910s. The father was frequently out of work and traveled long distances to other states to find employment. A visitor from the Hebrew Benevolent Society described his wife as a nervous woman, the house as filthy, and the children as poorly clad and fed. Upon recommendation, the children were moved to the H.O.A. Some years later the father found employment and the family was no longer in need of aid. The father gradually took back his children, but when he applied for Jacob's release the H.O.A. refused. The father promised to educate and provide for the boy, but the H.O.A. did not trust the parents. An investigation resulted in the conclusion that the other children should not stay in the family home either. In a letter to the superintendent, Jacob's father threatened to take the boy by force if his request was turned down. It is not clear whether a legal course was pursued in this case and whether the H.O.A. retrieved the other children, but Jacob did not return to his father's home. The boy, who was an excellent student, a leader among the children, full of initiative and very friendly, not only graduated from high school but also continued his studies under the auspices of the H.O.A.[82]

The Samuel Ready School had somewhat different relations with the children's parents. Like the H.O.A., the Ready School needed a good reputation as an educational institution in order to attract students, but it did not depend on the community for funds and did not hold a resident against her guardian's wishes.[83] Parents were expected to follow the rules of the school and were kept informed about their children's progress. Rowe's correspondence with them shows a great deal of delicacy and consideration.[84] Sometimes she was faced with more than one relative and very often with relatives who were not at peace with each other. Beyond the formal legal problem of which relative had the right of decision, there was the need to try to keep all relatives interested in the girl's welfare.

The correspondence between Rowe and relatives exposes other tensions and conflicts. The tone and vocabulary of the letters reveals differences in relationships on the basis of class and status. Letters from teachers, an architect, and a minister are friendly but assertive in tone, addressing Rowe as a colleague. Letters of widowed mothers serving as domestics or seamstresses are much humbler in tone, apologetic, respectful, and grateful. Conflicts and tensions tended to develop with the relatives in the first category.

Conflicts arose when relatives either bent the rules or tried to influence school policy. Tensions also surfaced when Rowe felt that relatives were neglecting their obligation toward one of "her" girls. She had to make decisions such as whether to allow three siblings to stay in their uncle's house, where only the older sister—a teenager herself—was in charge, because the uncle and his family abandoned the city for the country, leaving their nieces behind. In another instance, she had to write a letter to an aunt who, though she claimed it was difficult to part from her niece when she placed her in the school, nevertheless failed to make arrangements for the girl's summer vacations. The letters in the children's files reveal both Rowe's intense commitment to the girls and her restraint toward relatives who aroused her anger because they contain some original versions that were not sent. The sharpest one is her answer to the minister who tried to force the school to change its rules regarding church attendance. In the unsent letter, Rowe reminded the clergyman that the school was a charity institution and that his granddaughter studied and lived there for free. These lines were scratched out and the rest marked as a copy of the letter sent. No other letter in the files reminded a guardian that Samuel Ready was an orphanage. When parents tried to influence decisions, Rowe either cited the rules or refered the relatives to the trustees. In a few cases parents appealed to the trustees, and in a very few they were even successful, but in most instances differences were resolved in direct dealings with Rowe.[85]

But the school's community included more than the parents and other relatives of students. Rowe and the trustees cultivated relationships with religious and educational institutions. Streams of visitors passed through the Samuel Ready School. Many of them were ministers from various Protestant churches who came either to visit the Samuel Ready girls from their congregations or to learn from the school's experience how to open a school or orphanage or to improve an existing one.[86] The Johns Hopkins University sent students to examine the place. Journalists took interest in the school as scores of articles meticulously gathered and pasted into a scrap book by Rowe show.

The publicity and name the school gained had its rewards. Although the Samuel Ready did not solicit contributions, it nevertheless received large donations sometimes. A woman who knew about the school's work through one of her relatives left $26,470, a trustee's widow built a library for the school, and another trustee contributed a hall in memory of his wife.[87] Dr. Goucher, president of Baltimore Women's College, gave a scholarship for a Samuel Ready student to study at the Girls Latin School, a private school that prepared women for college.[88] Close connections with the Peabody Conservatory of Music and the Maryland Institute of Art helped the girls win scholarships for further studies. But the connections Rowe and the trustees developed with institutions, organizations, and individuals went beyond the city's churches and educational institutions. It spread into the business community, which for the Samuel Ready girls, was perhaps the most crucial connection because they depended on it for future employment.[89]

Business connections and ethnic and religious affiliations were important to young people seeking to learn a trade or to obtain employment. The H.O.A. superintendent and board of directors, which consisted mostly of businessmen, mapped the city's businesses and listed all those that would take H.O.A. graduates. In a ledger the superintendent listed in alphabetical order each business in which the H.O.A. successfully placed a graduate. The ledger contained hundreds of names representing a variety of industries and showed the thorough efforts of the H.O.A. to establish close connections with the business community.

But unlike the Samuel Ready School, the H.O.A. did not just need close connections with the business community; its existence depended on the community at large, especially on the Jewish community. Donations came from wealthy German Jews who had resided in Baltimore for several decades and also from poor Russian Jews. Some of the latter were no doubt the relatives of H.O.A. children.

Relating to the Jewish community involved more than simply soliciting funds; it required keeping the community informed about the orphanage and its work. The *Jewish Comment* recorded all celebrations of holidays and other events at the H.O.A. and urged the public to participate in them, including the children's Bar Mitzvahs, which occurred frequently. The most important event was commencement, which involved public examination of the children in Judaic studies as well as performances and awards. Special transportation was organized for the public, and the event was publicized in the *Baltimore Sun*, as well as in the Jewish press. The *Jewish Comment* reported on even relatively minor matters regarding the H.O.A., like the latest design the boys carved in their afternoon manual training and other educational developments. When the Baltimore public schools employed Miriam Adler, who had been placed at the H.O.A. through an arrangement with her dying adoptive mother, as a teacher, the *Jewish Comment* reported it. It was important to let the public know that the H.O.A. had educated the girl for the vocation she wanted and had fulfilled her mother's will.

The Dolan Home's relations with the outside world were somewhat different from those of the other institutions. The Dolan Home did not belong to St. Patrick's Parish, although it used its religious and educational facilities. Formally, St. Patrick's Orphanage was the parish orphanage, while The Dolan Home belonged to the entire Irish Catholic community. Theoretically, it should have belonged to the Irish Catholic in the city, but there is no evidence that it had close ties with any particular community. The superintendent complained that because the Dolan Home was endowed, it lacked church and community support.[90] The fact that the children partly came as boarders through recommendations of priests and trustees diminished the link with relatives' neighborhoods or communities. The children were often temporarily placed, or their parents changed residence, frequently being themselves boarders or domestics in other people's houses.[91] In addition, children who were committed through court order on account of neglect and abuse also lacked connections to their parents and relatives' neighborhood since ties between the two were not desirable.

The Dolan Home nevertheless had ties with the business community through the Young Catholic's Friend Society and the trustees of Dolan's will. From time to time these ties helped overcome financial crises, but they did not serve as adequate substitutes for community support. The children of the Dolan Home, unlike those of the H.O.A. and the Samuel Ready, left at the age of twelve if not earlier, and at that stage did not need placement or employment. The Catholic businessmen of Baltimore City could be of little help in the distant rural counties of Maryland where some of the children were placed. The rest of the children, being boarders and cared for by their own relatives and those sent to St. Mary's Industrial School, could not profit from the business community, at least not at the time of their release. Yet some community support was crucial for the Dolan Home, and the Sisters of the Holy Cross found it for a short period in the merchants of the Lexington Market.[92]

Unlike the H.O.A. and the Samuel Ready, which enjoyed continuous publicity, the Dolan Home was hardly mentioned in the Baltimore Catholic press. From 1880 to 1910, the *Catholic Mirror* was almost silent about it. In the same period, it lavished attention on St. Mary's Industrial School, St. Elizabeth's (for black infants) and St. Vincent's (for white infants). Dolan's endowment and his stipulation that the institution not be parish based isolated the home from community ties and support.

Whatever their economic base, all three orphanages had connections with their immediate neighborhoods. For the H.O.A. there were the stores, the school, the police station, and the employees who came to work from Calverton. The H.O.A. was part of the neighborhood of Calverton Heights—a Jewish institution in a Christian community. A few conflicts with neighbors appear in the records. The H.O.A. objected to the opening of a saloon across the street from the orphanage and to a change of hours of the neighborhood school. Otherwise, relations with the neighborhood were harmonious.[93]

A saloon directly across the street from the Samuel Ready School also presented a problem. For many years the school did not openly object to the saloon because the owner was a family man with children, as the trustees explained in a letter to the commissioner of the liquor board. But when the saloon was sold to a new owner, the school filed a complaint, citing the late night noise and the bad influence of the saloon on the sixty school girls.

Boys in the neighborhood presented a problem of another kind. They broke into the Samuel Ready garden to pick fruit and sometimes teased the girls verbally. Sneaking into the orchard at night stopped when the school installed a light at the edge of the garden, and daytime entry was ended when the girls chased the boys out with a gallant display of power. Picking unripe fruit was a favorite activity; ceding it to boys was unthinkable.

The Dolan Home probably confronted more trouble in relation to the immediate neighborhood because it was located in a tough part of East Baltimore. But its relationship with St. Patrick's parish helped to check neighborhood intrusions. The records indicate that a Dolan boy was once found in police custody (the charge is not reported) and that three girls were caught with boys from the neighborhood (improper sexual behavior is implied). An investigation by the trustees suggests that such incidents were rare.

When the H.O.A. felt that the city was closing in on it and that Calverton Heights was no longer pasture and trees, fresh air and peace, it moved to Baltimore County amid trees and open spaces.[94]

The Samuel Ready did the same. When North Avenue became busy and crowded, the school moved to Old Frederick Road.[95] As indicated earlier, the idea was not to isolate the children. Both the Samuel Ready and the H.O.A. benefited from the cultural and educational institutions of the city. But both institutions wanted beauty and quiet for their children, with space and clean air as well as a controlled environment without the influence of urban street culture.

The superintendents and boards of trustees encouraged relationships between children and their families and attempted to preserve family ties during the years of separation. The presence of siblings, the company of friends, the understanding and caring superintendents and staff in most cases diminished the pain of orphanhood and enabled children to have as "normal" a childhood as possible under the circumstances.

CHAPTER SIX

Life after the Orphanage

I N FACILITIES, education, and social life the three Baltimore orphanages studied resembled boarding schools. The Samuel Ready tried to instill in its students the notion that it was a boarding school, and the H.O.A. put a heavy emphasis on education as a vehicle for social mobility (see chapters four and five). But those who ran the orphanages and the children who lived in them were also aware of vast differences between the two types of institution. Children were conscious of family problems that often included indigence and a dependence on charity that spelled shame.

Orphanages had to ensure that upon being released children would be assisted in their initial steps into society. For some children, the family was able to help; others had to rely entirely on the institution's support. This chapter examines the process of releasing children, relationships between them and the orphanage after their release, and relationships between children and the community that once supported them and was expected to absorb them without prejudice as adults. It also attempts to trace the orphans' professional and personal lives after release.

The H.O.A. board of directors discussed the abilities and family circumstances of children proposed for release. It had to find employment for the children, a place to live, clothes, and some money to start life outside the sheltering walls of the H.O.A.[1] Sometimes preparations for discharging a teenager took weeks, even months. When a boy's employment and shelter were taken care of, the superintendent took him shopping for new clothes. Later that day the boy's friends eagerly examined his purchases.

The persons responsible for helping the girls were the Ladies of the Hebrew Orphan Aid Society. Clothes bought with the help of these ladies were not fancy or in the latest style and were not always liked. Dr. Freudenthal asked the board to give the girls money to buy whatever they liked, but the directors apparently turned his request down. The practice of shopping with the ladies continued long afterward.

Every child at the H.O.A. had a savings account. The superintendent deposited money that relatives saved for the children, money that children earned by working extra hours in the institution, and money they received when they won prizes for excellence at the end of the school year. These savings were important for the children upon leaving. For example, Simon Z. did not go to high school but worked outside the institution after he was fourteen. Because he was a full orphan, the H.O.A. kept him until he was seventeen and deposited his salary in the bank. When he left, he had a considerable sum of money. Aaronsohn's sister had a savings account at the H.O.A. that grew substantially because she won prizes. When the girl returned home and the family bought its first house, her prize money made the down payment.

Freudenthal objected to giving savings to relatives and requested the board to keep the money invested until the children reached maturity. The management of the H.O.A. thought that guardians ought to be satisfied to receive educated children who could help relieve the family's economic burden; the children's savings should serve only their own economic futures.

Returning home or becoming a boarder in other families was a harsh experience for some children. When Mr. Benjamin returned home, his father had remarried. His new stepmother treated him well, but his father was too strict. When asked why a child who endured Reizenstein's regime could not adjust to a disciplinarian father, Mr. Benjamin refused to discuss his father's behavior. His wounds had not healed.

For Aaronsohn, adjusting to a stepfather and a newborn brother was not as difficult as returning to a poor and filthy neighborhood and living without a routine.[2] Ilene B. left the orphange several times. She came to the H.O.A. first in the last years of Reizenstein's superintendency and again under Michael Sharlitt's superintendency. In between, she returned with her siblings to her remarried father and his new wife and lived several months in a crowded room above the chicken coop before going back to the H.O.A. She moved with the rest of the H.O.A. children to the new cottage orphanage (Levindale) but was placed shortly afterward in a foster home. Ilene B. did not adjust to her new home and felt exploited by her foster mother. She returned to Levindale, where she was very happy, but was placed again in an "opportunity home," which meant in this case, a rich family that treated her and her brother like strangers. She had to help the maid who took care of the baby and was not allowed to sit at table with the venerable doctor and his wife. In Levindale again, Ilene B. spent another happy period, which ended when she was considered old enough to go to work. The H.O.A. found her employment and boarded her in a home for working girls. At dinner her first evening there Ilene B. discovered that the other girls lacked manners, and she asked permission to eat alone in the kitchen. Although she stayed in the girls' home about two years and befriended some of the boarders, she could not reconcile her education and manners with theirs.

Ilene B. may appear to have been a problem child, perhaps stubborn and impudent. But she had a strong character, was a shy, bookish girl, an excellent student who graduated from Western Female High School, a violinist in the H.O.A. band, and an artist—a graduate of the Maryland Institute of Art. Her difficulty in adjusting to a new environment, as well as Mr. Benjamin's and Aaronsohn's, did not stem from their personalities but from the education they received and the life they led at the H.O.A.

The well-ordered asylum provided a middle-class education and manners and pushed children to achievements that gave them pride and self-confidence. It did not prepare them to return to the poor neighborhoods they came from. Beginning in Reizenstein's era, children learned housekeeping and home maintenance, including plumbing, electricity, and gardening, which were doubtless useful whether they lived with relatives or formed their own households.[3] But such preparations did nothing to mitigate the psychological and cultural shock some children experienced upon discharge from the orphanage.

For some the first job was a big disappointment. Finding jobs for graduates was not easy. The market was often limited and many businesses did not employ Jews; others had prejudices against graduates of an orphange.[4]

Aaronsohn's first job was clerking in a warehouse owned by a

son-in-law of one of the H.O.A. directors. He considered his fine
education, which included English, French, German, accounting, stenography, typing, as well as history and biology, wasted on a job
that any boy could fill. Aaronsohn did not know that Wilfred S.,
who graduated with him from Baltimore City College, failed to secure a job at all until he presented himself with a non-Jewish name.

Although the H.O.A. tried to secure the children's economic future, it could not protect them from society's cruelty toward children
from institutions. After Charles Dickens's *Oliver Twist* in 1838
evoked cries for reform in child care institutions, the public on both
sides of the Atlantic had a harsh image of orphanges. That image was
strengthened each time an institution did not meet standards or a
superintendent was accused of improper behavior.

Progressive Era literature perpetuated the image. The heroine of
Ann of Green Gables (1908) was raised in orphanages. Sometime
between the ages of eleven and thirteen she began living with families
who used her as a maid and a nurse for their children. Whenever a
family did not need her services any more, it returned her to the
orphanage. Her luck changed when two aging siblings, Matthew and
Marilla, requested an orphan boy to help them on the farm. By mistake Ann was sent. Though warned that children from orphanages
were ungrateful and could not be trusted, Marilla sent the girl to
school. Ann excelled and made Marilla proud by graduating from a
teacher's seminar and later from college. She became a teacher and a
writer. Particularly revealing is the author's explanation for Ann's
success. She came to Marilla at the age of thirteen with good reading
skills and a thirst for literature and poetry. She had no trouble entering school and excelled there immediately. Praising foster care and
describing Ann's fears of being returned to the orphanage, the novel
holds heredity responsible for her high level of education and her
good character. A real-life Ann would have gained her education in
the orphanage, but that explanation did not suit the author's agenda.
The orphan triumphed, but the orphanage retained a negative
image.[5]

These images haunted the graduates of the H.O.A. and other
orphanages. Ilene B. recalled that when she was told that she would
live in the Hebrew Orphan Asylum, she thought she would be in a
cell behind bars. When she entered public school, another student
offered her a peanut butter and jelly sandwich because she thought

that children in an orphanage would not have tasted peanut butter and jelly.

Mr. Benjamin was grateful for his and his siblings' H.O.A. education but was hesitant to talk about his childhood at the orphanage. Finally he explained that the stigma of being from an orphanage was so strong that he had decided not to tell anybody where he was raised. In his late eighties, he sat in a room full of trophies and documents that testified to his achievements, but he was determined that his sons, grandsons, and great grandsons would never know his secret. The stigma was not noticeable at the elementary school, but when he told his classmates at Baltimore City College that he came from the H.O.A., he felt that they considered him inferior. He felt the stigma even more keenly after returning home. When Mr. Benjamin applied for jobs, he was very careful not to mention his childhood at the H.O.A. Aaronsohn most likely did not tell his classmates at City College that he came from the H.O.A.[6]

Samuel Ready girls faced similar problems of finding employment and avoiding the stigma of having been raised in an orphanage. The process of release from the school was very much like the one at the H.O.A. Finding employment had top priority, and Miss Rowe used the trustees' connections as well as her own to place the girls in suitable jobs. She sought jobs for Ready School graduates that would enable them to be self-supporting and at the same time would suit their education and the school's expectations. A girl once asked her opinion about a position offered as a governess. Rowe's cross answer reminded the girl that she was trained as a dressmaker and questioned the girl's efforts to find a job in her profession. Being a nanny was considered low-paying, semidependent, and nonprestigious employment largely for uneducated blacks and immigrants.[7]

The first jobs some of the girls found indicate that connections were used. One worked at the office of the Charity Organization Society, of which Daniel C. Gilman, a trustee, was president. Another was a teacher in an orphanage. One girl was a dressmaker in a shop run by an alumna's aunt. The use of influence and connections is also apparent from the girls' letters asking Rowe for recommendations. When Rowe suggested that a girl should ask the president of the Ready School for a recommendation, the girl explained that a letter from Rowe would have more influence on the employer in question.

The school did not try to provide work for all the students it released but only for those who graduated from the full program, including the extra years of vocational education. Even then, Rowe tried to be sure a girl would fit a job and do credit to the school before she gave her a recommendation. In a letter to the girl who wished to become a governess, Rowe explained that she had a job suitable for her but hesitated to recommend the girl because she heard she was not able to cut and sew new models of clothes although she had been trained at school to do so. Rowe's insistence on accuracy and honesty in recommending her students derived from her conviction that the girls would benefit most if the school maintained a reputation for thoroughly preparing students for employment.[8]

During the 1900s Rowe tightened the process of selection for the school and concentrated more on academic ability. When these girls graduated, they were mainly situated in business and educational institutions as clerks and teachers. In June 1910, in the semiannual report, she was able to tell the trustees that all the graduates of that year had employment upon leaving the school.

Although letters to Rowe from graduates do not directly reveal disappointments about first jobs, hints are evident. One girl apologized that she had not written Rowe sooner and described her long workday in an office. Another described the hardship of opening an academy in a rural area and her exhausting work with a variety of students of different ages. Those trained to teach music, besides giving private lessons, had supplementary jobs as organists in churches. For women at the turn of the century it took long hours and hard work at low pay to be fully self-sufficient, especially when they had to support an elderly mother.

Returning home was probably difficult, too. Although letters written immediately after leaving do not describe disappointments and problems, there are many expressions of homesickness for the Ready School and wishes to visit the school.

Eleven-year-old Isabelle Pine probably felt what many seventeen- and eighteen-year-olds felt but did not express so openly. Isabelle returned home after her mother remarried. Two weeks later, Rowe received a letter from the girl's mother and another from her grandmother. Isabelle, according to the letters, had not stopped crying since she left the school because she could not adjust to conditions at home and to her stepfather. According to her grandmother, the stepfather did not know how to treat children. The girl's mother explained that she did not realize when she withdrew Isabelle that she would not be able to provide for her as well as Samuel Ready had. Both mother and grandmother pleaded with Rowe to let the girl return. Isabelle Pine's place had already been taken, and her mother had to reapply. Isabelle did not return. Two years later, a letter from the girl informed Rowe that she had finally adjusted and was happy at home. Isabelle Pine had spent five years at the school, from age six to eleven. The girls who graduated from the full program sometimes spent a longer time there. Their letters to Rowe register their disappointments and difficulties subtly. They often compare places visited to the Ready School, declaring that the former were not as beautiful or as clean as the Samuel Ready. Doubtless many girls were happy to be on their own after so many years of rules, regulations and supervision, but clearly it was not always easy to adjust to life on the outside.

Samuel Ready girls did not escape stigma even though their institution was called a school, not an orphanage. Susan Vault, a full orphan who was raised at the Samuel Ready from age five to sixteen, fell in love with a young man who wanted to marry her, but his father objected to the match. In a notebook in which Rowe detailed the girls' year of graduation, vocation, and marital status, Susan Vault is listed as married. Whether she married the young man whose father disapproved of her is not clear.

An attempt to combat the stigma was made as early as 1894, seven years after the school (then called an asylum) opened. The trustees petitioned the Maryland General Assembly to drop the word "asylum" from the name and substitute the word "school."

> The reason for this application was, that the children in this institution were receiving not only shelter, food and clothing, but were at the same time receiving an all-round education superior to that had at the public schools of the City of Baltimore. The superiority of this education had been several times demonstrated when the children from the Samuel Ready School competed with those from the public schools in public examinations, and elsewhere. But these children had found, when they stood in such competition, or when they made application to business places for positions through which to earn their living in the direction

for which they had been fitted and trained, that they were at a disadvantage, through a prejudice, perhaps unexpressed and undefined, against the graduate of an institution which went by the name of an "asylum." Hence the trustees determined that their wards, with whose education, both moral and intellectual, great pains were taken, should not suffer for such prejudice, whether it were reasonable or unreasonable, and that when they stood for examination, or as applicants for positions, they should stand, in all respects, upon the same footing as any others who stood by their side.[9]

Susan Vault left the Samuel Ready four years after the name of the institution was changed to "school," and yet she encountered prejudice.

The ambivalent feelings of elation at being at last on their own, with their families, self-supporting, and nostalgia for the old days, the "gang," the friendships, the sheltering place with all its joys and sorrows are evident in interviews of the H.O.A. graduates, in Aaronsohn's autobiographies, and in the Samuel Ready girls' letters after leaving the school. Mixed feelings also marked the H.O.A. graduates' attitudes toward the orphanage after they left. Some concealed their backgrounds from their employers, their schoolmates, and even their new families; but the same graduates visited the H.O.A., belonged to its alumni association, and greeted old friends at a reunion in 1968. Aaronsohn, who as a teenager hid his H.O.A. background, wrote extensively about his orphanage life afterwards. At a board meeting, Freudenthal raised the question of alumni visits to the institution. He described the situation of years before, when alumni flooded the place all year round, and suggested that graduates should be allowed to come only on visiting days and should receive a card to identify them. Some alumni apparently came to see their friends and siblings, and some came to consult Freudenthal.

Samuel Ready alumnae visits were regulated. The graduates had to let Rowe know they were coming before they arrived. Nevertheless, on some evenings more than one alumna sat at the teachers' table in the dining room.[10] Alumni of both Samnuel Ready and the H.O.A. were organized. A *Ready Record* column edited by one of the "old girls" kept the Samuel Ready community up to date on the whereabouts of alumnae and contributed articles on general subjects.[11]

On the first Saturday of the school year Ready alumnae traditionally prepared an entertainment for the new students. An issue of the *Ready Record* from 1910 reports one of many visits of the "old girls." The alumnae are described as sitting on a porch talking to Rowe, the Samuel Ready students as watching them from another porch, and the alumnae's eight children as enjoying the playground.

Alumnae provided inspiration and set an example for new students, and they served as an "old girls' network." When Eunice applied for a job in an office in which a former Samuel Ready girl held a position, Rowe contacted the alumna and obtained valuable information about the position. This allowed Rowe to prepare her new graduate for an interview and to write her recommendation in a way that would highlight the girl's ability and fitness for the particular job requirements. Moreover, alumnae filled all teaching positions at the Ready School—some as paid teachers, some as volunteers for afternoon classes in stenography and bookkeeping. The alumnae's strong bonds with the school helped keep tradition and preserve Rowe's spiritual influence on the school long after she died.

H.O.A. alumni filled similar functions as role models and as a network for graduates in search of work. The alumni organization, which was institutionalized in Reizenstein's era, formally met in the city, but informally the graduates returned for visits. Most stopped coming back when their friends and siblings and the superintendent they knew left.

When Dr. Freudenthal died, the H.O.A. alumni collected money to commemorate the superintendent. For the 1968 alumni reunion, the organizer made copies of Freudenthal's portrait, which had been given to the H.O.A. by his family after his death, and gave them to the gathered graduates. A woman who could not attend the reunion asked that the picture be sent to her so that she could show her children and grandchildren the father who had raised her.

H.O.A. graduates did not have a long-lasting relationship with Dr. Reizenstein, nor did he maintain ties with the asylum after he left. When the "Reformer" (as he was nicknamed by the children) died in 1939, only a few graduates came to his funeral. On the other hand, Michael Sharlitt, the superintendent who came to office in 1918 and served only two years, wrote in his autobiography that he had correspondence with H.O.A. graduates more than thirty-eight years after he left the orphanage. He recalled receiving "a unique set of tributes and framed resolutions of thankfulness" on his birthday in 1938; it was "signed by all graduates still resident in Baltimore." Sharlitt also described visits with H.O.A. graduates in various cities between 1920 and 1959.

The attitude of H.O.A. alumni toward the orphanage is best exemplified in the volunteer work of Selma Milner, a teacher. When the Spanish influenza epidemic passed through the H.O.A. in October 1918, she and two trained nurses worked devotedly until all the children were well again.[12]

No documentation of the Dolan Home's graduates' ties with the home after they left was found, although some references in the Minute Book suggest that there were contacts between the Sisters and the alumni and that the nuns knew their whereabouts. But the duration of the relationships, their extent, and the number of graduates included could not be determined from the scant evidence.

OF THE forty girls who entered the Ready School between November 1887 and January 1889, thirty-one (75.5%) stayed until they were sixteen or older. Five were dismissed by the school and four were withdrawn by parents. (One of the thirty-one was dismissed for disobedience at the age of seventeen, after five years at the school.) Of the thirty-one who left after age sixteen, twenty-six received a complete vocational education. Five did not win the extra years and left at the age of sixteen. Three of the five studied dressmaking.

Of the twenty-six who had a full vocational education, three graduated as music teachers, six in the business course (typing, stenography, bookkeeping), eight in the teaching course, six in dressmaking and sewing, one in straw work, and two in scientific cookery. Of the twenty-six, twenty-three worked in the field they were trained in, two who were trained as dressmakers went on to nursing school and worked as nurses. One who had a double training at school as a teacher of violin and piano and in scientific cookery chose to teach the latter.

The Samuel Ready School Alumnae Register has some details on the kinds of jobs the girls held. Beatrice Jones, who studied teaching and was a graduate of the state normal school, taught at a public school of Harford County until she married in 1903. Her schoolmate, Elizabeth Darling, who graduated with her from the Samuel Ready and the normal school also taught in the Harford public schools. Juliet Durant, a graduate of the 1897 class at the normal school, was a teacher in the Harvard School in Cambridge, Massachusetts, where her mother resided. Heidi Donaldson, the bright student who won a scholarship to Baltimore Woman's College and excelled in her studies, was a private tutor at the college after graduation (1899–1900) and taught in a Baltimore public school in 1900–1901 and at Western Female High School from 1901 to 1903. In 1903 she married and in the subsequent years raised four children. Beth Donaldson, her sister, who was also trained as a teacher, taught in public schools in Maryland counties and Baltimore City for six years and then took a teaching position at the Samuel Ready School, where she worked until she died in 1910. Carol Fleet was a teacher at St. Paul's Orphanage and later in Harford County and Baltimore City public schools. More graduates earned their living by teaching. The two students of scientific cookery worked as teachers, one in high school and one at the Samuel Ready School. Even some of those who completed the business course taught typing and stenography: Florence Delphy taught in the Frederick Seminary, and Edith Hullingood was "the first teacher of business at Samuel Ready School" until she married in 1900. Many graduates of the music course also earned their living by teaching. All together, at one time or another, fourteen of twenty-six graduates worked as teachers.

Seraphina Cook, a graduate of the business course, worked as a secretary at the Charity Organization Society and apparently liked her job because in 1900 she was still there. Other graduates frequently changed employment. Helen Hullingood, trained in the business course, served as a bookkeeper and a stenographer in six companies between graduation in 1895 and 1904, when she married. Five of the jobs were in Maryland and the last one in Alabama. Eleanor Been graduated in 1892 and worked in three companies in Baltimore and then in Atlanta, Georgia, where she married in 1902.

The dispersion of the Samuel Ready School's graduates across the United States might point to unusual confidence and initiative, especially among single women of the era. On the other hand, it might be the result of family and friends' connections.

Of six students of dressmaking, two became nurses and one was employed as seamstress at the Samuel Ready. The workplace of the other three is unknown. Twenty of the thirty-one graduates married. Rowe, who registered the girls' marital status, also kept newspaper clippings about their weddings. Most of the girls apparently married into the middle class. Florence Delphy, who graduated in 1890 in the business course, worked in 1891 as a secretary to the editor of a Frederick newspaper. Four years later she married him. Cathy Sullivan, who taught scientific cookery in Western Female High School, married the best friend of President Roosevelt's son-in-law. The groom, according to the newspaper, had worked in government service in Washington and was head of a department in the Bell Chesapeake and Potomac Telephone Company. He was also "very active in society."

There is little or no evidence of what became of the four girls who did not complete the program because their parents took them home. Harriet Jefferson wrote Rowe that she adjusted to her mother's new home, but the letter was written shortly after she was withdrawn at the age of ten and a half. Isabelle Pine, who left at the age of eleven after five years at the school, continued to write during the next two years, but there are no records of her later whereabouts.

Karen Logan, whose sister was a graduate of the Ready School, left at sixteen after four years. Although her sister kept close ties with Rowe and visited the school years after she left, Karen is not mentioned in her letters, except for the fact that she married.

Of the five girls who were dismissed by the school, there is information only for Mellisa Taller, who spent three and a half years at the school and was sent by her guardian to the House of Refuge. At nineteen, the girl wrote a letter repenting her behavior at the Ready School; she asked to be forgiven and allowed to tell her story to current students at the school. Rowe invited the girl to visit but received a reply that she would not be allowed such visits until she turned twenty-one. Six years in the House of Refuge sewing all day without any schooling was a big downfall for a former Ready School student. (The girl did not appear in the Baltimore City Directory or in the 1900 U.S. Census, and there was no mention of her in Rowe's notebook.)

In 1904 Rowe reported to the trustees on the school's progress in training orphan girls to be self-supporting. From 1887 to 1904, 185 of 600 applicants were admitted. Of this number, 60 were still at school in 1904. Between 1887 and 1904, 125 students left, but not all of them graduated. The school dismissed 41 (32 percent). Parents withdrew 13 (about 10 percent). The rest graduated. Eighteen (about 12 percent) left at the age of sixteen without vocational training.

Eight (about 6 percent) left at the age of seventeen, and 45 (about 36 percent) completed the full program. Of the 71 graduates, 21 (about 28 percent) married between the time they left and 1904. According to Rowe, the school had trained 67 girls to be self-supporting. (She counted most of the girls who graduated at sixteen in dressmaking as full graduates.)

Of the 67 girls about whom she informed the trustees, 20 took the business course (stenography, typing, and bookkeeping). Eighteen were trained as school teachers, 2 others to teach music, and 3 to teach cookery. Twenty-one were trained in dressmaking, 1 in embroidery, and 2 in millinery. Ten more graduates joined that number in 1904 at the time the report was made: 4 were trained in the business course, 3 in teaching, 1 in music, 1 in dressmaking, and 1 in drawing.

Of the girls trained in the business course, Eleanor Been earned the highest wage: $14 a week by working in a glass company in Baltimore. The highest wage among those who took the teaching course belonged to Juliet Durant, who earned $70 per month teaching in the Harvard School in Cambridge, Massachussets. Music teachers earned $1 per hour for lessons, and two of them (not in the sample) also had positions as organists in churches that yielded an income between $100 and $150 annually. Teaching in Baltimore public schools in 1900 brought an income of $50 a month. That is what Cathy Sullivan earned teaching scientific cookery at Locust Point Social Settlement.

Dressmaking, on the other hand, was not a rewarding job. The best salary recorded was $7 per week. One of the best compensations in this vocation belonged to Mellinda Gates (from the sample), who earned $5 a month plus full board by working at the Samuel Ready School. Those trained in embroidery and millinery did not earn better salaries than the dressmakers. The highest salary in embroidery was $4.50 a week and in millinery $30 per month. No wonder that six years after that report was made there were few graduates in dressmaking, embroidery, or millinery work.

The school's achievement in training seventy-seven girls to be self-supporting in sixteen years is impressive, especially if the competition for teaching jobs is considered. The *Catholic Mirror* of February 10, 1883, lamented that all Catholic mothers wanted their daughters to be teachers but that only one in a thousand could actually expect to fill such a position. Using connections to get teaching positions in the public schools was common at the time. The competition for secretarial jobs was also tough because middle-class parents arranged clerical jobs for their children.[13] The school gave the girls a good education and thorough preparation for work but also helped graduates to find jobs through connections. The girls' records of employment show their ability to find work and to support themselves. Furthermore, marrying into the middle class shows that they at least partially overcame the stigma attached to graduates of orphanages.

Yet the school's success was highly dependent on its selection process. Choosing the best applicants (only one of three), dismissing about a third of those admitted, and then graduating with full vocational education about two-thirds of those remaining gave the Samuel Ready School the best candidates for success—girls with motivation and ability. It is also doubtful that all twenty-one who were trained to be dressmakers (about 28 percent of the 77 graduates from 1887 to 1904) were entirely self-supporting women or that they had any measure of security. Judging from wages reported in 1904, they had to lean on some relatives for support or live very frugally.

The pattern at the H.O.A. differed, in part because the Hebrew asylum functioned mainly as a shelter or temporary home for children whose parents abandoned them, were sick, or died. Most parents requested the return of their children when they were between thirteen and fifteen and could be of some help in the family economy.

Of the forty-five children in my sample, only seven were not requested by their relatives between ages thirteen and fifteeen. Of the nineteen families the forty-five children belonged to, six took their children back less than a year after they entered the H.O.A., some because they moved to other states to be helped by relatives or Jewish communities there, some because their family circumstances changed. The six families reclaimed sixteen children. Another two girls left after two years, one to become a nurse in a family and one who was taken back by relatives. Of these eighteen children who stayed a short time at the H.O.A., only one was traced in later years in court records. Mina Nadler's landlady charged that her claim to be unable to pay a debt was groundless because she owned several houses. Mina Nadler and her siblings had been at the H.O.A. only a few months while her father, a farmer, recuperated from an illness. Her mother died, but her father took his children back. In the

H.O.A.'s book, poverty was not cited as a reason for admitting the Nadler children.[14]

Of the eleven families whose children remained more than three years at the H.O.A., eight withdrew their children before maturity. Five did so because of changing circumstances and three because they were urged to do so by the H.O.A. Most children in these families were between twelve and sixteen and were sent either to learn a trade or to work in order to help the family economy. These eight families had eighteen children at the H.O.A. Eight children were traced in the 1900 U.S. Census, seven boys and one girl. The Eders' two boys worked as "pant-hook maker" and "pants operator," Saul Solomon worked as a shipping clerk, Leon Gedanski as a huckster, Wolf Kurliz as a tailor, Morris Ulenberg as a cigarette maker, and fourteen-year-old Saul Ulenberg as an errand boy. Cayla Ulenberg, the only girl found in the census, was not employed outside of her uncle's home and probably helped her aunt in the house.

Three of the nineteen families left some of their children to be raised at the H.O.A. and removed others. They had thirteen children in the orphanage but only ten in my sample. Of the ten, the families withdrew three children when they turned fifteen. Mendel Semlin left to help his mother, who died shortly afterward. Described as a responsible teenager, Mendel Semlin was probably successful because years later when he requested the release of his young sisters, the H.O.A. discharged the girls to his custody. Aaron Miller was sent to live with his married older sister. Shortly afterward he went to a farm school in Pennsylvania. In the 1900s, however, he was listed in the Baltimore City Directory as a tailor. His sister, Lizzie Miller, was a student at the Western Female High School when her father applied for her and placed her with a married sister in New York. It is not known if she continued her schooling.

The H.O.A. trained seven of the forty-five children until adulthood, four girls and three boys. The four girls remained in the H.O.A. until they were eighteen or nineteen. Eta Semlin's training was dressmaking, and her first employment was at the H.O.A. She received full board and clothing plus $6 a month. A year later, Freudenthal asked the board to raise her salary to $10. In 1900, she was listed in the Baltimore directory as a stenographer. Similar changes were made by Joanna Miller, who at the age of eighteen was sent to Hutzler Brothers department store to learn dressmaking. Some years later she was listed as a stenographer. Her sister's vocation is un-known. The girl entered the H.O.A. when she was fifteen and when she left at eighteen was employed by Solomon Brothers; the records do not specify her role there. Henrietta Lurie was still at the H.O.A. in 1900. After graduating from the Western Female School and the state normal school, she secured a teaching position in the Balti-more City public schools. A bright student, Enoch Miller, graduated from City College and Hebrew Union College in Cincinnati and be-came a rabbi, first in Arkansas and later in Pennsylvania. Albert Sem-lin was a difficult boy both at the H.O.A. and in public school, where he was considered a slow student. Freudenthal asked the board to release him at the age of fifteen and send him to learn a trade. Albert Semlin went to live with his eighteen-year-old brother, Mendel. The records do not indicate in what trade he was trained. Louis Semlin was sent to a farm school upon reaching fourteen. In 1901 Albert and Louis Semlin were listed as tailors in the Baltimore City Directory.

Comparing the positions of the eight children who left the H.O.A. before they were sixteen to those who stayed to maturity points to the latter group's advantage. The seven children who stayed to matu-rity had more years of formal education and they obtained better jobs. Even if we do not consider the two talented children who had more than a high school education, the rabbi and the teacher, the children who stayed until maturity still had an advantage. The two girls trained to be dressmakers were able to change vocation because they could earn a living by working as dressmakers during the day while taking a business course in night school. Even the boy who went to a farm school and ended up working as a tailor had more choices in the job market than those who worked as unskilled la-borers in the clothing industry.

It could be argued that the children who returned home upon their relatives' request benefited from a warm family relationship that compensated for fewer years of formal education. But the warmth of relationships is questionable. Of the eight families that withdrew their children, six were traced in the 1900 U.S. Census. The six fami-lies together had fourteen children. In 1900 only six of those chil-dren, aged between twelve and twenty-two, lived with their families. The oldest of them might have been married, but some clearly chose not to live with their families. The Naphtali family, for example, took back four children after the father remarried a woman sixteen years younger than he. Three young children from his second marriage, but none from his first marriage, lived with him in 1900, although the youngest daughter from his first marriage was at that time only sixteen and not likely to be married. The guardian of the Ulenberg children (their uncle) took one boy at age thirteen and a boy and a girl at fifteen. But a year later the thirteen-year-old (then fourteen) was an inmate of the Boy's Home (an orphanage for working boys) and was listed in the U.S. Census as an errand boy. The boy limped and had a speech impediment. His elder brother, twenty years old in 1900, was boarding with somebody else.

The H.O.A. policy of providing a shelter for families in distress by helping raise their children temporarily was not always beneficial. Children who did not adjust to their home when they returned nonetheless lost the opportunity offered by the H.O.A. for better education and a better start in society.

The changes in H.O.A. policy between 1900 and 1920 toward more schooling for the children resulted in more graduates entering the professions. In 1908, David Hutzler, then president of the H.O.A., boasted that among the institution's graduates were many "shining lights" in the professions: lawyers, rabbis, teachers, social workers. Hutzler's claim could not be verified, but a trend toward higher education was apparent by the 1910s.[15] In 1911 the *Jewish Comment* published a list of H.O.A. children who won annual prizes that year. In interviews, Mr. Benjamin and Simon Z., who were at the H.O.A. during the 1910s, identified the professions of fourteen of the children on the list. Two became rabbis, one a pediatrician, one a dentist, one a lawyer, one a druggist. One girl graduated from college (major unknown), one girl became a teacher, and three were nurses. One graduate was a clerk, one served in the army and changed jobs frequently afterward, and one was a salesman. At that time (1911) there were ninety-three children at the H.O.A., and the twenty-eight prize winners comprised 30 percent of all children. One can argue that prize winners are achievers and therefore do not reflect the H.O.A. population. Indeed, they did not.[16] Moreover, not all the children on the list were achievers academically (prizes were given for sewing, cooking, and drawing, for example), and not all achievers won prizes that year. Three friends of Mr. Benjamin and Simon Z. did not appear in the list; two became lawyers and one an engineer.[17]

The 1900 U.S. Census reports that only 4 percent of all Americans were college graduates, yet during the 1910s at least 10.7 percent of H.O.A. graduates went on to graduate from college. Even if the number of college graduates in the United States during the 1910s rose to more than 4 percent, 10.7 percent is still an impressive ratio. Furthermore, it was also substantial in comparison to the norms among Baltimore Jews. The same page of the *Jewish Comment* that lists H.O.A. prize winners carries the names of Jewish graduates in law and medicine at the University of Maryland. Seven received degrees in law and seven in medicine. Other schools in Maryland also had Jewish graduates in law and medicine, perhaps another ten or twenty. The three lawyers and two physicians from the H.O.A. joined a small professional elite in the Jewish community.

In 1968, an H.O.A. graduate from a later period, a history teacher, organized a reunion of H.O.A. and Betsy Levy Home graduates. (Betsy Levy Home or the Hebrew Children's Sheltering Home [H.C.S.H.] was the "Russian" orphanage that merged with the H.O.A. in 1921). On the list he compiled with another graduate (also a history teacher) were one hundred people, of whom ninety-eight were still living. The reunion took place in the house of a prosperous businessman, a graduate who owned a printing shop. Eighty-four of the ninety-eight graduates invited showed up. Four more wrote letters regretting their absence. Bess Hammet, the last secretary of the H.O.A., said that she was surprised to see youngsters she recalled forty years ago as successful grown-ups with families of their own. Simon Z. expressed the same feelings. "After all" he said, "we were a bunch of bad boys." Mr. Benjamin was also surprised at the achievements of his fellow graduates. Some of his friends were not only successful but had left their mark on the community, like Rabbi W., whose opinions were respected in the Jewish community; Dr. F., who treated poor children in East Baltimore; and Mr. A., the wealthy businessman who contributed time and money to charity.

There were also a few failures. Jeanette Rosner Wolman, a lawyer, in 1918 was a social worker in charge of many of the families with children at the H.O.A. In an interview, she recalled three boys who were discharged as "incorrigible" and became criminals. One of them served a long term in jail.[18]

ALTHOUGH ONLY forty-five children from two of the orphanages (the Samuel Ready School and the H.O.A.) were traced in the years after they left the institutions, generalizations about their success in life can be made. The orphanages sent home teenagers capable of working and helping their families. They challenged and aided achievers among the orphans to pursue further studies and to excel. The number of students who not only graduated from high school but continued their studies afterwards is impressive, considering the educational norms of the era. Most graduates, as can be judged from the sources, integrated in society, had employment, and formed families of their own.

Graduates viewed the orphanage as their home and were grateful for their education, but they suffered from the stigma attached to child care institutions and as a result sometimes concealed their association with the orphanage.

CHAPTER SEVEN

Discarding the Orphanages

ORPHANAGES WERE under attack after 1893. Social workers accused them of not providing adequate education, facilities and care for their wards. They faulted them for being insensitive to individual children and particularly to their need for privacy. They charged that many children sheltered in orphanages could have been left at home because their families only needed financial support.[1] The charities that supported orphanages could have provided for the children's families and could have kept those families intact. As a result of these attacks orphanages tried to improve conditions and to adapt to the latest innovations in child care. Changes in facilities and programs strained their budgets and put many of them in financial difficulty. But the orphanages' worst enemy was their success. Changing child labor laws in many states and greater emphasis on schooling and vocational education made the orphanage popular for poor, single parents, many of whom regarded the orphanage as a boarding school that would give their children better opportunities.[2] The pressure on orphanages to admit children beyond their capacity created serious overcrowding, staff shortage, and financial strain. This chapter describes the problems orphanages faced and the process of discarding them during the century. It also makes some suggestions for the future of the institution.

THE PROBLEMS of the Hebrew Orphan Asylum were typical. In 1911, when the number of children at the H.O.A. rose above one hundred, the board of directors started to look for homes in which to place some of them. Although foster care had been used before, especially for infants and children who had difficulties adjusting to the orphanage, this time the search for families was a result of lack of facilities.³ In 1876, when the building was dedicated, its forty-four rooms were estimated to accommodate 150 children. But many of the rooms were used for educational purposes, and child care standards of 1910 required more space per child. As a result, the building could house only 130 children at most. Since the favored method of housing dependent children was now the cottage system, the directors aimed at building a new orphanage. In 1911, however, they renovated the old structure because they were not able to raise money for a new facility. Even a generous contribution for that purpose was not sufficient. In 1915, the directors asked the state for help in building cottages and also for an increased annual appropriation.⁴ To understand the state's policy in this matter, it is essential to take a small detour and explain the way it calculated subsidies for child care institutions.

The Board of State Aid and Charities investigated institutions that appealed for help and made recommendations to the Maryland General Assembly. In order to fulfill its task, the board defined guidelines for funding child care institutions. These reflected the general trend in charity, and especially in child welfare, to standardize methods of care and give money only to institutions that could be investigated and supervised and that would live up to their promises. The Board of State Aid and Charities had no power of decision and the Maryland Legislature sometimes disregarded its recommendations. But the work of the Board is important in understanding the considerations involved in appropriating money to a private child care institution.

Child care institutions were rated according to their facilities, educational system, and level of care. The Board of State Aid and Charities supported three groups of institutions graded as C, B, and A. The minimum requirements for a group C institution were (1) proper housing, including adequate segregation of sexes, (2) adequate supervision—at least one adult for each six children under two years of age and one for each twelve children above that age; (3) proper food and clothing and proper medical care for the sick; (4) religious instruction in the faith of the parents or guardians; (5) educational program equal to or better than the standard curriculum outlined by the state board of education for county schools and continuing at least through the fifth grade; (6) books that showed readily and accurately the family of each inmate and the whereabouts of all children placed out while under the control of the institution, the population of the institution, and income and expenditure according to the classification of the Board of State Aid and Charities, including a proper accounting of supplies raised or manufactured and used in the institution.

Group B institutions had to meet all the requirements of group C and, in addition, to employ a superintendent who was a well-trained and experienced children's worker. The institution had to give thorough medical examinations on admission and annually, to keep adequate medical records, to maintain a special room "for hospital purposes and detention ward for cases on admission until all danger of infectious disease is past," and to have a trained doctor or nurse resident in the institution. The staff had to investigate all children who applied and to keep case records (but case records could be kept by an agency approved by the Board of State Aid and Charities); it also had to follow up on children who were paroled or placed out. Finally, at least two kinds of vocational education for each sex had to be given to every child of twelve years and older.

Group A institutions had to fill all the requirements of groups C and B and, in addition, to give mental examinations (intelligence tests) and classify children on admission and annually thereafter. They had to use the cottage system and to provide three types of vocational education for each sex. Vocational classes had to offer shops and to have trained instructors for children age twelve and over. General education in the institution had to encompass at least elementary school through the eighth grade.

The state did not provide for all children in institutions. Children whose board was paid by parents or other individuals and organizations were not included. The per capita cost of a group C institution was estimated at between $50 and $260, with an average of $117 per child. Although those who set the standard did not believe that it was possible to meet the requirements of group C and spend only $50 per capita, they nevertheless set that amount as minimum. The proper charge for each child for an institution in group C, the board felt, was $200. The cost per capita for group B institutions ranged between $97 and $289, with an average of $186. The proper charge was estimated at $200, with an addition of $25 for each child who needed to be supervised after release. The charge for a child in a group A institution was estimated at $250.

The state in 1915 bore from 7 percent to 63 percent of the cost of maintaining and educating dependent children, with an average of 28 percent. In 1915, the recommendation of the Board of State Aid and Charities was to cover 30 percent of the cost per child in each category. In other words, if the cost of a child in a group B institution was estimated at $200, the state would pay 30 percent of that sum ($60) to the institution.

The board also pointed out that expenses could be reduced if institutions would follow the example of the Jewish Children's Bureau, which made "an accurate scientific investigation" of all children before they were placed and of those already in its institutions. The bureau found that a fifth of the population of its orphanages could be cared for at home without expense to the public. As a result, the number of children at the Russian orphanage (Hebrew Sheltering and Protective Association) was reduced from 106 to 80.

In its recommendation for the H.O.A., the Board of State Aid and Charities said that the orphanage "represents the highest grade of institutional work done in the State. It is planned to erect a new institution on the cottage basis and if done the asylum would easily rank in Class A." The board granted the H.O.A. more money than it had received in the previous year ($6,000 instead of $4,000) but refused to recommend $20,000 for construction. The explanation was that "as a matter of policy, it is not advisable to grant any appropriations to private institutions for building purposes."

The participation of the states in maintaining child care institutions varied considerably, but in 1910 the average state's support was estimated at 40 percent. In 1910 the tendency was toward "placing all benevolent institutions under government care." While states like Ohio and Pennsylvania built and supported child care institutions, Maryland continued to appropriate public money for private institutions to cover child care expenses only.[5] The level of appropriation in Maryland during the 1920s and 1930s remained lower than the national average and did not cover more than a third of the total population of dependent children in the state.[6]

The need for public subsidy affected all orphanages. It required them to accept uniform standards of care and to submit to supervision. It also exposed them to the charge that, because some institutions did not meet standards, orphanages were not appropriate for dependent children. An example of that approach was the study by William J. Doherty, the Second Deputy Commissioner of the Department of Public Charities in New York City. In addressing the 1915 national social workers' conference Doherty claimed that he had "an experience of fifteen years in handling the output of institutions and one year as a public official in dealing intimately with the methods entering into the conduct of children's institutions."[7] He did not conceal his opposition to institutions but explained that the only way to convince the public that institutional care was outdated was to provide concrete evidence rather than theoretical discussion. After twenty-two years of heated debate about child care institutions, Doherty admitted that attacks against them "lacked force because of the fact that they were based, not upon concrete evidence resulting from an extensive and exhaustive study but, quite generally, upon scattered instances of debatable conclusions."

He studied more than twenty private orphanages in New York and divided them into three groups. The first consisted of "exceptionally good institutions whose work is of such high type as to reflect credit not alone upon the institution itself but, likewise, upon the community where in they operate." He praised the superintendents of these orphanages as acting in "'loco parentis' to the children entrusted to their care." Not all the institutions he praised were cottage orphanages, but all—even those in the congregate system, which operated under serious environmental disadvantages—were "bending every energy to measure up to the standards of progressive and enlightened child care." Doherty's second group of orphanages were institutions "whose methods in operation are of such a low standard as to render them practically incapable of producing results worth while." In those of the third group "managers cling fondly to traditions and adhere tenaciously to methods of child care which long ago were thrown into the discard by progressive institutions."

Doherty painted a grim picture of institutions that failed to meet modern standards and faulted superintendents of these orphanages, who, according to him, were in most cases not social workers or educators. He blamed state and city authorities in New York for not supervising the institutions closely enough and not insisting on reform. He stated that financial problems were not the main cause of poor conditions in many institutions, but rather the attitudes of those in charge. As an example he cited the Hebrew Sheltering Guardian Society of New York, which "formerly . . . conducted an obsolete over-crowded congregate plant in the heart of the city. A few years ago the board of managers disposed of the city plant and removed to the county where there is now conducted a thoroughly modern, well-equipped, and progressive cottage orphanage, one of the best of its type in the country." Doherty's example tried to show that an educator, a trained social worker, was able to modernize an outdated institution. He failed to point out that the community raised a huge sum of money for the model cottage orphanage. Doherty ended his presentation on an optimistic tone, assuring his audience that as a result of his study and the state commissioner's supervision, the orphanages criticized had changed.[8]

Criticism of orphanages also came from superintendents of other institutions. The McDonogh School in Baltimore, for example, invited Dr. Rudolph Reeder, a superintendent of a New York orphanage, to inspect the school and suggest improvements. Superintendents of orphanages exchanged information and learned from each others' mistakes. But the intent of their criticism was to improve orphanages, not to close them down.

Critics like Doherty depicted foster care as a better answer than orphanges to dependent children's problems. According to its advocates, foster care gave children loving families and homes fully integrated in neighborhoods. They acknowledged that finding suitable families was sometimes difficult and that some children changed foster homes several times. But they believed that with effort, organization, and public information, the system would succeed. Besides, foster care was cheaper than the institution, they maintained.[9] Economic considerations, however, were not the reason given for preferring foster care. Supporters emphasized the benefits to the children, who would live in a family, learn to interact with the real world, and form affectionate bonds.

As early as 1921 problems in the foster care system were apparent. Sophia Van Senden Theis described the difficulties of finding suitable families, children who had to be placed several times, separation of siblings, lack of supervision, and child abuse in some cases.[10]

In the early 1920s, the Jewish community of Baltimore raised enough money to build a new cottage orphanage and achieved the highest standards of care prevailing at that time. The orphanage then resembled a boarding school. It had small rooms for two and three children each, and its residents attended public schools and had a rich extracurricular program including a band, music lessons, sports, dancing lessons, manual and vocational education, Hebrew school, clubs, entertainment, and cultural events. As Ilene B. testified, the children loved the new place in the country and enjoyed the activities planned for them. But the ideological trend that deemed orphanages outdated had been recognized by the Jewish community of Baltimore since 1911. Community leaders believed that they had to close the congregate institution and to have a cottage system in addition to an "efficient placing out system . . . until the placing system will be shown to meet all requirements of child-caring."[11] In the mid-1920s those requirements were probably considered sufficiently met because the community moved to make the placing-out system the exclusive method of child care. Orphans and their families resented and resisted the change. Bess Hammet, the last secretary of the H.O.A., described wrenching scenes in which children were called to the office and told that they had been selected for a foster family. Separation from siblings and friends was often entailed.

Most of the foster parents were poor and needed an extra income. Very often they had children of their own, and jealousy developed between the natural children and the foster child, who received gifts and new clothes on holidays from the foster care agency. The foster child's natural parents were dissatisfied with the arrangement because it highlighted their failure as parents, and they viewed the foster parents as rivals. Although social workers frequently implored synagogue congregations to accept foster children, finding suitable parents was a constant problem. The few middle-class homes that became available were what the agency called "opportunity homes." The case of Ilene B. shows, however, that such homes did not necessarily mean good relations between foster parents and children (see Chapter Five). For some, these relationships lacked warmth and affection and did not give the child a feeling of belonging. In other cases the children felt part of the family and were satisfied with the arrangement. Like orphanages, where some children adjusted and benefited and some did not, foster care was not the perfect solution for the dependent child. In 1930, Elias L. Trotzkey, the superintendent of Marks Nathan Home in Chicago, warned Jewish communities in the United States against the tendency to adopt every new notion in child care and particularly objected to the trend of abandoning orphanages. Instead, he suggested using orphanages and foster care side by side.[12] A similar warning in regard to discarding orphanages came earlier, in 1922, from a well-known social work researcher, Edward T. Devine, who reminded his audience of the advantages of an institution.[13] In 1949, Michael Sharlitt in his memoirs lamented that all the problems of foster care of the 1920s, which were supposed to be corrected, still existed. He referred to the lack of adequate supervision, a succession of homes for some children, and a lack of suitable homes as chronic problems. Sharlitt noted that "it was really surprising to read of the same hungers and criticism in foster home care that proverbially had been part of the running indictment against the old institution."[14]

By that time most Jewish communities abandoned child care institutions. The Baltimore Jewish community closed its orphanage in 1927; others were closed in the 1930s.

THE CATHOLIC community responded to the ideological trend toward foster care with mixed feelings and gradual change. Catholics already had placing-out agencies, and finding suitable Catholic homes was a pressing problem. The Children's Bureau of Catholic Charities placed 24 children in foster care in 1923, and 18 in 1924. These were children who did not have relatives interested in their welfare and for whom there was no hope of reestablishing parental homes. The Children's Bureau placed 137 children in institutions in 1923, and 119 in 1924. The 1933 census of dependent children does not reveal a great change in Catholic attitudes toward institutions. The same orphanages that operated in the 1920s were still accepting children in the 1930s, and the number of children in them did not decline. But there were more children in need of care during the 1930s, and the use of foster care was gradually growing. The Children's Bureau in 1933 reported 329 children in foster homes and 1,324 in institutions. The total number of dependent children in Maryland in that year was 4,249. Of that number 53 percent (2,283) were cared for in institutions and 47 percent (1,966) in foster homes. Catholic children were 57 percent of all dependent children in institutions in Maryland, but only 16 percent of those in foster homes. During the depression years the number of child care institutions in Maryland increased,[15] but Catholics did not found new institutions. Baltimore Catholics yielded to the ideological trend toward foster care, but they adopted the new system slowly.

In 1959, the Dolan Home was still operating at 1709 Gough

Street in East Baltimore and was still under the care of the Sisters of the Holy Cross. It had, however, a smaller number of children and a better financial base. In 1947, Catholic Charities invited experts in child care to inspect its institutions and suggest improvements. Mary Keeley's study found the same shaky financial ground that troubled the home in the 1890s and early 1900s. In 1947 the institution had twenty-four boys and girls between the ages of six and fourteen. The children represented only eight families, and all but one child had siblings in the institution. The population had not changed; it still consisted of boys and girls from several families. The children's records examined by Mary Keeley showed a lack of hope that their parental homes would be reestablished; some of them came either from other institutions (such as an orphanage for infants) or from foster homes. The staff was still overworked and was paid little more than in the early 1900s (in the 1940s the sisters annually received $200 each, compared to $100 in 1900). The dedicated sisters still spent many years at the orphanage. Of the superintendent, Mary Keeley wrote:

> The B.A. Degree was obtained at Manhattan College, and the graduate study at the University of Texas and Our Lady of the Lake College in San Antonio. The Sister Superior has been at Dolan Home for the past five years. She gives evidence of having vitality, interest and knowledge necessary to operate an institution serving children, and to her credit it ought to be pointed out that many excellent things are being accomplished at the Home, in spite of an almost impossible situation relative to plant, finances, and staff.

What the inspection revealed was not new. The staff was too small: three sisters and a part-time worker for twenty-four children. Three sisters and a laundress in the early 1900s had served thirty-five children and sometimes more.

Understaffing was not the only persistent problem the Dolan Home encountered; the small, old building and a shortage of funds had been part of the home's troubles almost since its foundation. The food budget was very low compared with other orphanages, even considering that some food was contributed. The Dolan Home was still located in a congested area and lacked adequate space for play. Yet Keeley found "an air of informality and freedom in the recre-

ational activities. . . . The children stand around and chatter freely
and they play the radio and dance in the study room." As in the early
1900s, Dolan Home children still attended the parochial school and
were raised in a religious atmosphere.

The recommendation of the report was to enlarge the financial
base of the institution, even if Father Dolan's will had to be contested
in court. Property that yielded little return should be sold and the
money more profitably invested. Two more sisters should be added
to the staff, or else the number of children admitted should be reduced. The Dolan Home's financial problems might be solved, the
report suggested, by merging the two institutions that had existed
side-by-side in the same building for so many years—St. Patrick's
Orphanage and the Dolan Home—and moving to a new area. Father
Dolan founded both institutions, the Sisters of the Holy Cross operated both, and both suffered from similar problems. Mary Keeley
suggested that, instead of two underfunded orphanages, one good
child care institution with adequate means would better serve Father
Dolan's intentions for the orphans of the community. In 1955, some
years after Keeley's study, Father Dolan's will was changed and his
assets consolidated to form a stronger financial base for the orphanage. Several years later, however, both orphanages were closed
and the children moved to another orphanage, Villa Maria, outside
the city.

The Dolan Home was only one of thirteen Catholic child care
institutions that Catholic Charities of Baltimore studied during the
late 1940s. Three of the institutions were schools for wayward children, and one was an institution for infants. Of the nine orphanages,
the Dolan Home and St. Patrick's Orphanage adjacent to it received
the harshest criticism. Some orphanages were praised for their
achievements, among them the St. James Home for Boys studied by
Grace A. Reeder of the Child Welfare League of America. This institution served boys who graduated from St. Mary's Industrial School
and had no homes to return to. Reeder explained the importance of
an orphanage for teenagers:

> It is becoming increasingly difficult to find foster homes even for chil-
> dren who do not present serious behavior difficulties and practically im-
> possible to secure good foster homes for children who do have such
> handicaps. The most important consideration, however, is that boys

who come into foster care at an age when it is difficult for them to accept substitute parents sometimes have to be placed and replaced in one foster home after another, [and] usually prove incapable of adjusting to any foster family home.

The St. James Home, according to the report, had single rooms and a wise and understanding staff. Moreover, the "unregimented atmosphere and the comparatively small group, all contributed toward the success of the program."

Mary Keeley also praised St. Francis Orphan Asylum, where thirty-three teenage black girls between the ages of twelve and eighteen were cared for by the Franciscan Sisters. The orphanage admitted girls of "bright or average mentality" and those "who can profit by the superior program of the institution." The study found that the St. Francis staff was the best educated of all orphanage staffs surveyed; members had professional training, college education, and teaching experience. Some sisters continued their education toward higher degrees. The orphanage seemed to be a model in terms of medical care, hygiene, diet, education, and extracurricular activities. It made good use of community facilities such as the YMCA swimming pool and a movie theater. Summarizing her report, Mary Keeley wrote:

> This institution operates very largely as a boarding school for girls. Obviously it has social services, as well as educational values to offer to the children under care. The whole institution is well equipped and attractive, and much seems to be done for the children. . . . The Sisters say that the girls prefer to stay through high school and certainly some unusual advantages are given these girls, with opportunities for foreign language training and many other special education opportunities.

Thus, within the centralized Catholic child welfare system in Baltimore of the 1940s and 1950s were a variety of institutions with different levels of care, just as in the 1890s and early 1900s. The difference between the 1940s and the turn of the century was that standards of care in the later period required a better educational program, better facilities, and more individual care. In the late 1950s, Catholic Charities closed down orphanages that could not meet standards, merged orphanages that faced financial difficulties, and moved orphanages from congested areas to better environments in order to improve its child care system.

The ethnic orphanage almost disappeared. Except for St. Leo, the Italian orphanage founded in 1913, there was not one orphanage with a distinct ethnic population. During the 1940s the Irish orphanages (St. Patrick and the Dolan Home) began to accept children of varying national backgrounds. The German orphanage (St. Anthony's) still existed in the 1920s and 1930s but does not appear in the reports of the 1940s. Orphanages, however, still differed in terms of race and gender. The 1933 U.S. Census of Dependent Children lists six orphanages for black children (housing 431 children, about 18 percent of all children in orphanages) in Baltimore. The majority were Catholic institutions for girls (five orphanages for blacks, four of which were for girls).

Protestant and nondenominational orphanages responded to the trend toward foster care either by closing their orphanages, making them temporary shelters until children could be placed in foster homes, or turning them into private schools. The Samuel Ready School took the latter course.

After Helen J. Rowe's death in 1919 and an interim period in which the general studies teacher, Clara H. Steiner, served as superintendent, the trustees selected Mary E. Krekel, a Samuel Ready graduate, to head the school. She entered the Ready as an eight-year-old full orphan in 1889 and graduated eleven years later with teaching certificates from the normal school and the Peabody Conservatory of Music. After a year of teaching privately and working as an organist in a church, she returned to Samuel Ready as a music teacher and remained on staff until her retirement in 1949. In 1922, she became superintendent. While she continued many traditions established in Rowe's era, she also made significant changes. The academic program expanded to include preparation of talented students for college. The institution was accredited by the Maryland Department of Education, and instruction in Latin became obligatory. Instrumental music was no longer taught only to the gifted but became a general requirement. The school tried to secure scholarships for its most promising students and enabled them to stay at the Ready School while taking courses at local colleges. During the depression, the school started charging students who were able to pay an annual fee of $50. In 1938, due partly to economic pressure and partly to the school's changing neighborhood, the trustees sold the property and built a new facility for eighty girls outside the city.

During the 1940s a new crisis threatened. For the first time the number of suitable candidates declined and enrollment dropped sharply. Between pensions and social security, which helped single parents raise their children at home, and foster care, which placed children in foster homes and used public schools for their education, institutions like Samuel Ready were left without students. Added to that problem was the poor state of the school's endowment, which had not kept pace with increasing costs. The trustees turned once more to McDonogh School for advice. McDonogh had its share of financial troubles in the 1920s, and its solution was to open the school to paying students. The advice of the McDonogh principal was to relocate the Samuel Ready School to McDonogh and institute a "program of coordinate education." McDonogh's trustees did not endorse the plan, but the Samuel Ready trustees moved in the direction McDonogh had taken. In 1947 they altered the school's charter to entitle paying students to enroll. In 1949, Mary Krekel retired, and Samuel Ready was no longer an orphanage. In 1950, the school opened to day students as well as paying students. For seventy-three years the Samuel Ready School had accommodated only boarders free of charge, but from 1950 on, it accommodated both paying and nonpaying boarders, as well as paying and full scholarship day students.

Economic strains continued to burden the school. In the early 1970s its boarding department closed. Ever-expanding academic costs and the increasing expense of boarding children caused a serious deficit. At that time the school no longer served white girls only but had a substantial number of black girls and both black and white boys up to fourth grade. In 1977, the trustees closed the institution altogether because expenditures had consumed the endowment. They sold the property and started a scholarship fund for needy girls from single-parent households to study in private schools in the Baltimore metropolitan area. The fund supported the Samuel Ready girls who transferred to three private schools in Baltimore. It now supports girls in five Baltimore private schools. The fund describes the girls it supports as "worthy and intelligent girls who need financial help to obtain an education that fully develops [their] capabilities." In 1987, the endowment, now called Samuel Ready Scholarships, Inc., provided for the education of thirty-four girls, of whom sixteen were from minority groups.[16]

Other private orphanages in Baltimore experienced the same financial troubles that depleted the Samuel Ready School's endowment. Some closed down, but some became successful private schools with rigorous academic requirements. McDonogh, St. Paul's School for Boys, and St. Paul's School for Girls fall into the latter category.

THE STORY of the orphanages had its twists. An institution born out of necessity was endorsed ideologically by reformers in the early nineteenth century, only to be abandoned by reformers at the turn of the twentieth century. Politically, the pendulum moved from left to right. At the beginning of the nineteenth century, advocates of orphanages were labeled reformers, and at the end of the century, they were conservatives. In the 1960s the institutions were repudiated by both sides of the political spectrum. Liberals viewed them as mechanisms of social control, and conservatives objected to their ever-expanding demands on public funds. The disappearance of the institutions had strong political implications for social workers as a professional group and for dependent children. Orphans became almost invisible; no longer in the public eye and without community ties, they were entirely dependent on social workers. Professional social workers, who dismissed the institutions without adequate research, doubtless had good intentions, as did the trustees of orphanages, but they were unable to form a better system of care for dependent children. Moreover, as several books on foster care show, the professionals were aware of the system's faults but claimed that there were no alternatives. They pointed out that the problems of foster care stem from inadequate resources allocated by the state, understaffing of foster care agencies, lack of suitable foster parents, and an increasing number of children needing the system. Ironically, these were the very problems opponents of orphanages cited when they declared that the institutions would never work: inadequate resources, understaffing, an increasing number of children in need, and insufficient bonding between adults and children.

From the experience of both systems, it is obvious that there is no easy or single solution for dependent children. The reformers of the late nineteenth century understood the importance of tailoring solutions to the child's needs and abilities. Since then society has moved continuously toward meeting each individual child's needs. Experience suggests that some children are better off in an institution and some in a foster home. But it also indicates that good institutions are expensive and that, even with a large endowment like the one the Samuel Ready School had, they can fail.

An alternative might be a foster home institution, a combination of both systems. In such an institution trained foster parents would preside over a large family in a good neighborhood. The children would benefit from such community institutions as a public school, a community center, a library, and social and medical welfare agencies. Foster care already has mini-institutions called "residential homes" or "group homes," but they are at present reserved for children waiting to be placed in foster homes or for children who did not adjust to previous placements. Training for foster parents also exists now. A foster home institution would essentially belong to the children in that it would be their permanent home throughout childhood. The professional foster parents might change from time to time, but the children would remain. When the adults in the home leave, the children need not adjust to a new school, new friends, and a new environment. This arrangement, like orphanages, would allow siblings to be placed together and would thus help to preserve family ties. A small institution in a good community can also benefit from volunteers' work, which can be valuable when long-term bonds are established between the volunteers and the children. Any institution, large or small, runs the risk of stigmatizing the children, but the stability such an arrangement would bring to children's lives and the feeling of belonging promise to be of no less importance.

Child care institutions in the past experimented with new ideas and were constantly under criticism and supervision that forced them to change. Older institutions included professionals and semiprofessionals, paid managers and volunteers—and the tension and exchange of ideas between them profited the orphanages. It is worth looking more deeply at the experience of the orphanage for guidance, and perhaps the best way to begin is to talk to the people it graduated.

INTRODUCTION

1. Based on Michael Aaronsohn's autobiographical book, *Broken Lights* (Cincinnati: Johnson and Hardin, 1946) and an interview with Wilfred S. February 17, 1988. Names of interviewees who wished to remain unidentified and names of children at the orphanages are disguised.

2. For a discussion of the relations between home ownership and middle-class status, see Stephan Thernstorm, *The Other Bostonians* (Cambridge, Mass.: Harvard University Press, 1973), p. 98.

3. David J. Rothman, *The Discovery of the Asylum* (Boston: Little, Brown, 1971), pp. 206–36.

4. William Raspberry, "What to Do about Foster Care?" *Washington Post*, October 4, 1989, p. A27.

5. Susan Tiffin, *In Whose Best Interest? Child Welfare Reform in the Progressive Era* (Westport, Conn.: Greenwood Press, 1982).

6. LeRoy Ashby, *Saving the Waifs: Reformers and Dependent Children, 1890–1917* (Philadelphia: Temple University Press, 1984), pp. 4–5, 8–10.

7. Aaronsohn, *Broken Lights*; Eileen Simpson, B. *Orphans, Real and Imaginary* (New York: New American Library, 1987); Frances Garate, *St. Anne's Orphanage* (Moore Haven, Fla.: Rainbow Books, 1984).

8. Patricia T. Rooke and R. L. Schnell, *Discarding the Asylum: From Child Rescue to the Welfare State in English-Canada (1800–1950)* (New York: University Press of America, 1983), pp. 134–35, 137.

9. Ashby, *Saving the Waifs*.

10. Susan Whitelaw Downs and Michael W. Sherraden, "The Orphan Asylum in the Nineteenth Century," *Social Service Review* 57 (June 1983): 272–90.

11. Ashby, *Saving the Waifs*, p. 9.

12. Speeches aimed at children, for example, emphasized their ability to overcome deprivation, while those aimed at contributors stressed the children's helplessness and misery.

13. Barbara M. Brenzel, *Daughters of the State: A Social Portrait of the*

First Reform School for Girls in North America, 1865–1905 (Cambridge, Mass.: MIT Press, 1983), p. 78.

14. Bruce William Bellingham, "Little Wanderers. A Sociohistorical Study of the Nineteenth Century Origins of Child Fostering and Adoption Reform Based on Early Records of the New York Aid Society" (Ph.D. diss., University of Pennsylvania, 1984). Like Bellingham, Michael Sherraden explained the growth of child care institutions in the nineteenth century as a solution to "oversupply child labor," that is, to teenage unemployment. "The Orphan Asylum," *Social Service Review* 57 (June 1983): 272–90.

15. For example, Anthony Platt, *The Child Savers—The Invention of Delinquency* (Chicago: University of Chicago Press, 1974, and Robert Mennel, *Thorns and Thistles: Juvenile Delinquents in the United States, 1825–1940* (Hanover, N.H.: University Press of New England, 1973).

16. *Proceedings of the National Conference of Charities and Corrections at the Forty-second Annual Session Held in Baltimore, Maryland, May 12–19, 1915* (Chicago: Hildmann Printing Co., 1915), pp. 174–93.

17. Stanley F. Bonner, *Education in Ancient Rome: From the Elder Cato to the Younger Pliny* (Berkeley and Los Angeles: University of California Press, 1977), p. 17.

18. *Jewish Encyclopedia*, 1903, s.v. "orphans"; *Encyclopedia Judaica*, 1971, s.v. "orphans."

19. *Enciclopedia Cattolica*, 1948, s.v. "Orphanotrofio" by Celestino Testore. Michael Mollat, *The Poor in the Middle Ages*, trans. Arthur Goldhammer (New Haven: Yale University Press, 1978), pp. 288–89.

20. Rev. P. A. Baart, *Orphans and Orphan Asylums* (Buffalo: Catholic Publication Co., 1885), pp. 22–23.

21. See Joseph Robins, *The Lost Children: A Study of Charity Children in Ireland, 1700–1900* (Dublin: Institute of Public Administration, 1980), p. 271.

22. Dorothy Zietz, *Child Welfare: Principle and Methods* (New York: Wiley, 1959), pp. 41–43. Lothar L. Tresp, "The Salzburger Orphanage at Ebenezer in Colonial Georgia," in *Americana Austriaca, Beitrage zur Amerikakunde* (Vienna: W. Braumüller, 1974) 3:190–234.

23. U.S. Department of Commerce, Bureau of the Census, *Benevolent Institutions, 1910* (Washington, D.C.: Government Printing Office, 1913), p. 108.

24. Rothman, *Discovery*, p. 207; Francis E. Lane, *American Charities and the Child of the Immigrant* (New York: Arno Press, 1974 [1932]), p. 103. According to institutional records and reports of the U.S. Bureau of the Census in 1880, 60,000 children were in institutions and by 1910, 123,000. See Downs and Sherraden, "The Orphan Asylum in the Nineteenth Century," p. 273.

25. Catholic orphanages accounted for 54 percent of all such institutions in the United States in 1902. Homer Folks, *The Care of Destitute, Neglected and Delinquent Children* (New York: Charities Review, 1902), p. 60. In 1890, according to the U.S. Census, among registered members of churches,

Catholics were 33 percent, but in the general population only about 10 percent (their actual percentage in the population might have been higher because some were not members of a church). *Compendium of the Eleventh Census: 1890* (Washington, D.C.: Government Printing Office, 1892–97), pp. 298–99, table 6.

26. See Homer Folks, "Dependent Children," in *The Care of Dependent, Neglected and Wayward Children, Being a Report of the Second Section of the International Congress of Charities, Correction and Philanthropy, Chicago, June 1893*, ed. A. G. Spencer and C. W. Birtwell (Baltimore: Johns Hopkins University Press, 1894), p. 69. U.S. Senate, *Proceedings of the Conference on the Care of Dependent Children* (held at Washington, D.C.), January 25–26, 1909 (Washington, D.C.: Government Printing Office, 1909).

27. *Social Work Year Book, 1929* (New York: Russell Sage Foundation, p. 134.

28. Marvin Lazerson and W. Norton Grubb, eds., *American Education and Vocationalism: A Documentary History, 1870–1890* (New York: Teachers College Press, Columbia University, 1983), pp. 17–30, trace the struggle over adopting vocational education in the public school during the 1910s. The Samuel Ready School had an industrial program in 1877, and other orphanages started industrial programs even earlier. See Helen J. Rowe's letters to E. G. Perine while touring child care institutions in 1886–87, in Samuel Ready School Archives.

29. Rothman, *Discovery*; Brenzel, *Daughters*, pp. 47, 104, 122–23, 148–55, 166.

30. Brenzel claimed that social Darwinism affected that view. See *Daughters*, p. 108.

31. A good example of this attitude is the Sisters of the Holy Cross, who ran the Dolan Children's Aid Society in Baltimore. They scrubbed floors, begged for food in the market, and raised forty children in a difficult environment. They worked for years and were paid the meager sum of $100 a year, which was barely sufficient for their annual trip to their convent in Indiana. Other superintendents and trustees were equally dedicated. Their devotion is discussed in subsequent chapters.

32. In the fifth report of the Federated Jewish Charities from 1912, the Hebrew Benevolent Society revealed the philosophy regarding poor Jews: "Jewish cases, were to a large extent the result of lack of opportunity, difficulty of securing a foothold in new surroundings, and physical breakdown under strange conditions and in new occupations." Both reports are in the Maryland Jewish Historical Society, Baltimore.

33. *Jewish Encyclopedia*, s.v. "orphan"; *Encyclopedia Judaica*, s.v. "orphans."

34. E. L. Trotzkey, *Institutional Care and Placing Out* (Chicago: Marks Nathan Jewish Orphan Home, 1930), p. 12.

35. From 1881 to 1920, 1,639,240 Jews came to the United States from Eastern Europe. Isaac M. Fein, *The Making of an American Jewish Commu-*

nity: The History of Baltimore Jewry from 1773 to 1920 (Philadelphia: Jewish Publication Society of America, 1971), p. 147.

36. "The Wrong of Immigration," *Jewish Chronicle*, Baltimore, October 1, 1875.

37. "The Committee of the United Charities," *Jewish Exponent* (published in Philadelphia but carried Baltimore news), December 4, 1891.

38. "Jewish Orphan Asylum, Cleveland, Ohio," *Jewish Comment*, Baltimore, May 25, 1906, p. 12.

39. Baart, *Orphans*, p. 240.

40. Marguerite T. Boylan, *Social Welfare in the Catholic Church* (New York: Columbia University Press, 1941), p. 20.

41. Francis E. Lane, *American Charities and the Child of the Immigrant* (New York: Arno Press, 1974), p. 105.

42. George Paul Jacoby, *Catholic Child Care in Nineteenth Century New York* (New York: Arno Press, 1974), p. 148; Lane, *American Charities*, p. 106.

43. See "Colored Nuns," *Catholic Mirror*, Baltimore, October 11, 1884, p. 2.

44. See for example, "The St. Elizabeth Home," *Catholic Mirror*, Baltimore, October 11, 1884, p. 2; December 14, 1907, p. 4.

45. Leonard Albert Stidley, *Sectarian Welfare Federation among Protestants* (New York: Association Press, 1944), pp. 1–25.

46. *Ready Record*, 1 (April 1, 1892): *Thornwell Orphanage: Its Principles and Product* (Clinton, S.C.: Thornwell Orphanage, 1942), p. 22.

47. See Rabbi Stephen S. Wise's speech attacking the distinction between worthy and nonworthy in *Proceedings of the Thirty-sixth National Conference of Charities on Correction Held in the City of Buffalo, New York, June 9–10, 1909* (Fort Wayne, Ind.: Fort Wayne Printing Co., 1909).

48. The "German" orphanages in various cities were established during the 1860s and 1870s. The "Russian" orphanages appeared first in the 1890s and 1900s.

49. Jay P. Dolan, *The Immigrant Church: New York's Irish and German Catholics, 1815–1865* (Baltimore: Johns Hopkins University Press, 1975), pp. 135–38; Simpson, *Orphans*; Garate, *St. Anne's Orphanage*, describes Italian orphanages.

50. On a Swedish orphanage see Ann Freebers Mandolini, "A Commitment to Faith and Heritage," *Swedish American Historical Quarterly* 5 (January 1984): 55. On an Indian orphanage see Kathleen Garrett, "The Cherokee Orphan Asylum," *Bulletin of the Oklahoma Agricultural and Mechanical College* 50 (August 1, 1953): 3–38. On black orphanages see John C. Chilton, *A Jazz Nursery, The Story of the Jenkins Orphanage Band* (London: Bloomsbury Book Shop, 1980); *Admission Record Indianapolis Asylum for Friendless Colored Children, 1871–1900*, transcribed and arranged by Jean E. Spears and Dorothy Paul (Indianapolis: Indiana Historical Society, 1978); *Sixteenth Annual Report of the Home for Destitute Colored Children* (Philadelphia: William P. Kildare, 1871).

51. Dieter Cunz, *The Maryland Germans* (Princeton: Princeton University Press, 1948).

52. Dolan, *The Immigrant Church*, pp. 133–37.

53. The Jenkins Orphanage is an example of an orphanage organized by blacks, while the Indianapolis Asylum for Friendless Colored Children was organized by the Friends Society in Indiana. The report of another orphanage speaks to other black orphanages' problems: "We need better school house facilities; we have the land for erection of an industrial school building but have no endowment fund, and are often compelled to make a perpetual struggle for a bare subsistence." *Twenty-ninth Annual Report of the Brooklyn Howard Colored Orphan Asylum Society*, September 30, 1898 (Brooklyn: Tremlett and Co., 1898). Brooklyn Howard was a black community orphanage and was considerably poorer than the New York Colored Orphan Asylum, which was organized, financed, and run by whites. Carleton Mabee, *Charity in Travail: Two Orphan Asylums for Blacks* (Cooperstown, N.Y.: New York State Historical Association, 1974), pp. 55–77.

54. Kathleen Garrett, "The Cherokee Orphan Asylum," p. 30.

55. Stephen Steinberg, *The Ethnic Myth* (New York: Atheneum, 1981), p. 227. "The Wrongs of Immigration," *Jewish Chronicle*, Baltimore, October 1, 1875.

56. Paul L. James, *Pennsylvania's Soldiers Orphan Schools*, 3d ed. (Harrisburg, Pa.: Lane S. Hart, 1877). *Biennial Report of the Military and Naval Orphan Asylum at Bath, Maine* (Waterville, Maine: Sentinel Publishing Company, 1909).

57. The Orphan Asylum of the City of Brooklyn is an example of a city institute (*Manual of the Orphan Asylum Society of the City of Brooklyn* [New York: The Society, 1899]). The State Orphans Home in Atchinson, Kansas, is an example of a state institute (*Thirty-third Biennial Report of the State Orphans Home* [Topeka: State Department of Social Welfare, 1952]). The orphanages in Maryland were all private but some received financial aid from the state. See Chapters One and Six.

58. For the professionalization of the field see Roy Lubove, *The Professional Altruist: The Emergence of Social Work as a Career, 1880–1930* (Cambridge: Harvard University Press, 1965). Literature about the new professional child care workers includes: Rudolph R. Reeder, *How Two Hundred Children Live and Learn* (New York: Charities Publication Committee, 1910); and Adele S. Jaffa, *A Standard Dietary for an Orphanage* (Sacramento: California State Printing Office, 1915).

59. Reeder, *How Two Hundred*, pp. 45–71.

60. "Should an institution for dependent children maintain its own schools, or send its wards to the public school?" The question posed in ibid., pp. 117–21, sums up the reformers' debate.

61. Ashby, *Saving the Waifs*, p. 5.

62. *Proceedings, National Conference of Charities and Corrections, Forty-second Annual Session*, pp. 174–93.

CHAPTER ONE

1. James B. Crooks, *Politics and Progress: The Rise of Urban Progressivism in Baltimore, 1895 to 1911* (Baton Rouge: Louisiana State University Press, 1984), pp. 156–62. Other methods of caring for dependent children were placing them in families or supporting them at home.

2. Michael S. Franch, "Congregation and Community in Baltimore, 1840–1860" (Ph.D. diss., University of Maryland, 1984), table 15.

3. Some of the orphanages, such as the Dolan's Farm School for Boys founded in 1849, merged with others or disappeared. U.S. Department of Commerce, Bureau of the Census, *Benevolent Institutions, 1910*, 2d ed. (Washington, D.C.: Government Printing Office, June 1914), pp. 108–9.

4. Isidor Blum, *The Jews of Baltimore* (Baltimore: Historical Review Publishing Co., 1910), p. 20.

5. Jewish Family and Children's Bureau, *A Century of Understanding, 1856–1956* (Baltimore: Associated Jewish Charities, 1956).

6. Alexandra Lee Levin, *The Szolds of Lombard Street: A Baltimore Family, 1859–1909* (Philadelphia: Jewish Publication Society of America, 1960), pp. 7, 352.

7. "Local Matters," *Baltimore Sun*, November 13, 1874. *The Gazette*, Baltimore, October 23, 1876, p. 4, and G. W. Howard, *The Monumental City* (Baltimore: J. D. Ehlers, 1889), p. 621.

8. Michael Aaronsohn, *Broken Lights* (Cincinnati: Johnson and Hardin, 1946), p. 13.

9. Michael Aaronsohn, *That the Living May Know* (Cincinnati: Johnson and Hardin, 1973), p. 212.

10. *Address Delivered by William S. Rayner, Esq. at the Dedication of the Hebrew Orphan Asylum, May 8, 1873* (Baltimore: Deutch and Co., 1873) in Enoch Pratt Free Library, Baltimore.

11. LeRoy Ashby, *Saving the Waifs: Reformers and Dependent Children, 1890–1917* (Philadelphia: Temple University Press, 1984), p. 7. Barbara M. Brenzel, *Daughters of the State: A Social Portrait of the First Reform School for Girls in North America, 1865–1905* (Cambridge, Mass.: MIT Press, 1983), p. 137.

12. The collective description is based on biographies. Blum, *Jews of Baltimore*, describes some board members in detail and lists others as members of various social clubs and philanthropic organizations. See esp. pp. 165, 169, 187, 237, 270, 407.

13. Ibid., p. 99; Aaronsohn, *That the Living*, p. 23; H.O.A. minute book.

14. A good example of this trend is Abraham Cohen, a graduate of City College who earned a Ph.D. in mathematics from Johns Hopkins University. He became a professor of mathematics at Johns Hopkins and served on the board of the H.O.A. from 1898. Blum, *Jews of Baltimore*, p. 149.

15. For the standard of education in the orphanage during the 1870s see Nurith Zmora, "A Rediscovery of the Asylum: The Hebrew Orphan Asylum through the Lives of Its First Fifty Orphans," *American Jewish History* 77

(March 1988): 452–75. The standard of education in the H.O.A. from 1900 to 1910 is discussed in Chapter Four.

16. Alexandra Lee Levin, *Vision: A Biography of Harry Friedenwald* (Philadelphia: Jewish Publication Society of America, 1964); Blum, *Jews of Baltimore*, p. 203.

17. Alexandra Lee Levin, *Dare to Be Different: A Biography of Harry H. Levin* (New York: Bloch, 1972).

18. An example is the case of Albert, who had conduct problems and was brought before Mr. Schloss twice.

19. The rabbis were A. Herffman (Hoffman), J. Gabriel, A. Sonn, S. Freudenthal. The social workers were M. Reizenstein, M. Sharlitt, and J. Kepecs.

20. *Jewish Comment*, Baltimore, June 10, 1910, pp. 1, 2.

21. Aaronsohn, *Broken Lights*, p. 28.

22. The work of Mrs. Freudenthal and her daughter, Dora Freudenthal, is described in a newspaper article about the H.O.A.: "All in a Happy House," *Baltimore American*, May 20, 1894.

23. The young daughter, Ray, was the kindergarten teacher in the first decade of the century.

24. In 1882 there were fifty-eight children in the H.O.A.; in 1907, seventy-eight; in 1909, ninety-two.

25. Although these philanthropic institutions belonged to two different organizations, one of German Jews and the other of Russian Jews, contributions very often came from the same sources.

26. In 1908, the Federated Jewish Charities brought all charitable organizations of the German Jews in Baltimore under one roof.

27. Michael Sharlitt, *As I Remember: The Home in My Heart* (Shaker Heights, Ohio: Belle Paire Jewish Children's Home, 1959), pp. 29–93.

28. Frances S. Meginnis, *Samuel Ready . . . The Man and His Legacy* (Baltimore: University of Baltimore, 1987), pp. 12–18. Langsdale Library Special Collections, University of Baltimore.

29. Hugh F. Burgess, Jr., and Robert C. Smoot III, *McDonogh School: An Interpretive Chronology* (Columbus, Ohio: Charles F. Merril, 1973), pp. 43, 111.

30. Miss Rowe appointed all the staff at the Samuel Ready School, and when she was not satisfied with the appointed persons she either fired them or forced them to resign. The board rejected Rowe's advice in the case of Rachel, a student who was not reappointed. Miss Rowe felt sorry for her mother and grandmother and wanted to reverse her decision. The trustees disagreed.

31. The S.R.S. minute book, p. 50, reports a new trustee: "Mr. Hurst nominated Mr. George W. Corner Jr. of the firm of Rouse Hempstone J. Co. and son of Mr. George W. Corner, for 33 years a trustee and for 13 years a president of the Board, to fill the vacancy." Mr. Hurst himself was a second-generation trustee whose father, John E. Hurst, served on the board before him. E. G. Perine was the son of David M. Perine, who wrote the charter of the Samuel Ready Orphan Asylum. Daniel C. Gilman and Charles H. La-

trobe were trustees from the early years of the Samuel Ready School until their deaths.

32. "Blanchard Randall," *Baltimore Sun*, August 26, 1942. This class of gentlemen donated some of Baltimore's best cultural institutions, such as the Enoch Pratt Free Library.

33. John E. Hurst, 1832–1904, Dilenan Hayward file in Maryland Historical Society.

34. "E. Glenn Perine Dies at Age of 93 Years," *Baltimore Sun*, June 16, 1922.

35. "Wilton Snowden Obsequies Today," *Baltimore Sun*, July 26, 1930.

36. *History of Baltimore*, by various contributors (New York: 1912), pp. 401–2. Albert E. Denny, "Gilman: The Man Who Shaped Hopkins' Destiny," *Evening Sun*, July 6, 1987.

37. A good example of the role of the trustees in handling the institution's finances is the February 1, 1911, meeting at which Miss Rowe's salary was discussed. The debate was extensive, but finally Miss Rowe received an increase.

38. Rev. James Dolan's last will and testament, Register of Wills, 1870, Book 36, Folio 26/27/28, Baltimore City Court.

39. "Young Catholics' Friend Society," *Catholic Mirror*, Baltimore, April 26, 1890, p. 5. (The name of the association appears differently in different places: "Young Catholic's Friend Society," "Young Catholics Friend Society," and "Young Catholic Friends' Society." I use the first form.)

40. Dolan's will specifies what kind of orphanage he wanted in the item referring to the St. Patrick's orphanage: "said boys and girls to be kept at said asylum or school until of twelve years of age and no longer, and then . . . bound or placed in some good Catholic families." The executors of the will applied these guidelines to the Dolan Children's Aid Society.

41. The Executive Committee gave the sisters guidelines for registering the children and keeping the books after they discovered that the books were not kept well.

42. The trustees were eleven persons from various parishes. For example, Thomas Foley Hiskey, the secretary in 1896, was from St. Martin Branch of Y.C.F.S., E. J. Codd, the treasurer at that time, was from St. Patrick Branch, Simon I. Kemp was from St. Vincent. The Executive Committee were three members from the board who served for three months. Every member of the board served a quarter of a year on the Executive Committee.

43. "Death of Dr. Chatard: Well Known Catholic Physician Passed Away," *Catholic Mirror*, September 1, 1900.

44. Michael A. Mullin, Bar Association Report 1914, in Dilenan Hayward file, Maryland Historical Society.

45. Edward J. Codd, 1900 U.S. Census, Maryland Population E.d. 104, p. 106 line 4; RG3 series 1, Box 87, Doc. 758, in Baltimore City Archives. E. J. Codd, Michael A. Mullin, George F. Rosensteel, Simon I. Kemp were born in Maryland, but their parents were Irish. James. R. Wheeler and Michael Eagan were born in Ireland. Except for Dr. Chatard, who was of French origin but born in Maryland, all the members of the trustees during the 1890s and

early 1900s were of Irish descent. Based on 1900 U.S. Census, Maryland Population. The following line from an obituary from Michael A. Mullin shows the importance of ethnicity in his life: "He was a member of the Maryland Historical Society, and president of the Hibernian society of which he was a member for forty-nine years; he devoted a great deal of his time and talents to the Irish cause." Michael A. Mullin, Dilenan Hayward file, Maryland Historical Society.

46. Some members of the H.O.A. board are listed as members of the Phoenix Club (a social club). Some also belonged to the Suburban Club (a sports club). Jews contributed money to German charities in the city and were considered part of the German colony. Rev. John Gottlieb Morris, *The Germans of Baltimore* (Baltimore: 1893), p. 18.

47. James B. Crooks, *Politics and Progress: The Rise of Urban Progressivism in Baltimore, 1895–1911* (Baton Rouge: Louisiana State University Press 1984), pp. 176, 228, 229.

48. Blum, *Jews of Baltimore*, pp. 80, 192.

49. W. S. Rayner, an H.O.A. director, served as one of the managers of the House of Refuge. Simon I. Kemp from the Dolan Home and Joseph Friedenwald, a former H.O.A. president, were both trustees of the almshouse in 1886 (City Council of Baltimore RG-16/S1, 1886/180, in Baltimore City Archives).

50. Dr. Chatard, for example, was involved with two orphanages: St. Mary's Orphan Asylum and the Dolan Home. His wife was an officer of St. Elizabeth Orphan Asylum. The wives of most of the directors of the H.O.A. belonged to Hebrew Orphan Ladies Aid Society, which helped supply the H.O.A. with clothes and linen.

51. Meginnis, *Samuel Ready*, p. 17.

52. Ibid., p. 15.

53. In the annual report for 1911 of the Kelso Home (in the Maryland Historical Society), approximately two hundred dollars was spent on each of the forty-three girls in the home. The Hebrew Orphan Asylum also spent two hundred dollars for each child annually. Both institutions sent their children to the public schools, and in both institutions doctors treated the children without pay.

54. "Many are the advantages enjoyed by 'Ready' girls today to which we of 1887 were strangers." "A Retrospect: Impressions of Three 'Old Girls'," twenty-fifth anniversary of the Samuel Ready School.

55. *Ready Record* 1 (February 5, 1892): 1 has a description of the new dormitory; 4 (November 1, 1895): 1 describes the new library. Both were trustees' donations. The trustees and their friends made more donations later (Ross legacy, 1897; Lyon's Hall, 1905).

56. St. Patrick's School was the first parochial school in the United States. It opened in 1815 and was free of charge, supported by contributions. *Sisters of the Holy Cross Centenary, 1859–1959, St. Patrick's Girls School and Orphanage.*

57. Legacies and donations were listed under "sinking fund account" in the annual reports of the H.O.A.

58. In 1903, the list of members and annual contributors included more than 650 members who contributed between $5 and $100.

59. This organization raised money only in the first years of the H.O.A.'s existence. Blum, *Jews of Baltimore*, p. 121.

60. Meginnis, *Samuel Ready*, pp. 31, 33; Blum, *Jews of Baltimore*, p. 99; H.O.A. annual report, 1906.

61. Baltimore City Court, Equity Docket 1904, file 44A, p. 384.

62. The decision is given in a note attached to Jacob's registration and bears the date, December 9, 1918. The siblings' records show that they did not return to the institution. Jacob was admitted in 1915 on account of neglect.

63. For example, Alice, age eight, was admitted to the H.O.A. in May 1908 on account of "immoral condition in the house of parents," through a juvenile court order. A year later on April 1, she returned to her mother again by a juvenile court order.

64. The city of Baltimore and the state assembly contributed toward maintaining child care institutions. This subject is discussed in Chapter Seven.

CHAPTER TWO

1. Michael Aaronsohn's mother emigrated from Russia to the United States as a young bride and worked in "the field and the factory" before giving birth to three children within the first six years of her marriage. She was probably in her midtwenties when she was widowed. Michael Aaronsohn, *Broken Lights* (Cincinnati: Johnson and Hardin, 1946), pp. 9–12.

2. Tamara K. Hareven and Randolph Longenbach, *Amoskeag* (New York: Pantheon Books, 1978), p. 180; David M. Katzman, *Seven Days a Week* (New York: Oxford University Press, 1978), p. 44.

3. Alice Kessler-Harris, *Out to Work* (Oxford: Oxford University Press, 1982), p. 124.

4. The population of the three orphanages contained more fatherless children than motherless children. For example, in the Samuel Ready School there were thirty-six half orphans. Of those, thirty-two were fatherless, and only four were motherless. The disproportion may be due to economics. Fathers who lost their wives were still breadwinners and in a better position to hire helpers to cook and clean than widows who had not been wage earners before their husbands died and were therefore without specific training or employment.

5. The orphanages' records read, for example: "[Received] by request of Rev. Foley—St. Martin church" or "referred to by the Hebrew Benevolent Society." For all three institutions, parents applied directly to the trustees or directors.

6. For example: Edward Allen, "committed by M. A. Canton J.P. [justice of the peace] on account of the poverty of his mother."

7. The 1890 U.S. Census did not list the agencies through which children entered orphanages, but the 1910 census of benevolent institutions did. Since reformers after 1890 increasingly paid attention to proper child care and problems of child abuse, we would expect more children by 1910 to enter

orphanages through agencies such as the juvenile court or societies for preventing cruelty to children. Yet the majority of children in orphanages in 1910 were admitted by their parents. In the thirty-six institutions in Maryland, 1,106 children were admitted through four sources: public officials (168), officials of the institutions (trustees) (113), child-placing societies (like the Society for Preventing Cruelty to Children) (70), and relatives and friends of the children (755). That is, 68 percent of the children in Maryland's orphanages were admitted directly by relatives. A similar distribution is shown for the three Baltimore institutions studied in Table 1.

8. The Dolan Home record book described the reason for the admission of five-year-old Jeremy Deane in these words: "This child was abandoned by both his parents and was committed by Mr. Cusmyre, Northern Central District Station." Cory McDonald was committed through the intervention of Mr. Palmer from the Society for Preventing Cruelty to Children because "the child's parents being dead left [him] without a home."

9. "Mary suffering through neglect and bad habits of her mother was committed by Columbus Hobbs J. of P." Leni Guy, "suffering through neglect of his father, Gordon Guy, not restrained from habitually begging" (Dolan Home record book).

10. During 1888, few admissions were registered in the Dolan Home record book. I took the admissions of the subsequent year and added them to the children who were already in the home.

11. Department of Commerce, U.S. Bureau of the Census, *Benevolent Institutions, 1890* (Washington, D.C.: 1895). Table 284 lists 26,282 Irish-born parents, 11,737 of German birth (Bavaria, Austria, Bohemia, and Prussia appear separately in the table), 884 Russian-born parents, 497 parents born in Poland. (Poland was not an independent state in 1890. Because Jews arriving from Poland were not always registered as Poles, but sometimes as Russians, I combined the two groups.)

12. U.S. Census, *Benevolent Institutions, 1890*, table 282—Maryland. It should be mentioned, however, that blacks, Chinese, Japanese, and Native Americans appear in these tables separately. There were 283 black parents in Maryland (4,102 blacks and 972 of Asian origin in the United States).

13. The census shows 1,226 males and 2,048 females.

14. According to the 1890 U.S. Census, Population, Part 3, table 6, p. 298 (churches), Maryland had 379,418 members of all churches, of which 141,410 were Roman Catholics. In the U.S. population of 1890 (62,622,250), there were 6,231,417 Catholics (about 10 percent). The estimated number of Jews in Baltimore in 1900 was between 50,000 and 60,000 (about 10 percent of the city population). Between 1890 and 1910 about 2 million Russian Jews immigrated to the United States. In 1900 Jews were about 2 percent of the population.

15. Although there was no registration of a child's religion, those committed through a court had to be Catholics because judges tried to place children in institutions of their faith. Parents who used the intervention of priests probabaly belonged to their parishes.

16. Three children admitted by the intervention of the Society for Preven-

tion of Cruelty to Children (as it was registered in the records), as well as two children sent by Father Dominick from the St. Mary's Industrial School, were probably committed by the court. The Dolan Home record book registered Father Dominick's complaint about sending children to his institution without legal commitment, and it is likely that he secured the proper documents for the children he placed in the Dolan Home.

17. One full-orphan child entered the Dolan Home for a year, because "his sister could not control him."

18. Kristine Irin was committed by Squire Samner through the intervention of her father because "the child was destitute and suffering from the bad habits of her mother." A year later the father received the child.

19. Kelley Hobban had a living mother but was placed in the Dolan Home by her guardian. Between October 8, 1888, and September 1893, she was admitted and released four times.

20. None of the children in my sample fall into this category, but such cases are cited in the Dolan Home book.

21. It is possible that the child was returned to his mother because she was very sick. Five months later, the eleven-year-old boy returned to the home because his mother had died.

22. Three had unclear legal status, and five (25 percent) were committed by their parents through a court's order.

23. Four of the five children committed that way returned to their mothers upon the mothers' request. In the case of the fifth child (Chris Alvin), it is not clear if his mother was alive, because his previous residence with his mother was the Bay View Hospital.

24. A seven-year-old girl was placed by her father through a court order. Her mother is labeled as having "bad habits," and it is not clear that the labeling was part of a litigation between the parents. The father took the girl a year later with the consent of the Dolan Home and upon the recommendation of a priest.

25. Christopher Lasch in *Haven in a Heartless World, the Family Besieged* (New York: Basic Books, 1977), p. 8, claimed that "between 1870 and 1920, the number of divorces increased fifteen fold. By 1924, one of every seven marriages ended in divorce."

26. The Watts brothers had an older married brother and a sister, herself a graduate of the Dolan Home. The brother took one of the boys to his home, but the child ran away and the brother committed him to the House of Refuge.

27. Five families had two children each in the H.O.A. Three families had three, three families had four, and two families had five children there. Six children had no siblings in the orphanage, though the younger sister of one of these was admitted in 1889.

28. Both parents of twelve and one parent of sixteen children were born in Russia or Poland. Both parents of one child and one parent of sixteen were born in Germany. Both parents of four children and one parent of five children were born in Baltimore. One child's mother was born in New York. The birthplace of sixteen parents was unknown.

29. Eight fathers were found in the Baltimore City directories for 1880–94. Two fathers died in Russia before the families came to the United States.

30. In the Miller family, the father was a teacher and the mother ran a store. They moved in 1886, 1887, and 1888. Even before 1886, there is a different address each year. For none of the children is the family address upon release the same as the one upon admission.

31. The high number of desertions points to the economic distress and cultural shock experienced by Jewish immigrants from Russia and Poland. All the fathers in these families were Russian or Polish, and three of them moved more than once after they left Russia. Only two reappeared.

32. The uncle, who became the guardian of all five children, had a large family of his own.

33. In one case the deserting father reappeared and took his three daughters back. Three parents remarried. The rest took their children when their economic and domestic situations improved.

34. LeRoy Ashby, *Saving the Waifs: Reformers and Dependent Children, 1890–1917* (Philadelphia: Temple University Press, 1984), p. 24.

35. The by laws of the H.O.A. left age of admission and release open, probably because Jewish law requires the community to take care of orphans until they are self-supporting, regardless of their age. For example, a handicapped orphan who cannot support himself is the community's dependent for life.

36. Whether the age of release for a boy was thirteen (three boys), fifteen (two boys), or sixteen (one boy), seems to have depended not only on family circumstances but also on the child's scholastic achievement. The relationship among age, education, and gender is discussed in Chapter Four.

37. When a death (or permanent hospitalization) of a mother occurred, the small children, three years and older, were placed in the H.O.A. with their school-age siblings. When the mother survived, the young siblings remained with her. In one case, the remaining parent was hospitalized, and in another the mother died shortly after the father. In these cases a foster home was secured until the children attained the age of three years. The teenage siblings in all cases stayed with their parent or relatives.

38. The undertaker, the small boat owner, and the farmers might be considered small entrepreneurs if they employed other workers. I included them among the manual workers because there was no evidence that they employed anybody and their widows' financial situation indicates that they probably worked alone.

39. Twenty of the forty had siblings in the school. Of the twenty, seventeen had one sister and three had two sisters at Samuel Ready.

40. Most of the girls attended public schools near their homes. Three (including two sisters) studied with private teachers. There are many references to church affiliation and activities in the files, either by Rowe, who noted with a pencil a child's denomination, or in letters of recommendation from ministers, or in letters to Rowe describing church activities during summer vacations.

41. Telephone interview with Hyman Warsaw, January 19, 1988.

42. Aaronsohn, *Broken Lights*, p. 11.

43. In another file, a letter of recommendation from a family pastor praised a poor widow of a physician who was left with four small children and managed for years to keep them with her by working as a seamstress. But the town had only an elementary school, and the widow wanted her daughter to have further schooling.

CHAPTER THREE

1. Cathy Sullivan, "A Retrospect: Impressions of Three 'Old Girls'," twenty-fifth anniversary of the Samuel Ready School.

2. William T. Howard, Jr., M.D., *Public Health Administration and the Natural History of Disease in Baltimore, Maryland, 1797–1920* (Washington, D.C.: Carnegie Institution of Washington, 1924), pp. 147–56.

3. LeRoy Ashby, *Saving the Waifs: Reformers and Dependent Children, 1890–1917* (Philadelphia: Temple University Press, 1984), pp. 27–29.

4. Rudolph R. Reeder, *How Two Hundred Children Live and Learn* (New York: Charities Publication Committee, 1910), pp. 45–71.

5. Elizabeth C. Putnam, an advocate of modest care, recommended foster care over the orphanage for "its deterrent effect" on parents, who often exaggerated their need in order to place their children in luxurious orphanages. Isabel C. Barrows, ed., *Proceedings of the National Conference of Charities and Correction at the Seventh Annual Session Held in Baltimore, Maryland, May 14–21, 1890* (Boston: Press of Geo. H. Ellis, 1890), p. 195. See also Col. William Allan, *The Organization of the Samuel Ready Asylum for Female Orphans, A Letter from Col. William Allan, Principal of the McDonogh School to the Trustees* (Baltimore: S.R.S. Trustees, 1883), p. 16, in Maryland Historical Society, Baltimore.

6. In 1946, when the orphanage housed only twenty-four children, Keeley's study showed that it was crowded. With thirty children, space must have been very limited.

7. *Baltimore Sun*, November 13, 1874, p. 1; Jewish Family and Children's Bureau, *A Century of Understanding, 1856–1956* (Baltimore: Associated Jewish Charities, 1956).

8. Michael Aaronsohn, *Broken Lights* (Cincinnati: Johnson and Hardin, 1946), p. 13; *Baltimore Sun*, November 13, 1874, p. 1; *The Gazette*, Baltimore, October 23, 1876, p. 4; *The Herald*, Baltimore, October 23, 1876, p. 4; G. W. Howard, *The Monumental City* (Baltimore: J. D. Ehlers and Co., 1889), p. 631; *American Architect and Building News* 25 (March 30, 1889):150.

9. *Jewish Chronicle*, October 23, 1876.

10. *Baltimore American*, May 20, 1894.

11. The architecture of the building, its location, and its modernization in later years interested the Jewish community at large. For example, after the building burned down in 1874, a committee was formed to examine several locations for the orphanage. "After much debate it was resolved to rebuild

on the old grounds" (*Jewish Comment*, February 19, 1875). On February 9, 1912, the *Jewish Comment* informed its readers that "the most imperative demand that confronted the officers and directors of the Hebrew Orphan Asylum during 1911 was the physical rehabilitation of the institution which required modernization in a number of particulars." It went on to describe each problem.

12. *Jewish Comment*, February 9, 1912; also superintendent's report.

13. Sanborn Map Company, *Sanborn Fire Insurance Maps, Md., 1901, 1914* (Teaneck, N.J.: Chadwyck-Healey, 1983).

14. Aaronsohn, *Broken Lights*, p. 15.

15. *Jewish Comment*, December 16, 1910. See also Reeder, *How Two Hundred*, p. 67.

16. Frances S. Meginnis, *Samuel Ready . . . The Man and His Legacy* (Baltimore: University of Baltimore, 1987), pp. 18–19, 21.

17. *Ready Record* 1 (February 5, 1892): 1.

18. Another girl wrote a year after she left the school that the flowers, trees, and grass at her new home reminded her of the Ready School.

19. Aaronsohn, *Broken Lights*, p. 39.

20. Howard, *Public Health Administration*, p. 20.

21. Ruth Schwartz Cowan, *More Work for Mothers, The Ironies of Household Technology from the Open Hearth to the Microwave* (New York: Basic Books, 1983), p. 162. Also interviews.

22. Meginnis, *Samuel Ready*, p. 15.

23. Michael Aaronsohn, *That the Living May Know* (Cincinnati: Johnson and Hardin, 1973), pp. 21–22.

24. Michael Sharlitt, *As I Remember, the Home in My Heart* (Shaker Heights, Ohio: Bellefaire Jewish Children's Home, 1959), p. 21; Aaronsohn, *Broken Lights*, p. 15; Eileen Simpson, *Orphans, Real or Imaginary* (New York: New American Library, 1987), pp. 145–47; Frances Garate, *St. Anne's Orphanage* (Moore Haven, Fla.: Rainbow Books, 1984), p. 48.

25. " 'Going to City College' signified bread spread with butter, instead of molasses, and two eggs for breakfast each school day." Aaronsohn, *Broken Lights*, p. 32.

26. Simpson, *Orphans*, pp. 145–47.

27. Sharlitt, *As I Remember*, p. 21.

28. Cowan, *More Work*, pp. 164–65.

29. "School Children Well Nourished," *Jewish Comment*, April 28, 1911.

30. Spargo claimed that many children were going to school hungry, were underfed and suffering from various illnesses related to malnutrition. As a result of the controversy the book raised, communities started organizing meals for children in the public schools. John Spargo, *The Bitter Cry of the Children* (London: Macmillan, 1906), pp. 57–124.

31. On March 1, 1911, Superintendent Reizenstein complained before the board of directors that girls' chores interfered with their school and enrichment program because they had to serve three meals. His description of the girls' schedule reveals some of the H.O.A.'s menu: "some of these girls must butter the bread for breakfast (four pieces for each of the 103 children) pour

out the coffee, etc. . . . When they return at noon they serve the soup for dinner; and later, the meat, potatoes and vegetables. . . . At 4.30 P.M. some of the girls are needed to butter the bread for supper. Later they must serve the cereal, or other supper, pour out the tea or coffee, etc."

32. "Mamma, everything's fine out here. We've got a lot of boys to play with. . . . But, gee Mamma, I wish they'd give us more to eat." Aaronsohn, *Broken Lights*, p. 15.

33. For example, Freudenthal wrote in his report from May 1893: "thanks to Mrs. Joel Gutman for a dinner and fruit given to our children in honor of her daughters marriage, . . . [to] The Mrs. Lena Hecht Society [for] a treat to our children consisting of cakes and candies."

34. Aaronsohn, *Broken Lights*, p. 42; *That the Living*, p. 39.

35. "Mrs Eden, being remarried since December last visiting her children on our last Visiting Day Sept. 1st and infringing upon the rules of our institution by feeding her children with not very wholesome fruit, candy and cakes and being reprimanded for the same became very impudent in presence of all the children and strangers." H.O.A. superintendent's report.

36. *Ready Record* 1 (March 4, 1892): 5.

37. Aaronsohn, *Broken Lights*, p. 23; interview with Simon Z.

38. *Ready Record* 1 (February 19, 1892): 5.

39. In the Dolan Home in 1890, the expenditure for food for thirty-six children was $220 for three months. The sisters solicited gifts of food worth $35 per month. All together food at the orphanage cost about $1320, or $36.6 per child, a year ($3 a month per child). The H.O.A. in 1883 spent $3,548 for "Household Expenses and Marketing, including cost of cow and feed, sundry Expenses, Bread, Meats, and Other Provisions and Groceries." At that time the H.O.A. sheltered 51 children. The expenses per child (without outside contributions of food) were $69 (about $5.8 per child a month). In the Samuel Ready, in 1888, provisions and servants' wages appear under the same item and amount to $3,664. In order to estimate the sum spent on provisions, I assumed that servants' wages at Samuel Ready were similar to those at the H.O.A. and deducted $885 (servants' wages at the H.O.A.) from the Samuel Ready total. The Samuel Ready probably spent about $2,779 on provisions for its 45 students, or $61.70 per child (about $5 a month per child).

40. Cowan, *More Work*, p. 65.

41. "The seamstress is busy fixing the spring and summer dresses. . . . The girls are interested in making waists and new-style white aprons. The aprons are for the small girls, and are prettiest [*sic*] than any made before." *Ready Record* 2 (March 24, 1893): 1; also (March 18, 1892): 4.

42. Aaronsohn, *Broken Lights*, pp. 31, 33.

43. In 1883, when clothing expenses for each child were $17, the contributions list shows 13 dozen underwear, 23 skirts, 7 pairs of knit stockings, 24 boys' suits, 10 boys' hats, shoes, hats for all the girls. All contributions, except for the knitted stockings, came from businesses.

44. Howard, *Public Health Administration*, p. 65.

45. Cowan, *More Work*, pp. 162–63.

46. Interview with David "Dutch" Baer, June 12, 1980, Oral History Project, Maryland Jewish Historical Society. Wilfred S. and Harry S. gave similar descriptions of bathing and toilets in their homes. See also Cowan, *More Work*, pp. 160–72.

47. The Samuel Ready School provided lessons in washing and ironing. *Ready Record* 1 (March 3, 1892): 3; 19 (March 18, 1910): 5.

48. Aaronsohn, *Broken Lights*, p. 41.

49. Howard, *Public Health Administration*, pp. 151–52.

50. Freudenthal reported on March 1906: "The health of our children has been good except that 3 of the Dayan's children have the whooping cough, have isolated them and so far our children have not caught the disease." A child with diphtheria was also successfully isolated.

51. Aaronsohn, *Broken Lights*, p. 14.

52. Garate, *St. Anne's Orphanage*, p. 24.

53. Reeder, *How Two Hundred*, p. 169.

54. Spargo, *The Bitter Cry*, p. 39.

55. Lauren Keller left the school in 1892 at the age of twenty. Five years later she wrote Rowe from the hospital that she was impatient to leave and rest for a few days at the Ready School. In a previous letter Rowe had advised her not to have an operation but to wait for further examinations. Beatrice Jones informed Rowe that she had recovered from diphtheria and was feeling much better. Her letter was sent to Rowe six years after she left the school.

56. The reasons for the school medical examination can be clearly understood from the discrepancies so often found in students' files between what the family doctor wrote and what the Ready School physician's examination showed. Family doctors tried sometimes to conceal health problems not only of the children but also of the parents, fearing an impediment to admission. For example, instead of writing that a father died of consumption, the family doctor attributed the death to a long case of pneumonia (eighteen months). The mother died from pneumonia, according to the doctor's report, but suffered only five to six months.

57. The age of the girls suggests that Rowe thought that health problems would render the extra two years of vocational education, which were optional, too difficult for them.

58. Freudenthal complained that he could not hire responsible nurses or keep them employed. In 1905 he suggested a raise in salary in order to attract good nurses. The records show that some children requiring constant care stayed in the H.O.A.

59. "I am sorry to report that one of our children Samuel Horowitz, 11 years old has been down with Pneumonia since January 26, it was a severe case and a trained nurse had to be employed; with the help of our Heavenly Father, the untiring attention of our physician Dr. Harry Adler and constant care and nursing the boy recovered so that by January 31 the nurse could be discharged, the rest of our children enjoy good health." H.O.A. superintendent's report.

60. See Isidor Blum, *Jews of Baltimore* (Baltimore: Historical Review Publishing Co., 1910), p. 55.

61. Alexandra Lee Levin, *Vision: A Biography of Harry Friedenwald* (Philadelphia: Jewish Publication Society of America, 1964).

62. Michael Teller, "The American Tuberculosis Crusade, 1889–1917; The Rise of a Modern Health Campaign" (Ph.D. diss., University of Chicago, 1985). "An Indiana study revealed that 42.3 percent of the children in three institutions were orphaned by tuberculosis; a New York investigation attributed 52 percent of the orphan asylum population in one city to the disease" (p. 87).

CHAPTER FOUR

1. Report of the Baltimore Public School Commissioners from 1890, p. 65, and 1912, p. 63. Maryland Historical Society, Baltimore.

2. Wayne E. Fuller, *The Old Country School: The History of Rural Education in the Middle West* (Chicago: University of Chicago Press, 1982).

3. Mary Antin, *The Promised Land* (Boston: Houghton Mifflin, 1912), pp. 26–27.

4. Stephen Steinberg, *The Ethnic Myth: Race, Ethnicity and Class in America* (New York: Atheneum, 1981), pp. 227–28. See also Michael Olneck and Marvin Lazerson, "The School Achievement of Immigrant Children, 1900–1930," *History of Education Quarterly*, 14 (Winter 1974): 424.

5. The school census of 1888 reported that of the 110,231 school-age children in the city, some 20,000 had not been in school for three years. Report of the Baltimore Public School Commissioners, 1890, p. 65, in Maryland Historical Society.

6. Michael Aaronsohn, *That the Living May Know* (Cincinnati: Johnson and Hardin, 1973), p. 28. Also interview with Wilfred S.

7. *Baltimore Public School Commissioners, 1912*, p. 63. Robert Bremner, *Children and Youth in America: A Documentary History* (Cambridge: Harvard University Press, 1971), 2:1125–29, 1333–36, focuses on the questions of "Americanization" and education in a democracy. See also discussion of John Dewey's Progressive ideas in Lawrence A. Cremin, *The Transformation of the School; Progressivism in American Education, 1826–1957* (New York: Vintage Books, 1964), pp. 123–24.

8. Francis Newton Thorpe, "Manual Training as a Factor in Modern Education," *Century Magazine*, October 1889, pp. 920–27.

9. Calum M. Woodward, "The Print of Manual Training," in *American Education and Vocationalism: A Documentary History, 1870–1970*, ed. with introduction and notes by Marvin Lazerson and W. Norton Grubb (New York: Teachers College Press, Columbia University, 1974), pp. 60–66.

10. Ruth Schwartz Cowan, *More Work for Mothers: The Ironies of Household Technology from the Open Hearth to the Microwave* (New York: Basic Books, 1983), chapters 4 and 6; Lazerson and Grubb, *American Education and Vocationalism*, pp. 10, 17, 114–15.

11. Felix Adler, "The Democratic Ideal in Education," *Century Magazine*, October 1889, pp. 927–30. Recent historians argue that the opposition was

right: "Working-class students have been channeled into vocational tracks, young women into traditional female courses such as cooking and sewing, and middle-class students into the academic course." Harvey Kantor and David B. Tyack, *Work, Youth and Schooling: Historical Perspectives on Vocationalism in American Education* (Stanford, Calif.: Stanford University Press, 1982), p. 9.

12. Ileen A. Devault, "Sons and Daughters of Labor: Class and Clerical Work in Pittsburgh, 1870's–1910's" (Ph.D. diss., Yale University, 1985); Marguerite Renner, "Who Will Teach? Changing Job Opportunity and Roles for Women in the Evolution of the Pittsburgh Public Schools, 1830–1900" (Ph.D. diss., University of Pittsburgh, 1981).

13. Interviews with Wilfred S. and Bess Hammet.

14. Col. William Allan, *The Organization of the Samuel Ready Asylum for Female Orphans; A Letter from Col. William Allan, Principal of McDonogh School, to the Trustees* (Baltimore: S.R.S. Trustees, 1883), p. 12. Maryland Historical Society, Baltimore.

15. *Ready Record* (March 18, 1892): 3.

16. Frances S. Meginnis, *Samuel Ready . . . The Man and His Legacy* (Baltimore: University of Baltimore, 1987), p. 28. Department of Special Collections, Langsdale Library, University of Baltimore.

17. See "Happy Young Girls, A Model Training School," *Baltimore Sun*, May 16, 1889; "Training Girls to Care for Themselves," *Baltimore Sun*, January 29, 1889; "A Girls' Training School," *Jewish Messenger* (New York), June 7, 1889.

18. "Each week the girls' reports are taken and on Friday evening their average made out. If the average made is nine or over the girl's name is put on the roll of honor, if it is below nine her name goes on the 'work list' which is a great disgrace." *Ready Record* 1 (March 4, 1892): 3.

19. Baltimore Public School Commissioners, 1900, pp. 55, 76, Maryland Historical Society.

20. Aaronsohn, *That the Living*, pp. 12, 16; *Broken Lights* (Cincinnati: Johnson and Hardin, 1946), p. 26; see also *Jewish Comment*, June 7, 1911.

21. Aaronsohn, *That the Living*, p. 72.

22. Meginnis, *Samuel Ready*, p. 29.

23. "The large girls are taught washing and ironing. They iron an hour every week and wash twice a month." *Ready Record*, March 4, 1892.

24. Meginnis, *Samuel Ready*, p. 29.

25. In a commencement speech in 1909, E. Glenn Perine detailed the vocations for which the girls were prepared: "113 have left fitted to earn their own living. Business course—38, sewing and dress making—33, teachers in public school—26, teachers of music—6, nurses—5, teachers of cooking—2, millinery—2, drawing—1."

26. That children and relatives were involved in the decision is clear from a distressful letter. A girl reminded Rowe that her aunt was present at a consultation at which all agreed that the girl would teach music. The aunt now wanted her niece to do something else.

27. An example is Enoch Miller. "Enoch Miller having passed the 8 grade in the Public School his average being 90 will attend City College Sept. next." On February 1, 1895, Freudenthal wrote in his report, "Would respectfully suggest that arrangements be made now for Enoch Miller to enter college next fall, he is, in my opinion, far enough advanced to be admitted."

28. For example: "Wolf Kurliz, Aaron Eder having reached the age of 14 years and not being talented enough to pursue their studies in the Public School, I would respectfully recommend their discharge from the Institution." The request was made on December 1, 1893. Aaron Eder was discharged on April 15, 1894. Wolf Kurliz was discharged on October 8, 1894. Both returned home. Wolf Kurliz was employed by "Our Director Isaac Blum Esq." Aaron Eder was discharged as "incorrigible"; no employment was mentioned.

29. A letter to the president and directors of the H.O.A. from December 10, 1910, says, "I hereby accept full charge of, and responsibility for my son, Samuel Selzers, and absolve you from taking care of him in the future. I shall send him to school. Thanking you for the care and attention that you have given him."

30. For example: "The Eder children ought to be returned to their parents. G. Gerber ought to be sent to his father in Washington D.C. who is fully able to take care of him. The Wilkovitz children should be discharged as their parents are living together." Superintendent's report, November 1, 1893.

31. In two samples taken from the H.O.A.'s population—one in 1873 (50 children) and the sample from 1899 used in this book (45 children)—there were no more than three girls at a time beyond sixteen in the institution. For analysis of the first sample (1873) see: Nurith Zmora, "A Rediscovery of the Asylum: The Hebrew Orphan Asylum through the Lives of Its First Fifty Orphans," *American Jewish History* 77 (March 1988): 452–75.

32. "Steps should be taken regarding Simon S., Larry S. and Matilda A. . . . As to the first two it would be advisable to ascertain what branches of studies they want to pursue. . . . As to Matilda A.—she wants to qualify herself as a teacher."

33. One of the two students underwent an eye operation that year (superintendent's report, March 1, 1898). It is possible that the boys did not pass their examinations for the second year. Only a quarter of those enrolled in the city public high schools finished the full course of studies in 1900.

34. Western High is one of two public high schools in Baltimore exclusively for girls, as City College and the Polytechnic Institute are exclusively for boys. Some H.O.A. girls without a high school education went to business or nursing schools.

35. Henry B. Waskaw, "I Remember: Two Different 'Rulers' at Jewish Orphan Home," *Baltimore Sun Magazine*, June 6, 1980.

36. During the 1890s the H.O.A. had two rabbinical students in different colleges. Their progress was frequently mentioned as well as their visits to the institution.

37. During the 1870s there were between thirty and forty children at one time in the Hebrew Orphan Asylum. This number rose to sixty to seventy during the 1890s and eighty to ninety during the early 1900s. After 1900 the majority of the children in the orphanage were Russian Jews.

38. "With the Hebrew Sheltering Society we have entered into an arrangement by which orphans and semi-orphans shall be referred to us, while cases needing temporary treatment will be sent to that organization." *Jewish Comment*, February 9, 1902, p. 2.

39. H.O.A. ninth annual report, 1915, p. 87.

40. An example of Freudenthal's policy with respect to vocational education is his request that the board of directors make inquiries about "the cost of establishing a printing press (hand-press)" and also give instructions in printing to "such of our children who show aptness."

41. In 1911 Daughters in Israel, an organization that founded a home for working girls, offered to take in the older girls of the H.O.A. and instruct them in domestic science. A committee of the H.O.A. accepted the offer only "for such girls over fourteen whom it would be inadvisable to keep longer in school. Those who make satisfactory progress in school ought to be allowed to complete their grammar school education." Sewing and cooking were part of the manual training at the H.O.A. but obviously were not considered training for a job. In the summer of 1915, Reizenstein added sewing and darning courses for boys. The change in orientation toward the professions and emphasis on academic studies are discussed in Chapter Six.

42. The *Jewish Exponent* (which was published in Philadelphia but circulated in Baltimore and also carried Baltimore news, reported that Rabbi Fleishman, the superintendent of the Jewish orphanage in Philadelphia, told the orphans in his December 30, 1889, sermon that "no man who depends entirely upon his hands earns more than two to three dollars a day at the very highest and certainly is not highly respected or honored in the community. . . . If we desire to occupy a position of trust or responsibility," he added, "with corresponding good pay for our work, we must learn, we must improve our minds." *Jewish Exponent*, December 30, 1887, p. 9.

43. See Bruce William Bellingham, "Little Wonderers: A Socio-Historical Study of the Nineteenth Century Origin of Child Fostering and Adoption Reform, Based on Early Records of the New York Aid Society" (Ph.D. diss., University of Pennsylvania, 1984), p. 68. (The word "adopted" appears in the Dolan Children's Aid Society minute book with a quotation mark.) A Maryland statute for adoption became law in 1892. *West's Maryland Law Encyclopedia*, s.v. "adoption."

44. LeRoy Ashby, *Saving the Waifs; Reformers and Dependent Children, 1890–1917* (Philadelphia: Temple University Press, 1984), pp. 23–25.

45. For example, a priest in Charles County depicted a child as having turned bad, but an investigation by the Dolan Home showed that the boy was ill treated.

46. "Under the Amended Charter of this Corporation Judges of Courts and Magistrates were authorized to commit minors to our care, parents be-

ing permitted to elect between this institution and the House of Refuge."
"The Memorial of St. Mary's Industrial School for Boys of the City of Baltimore," 16 SI, 1879; 729, in Baltimore City Archives.

47. Grace A. Reeder, "Memorandum Report of Study of St. James Home
for Boys."

48. "St. Mary's Industrial School . . . had at this time four hundred and
five boys in its custody, of which 375 were committed by Judges of Courts
and the various Magistrates of the State" "Memorial of St. Mary's Industrial
School." St. Mary's returned children from the Dolan Home on the ground
that they had not been properly admitted.

49. Barbara Brenzel, *Daughters of the State*, p. 78.

50. Some children attended parochial schools, others only Sunday
schools, and some only celebrated holidays.

51. In a letter about admitting a Jewish girl to the Ready School, Perine,
secretary of the board, wrote: "There is nothing in the charter to prevent the
admission of children of Hebrew birth." In the introduction to the Dolan
Home minute book, the board of trustees declared, "This charity is general
in its character, affording an asylum to waifs or indigent children from all
parts of the city, and of all creeds."

52. Rowe marked on the children's applications the church the family
belonged to, when it was not Methodist Episcopal. The presence of Catholic
girls in the school is apparent from letters in students' files. Several graduates
from the 1920s mentioned two Jewish girls in their class in conversations on
November 1, 1987, at the celebration of the school's one hundredth anniversary.

53. See *Address of Wm. S. Rayner, Esq. at the Dedication of the Hebrew
Orphan Asylum of Baltimore, May 18, 1873* (Baltimore: Deutsch and Co.,
1873), p. 6. Enoch Pratt Free Library, Baltimore.

54. William S. Rayner was a Reform Jew, and Benjamin Szold was a
Conservative. Michael Aaronsohn, the H.O.A. graduate who wrote about
his life there, came from an Orthodox family like many other Russian Jewish
families that arrived at the turn of the century. See Isaac Fein, *The Making of
an American Jewish Community* (Philadelphia: Jewish Publication Society of
America, 1971), p. 166.

55. The sermons of the first superintendent of the H.O.A., Rabbi
Abraham Hoffman, were written in German (six of them are in the Maryland Jewish Historical Society). German was dropped from the H.O.A. curriculum in 1902 in accordance with Freudenthal's request.

56. Aaronsohn, *That the Living*, p. 14.

57. Aaronsohn, *Broken Lights*, pp. 20–21.

58. The superintendent's report for October 23, 1913, states: "Memorial
services for the following benefactors of this institution are scheduled for
November. Nov. 2—Edward Oppenheimer, Nov. 8—David Ambach."
(Many of the people listed had been directors or relatives of directors of the
H.O.A.)

59. Aaronsohn, *Broken Lights*, p. 21; *That the Living*, p. 10.

60. Frances Garate, *St. Anne's Orphanage* (Moore Haven, Fla.: Rainbow Books, 1984). Eileen Simpson, *Orphans, Real and Imaginary* (New York: New American Library, 1987).

61. Aaronsohn, *That the Living*, p. 19.

62. Joseph M. Hawes, *Children in Urban Society, Juvenile Delinquency in Nineteenth-Century America* (New York: Oxford University Press, 1971). G. Stanley Hall is quoted on pp. 206–7.

63. Rudolph R. Reeder, *How Two Hundred Children Live and Learn* (New York: Charities Publication Committee, 1910), p. 55.

64. The Report of the Public School Commissioners of the City of Baltimore, 1900, Extracts from the Rules, Articles XIV (sessions) and XV (recess), p. 157. Maryland Historical Society.

65. Hawes, *Children in Urban Society*, p. 13.

66. Otto T. Mallery, "The Social Significance of Play," *Annals of the American Academy of Political and Social Science* 35 (January–June 1910): 368–73. In the same volume see Victor Von Borosin, "Our Recreation Facilities and the Immigrant," pp. 357–67, and Amalie Hoffer Jerome, "The Playground as a Social Center," pp. 345–48.

67. The connection between juvenile delinquency and lack of play time and space appears extensively in the literature of the Progressives. U.S. Department of Labor, Children's Bureau, *Facilities for Children's Play in the District of Columbia* (Washington, D.C.: The bureau, 1917), p. 16. Andrew G. Truxal, who investigated the subject in Manhattan, in 1920, came to the conclusion that "a certain amount of association between recreation areas and juvenile delinquency appears to exist." *Outdoor Recreation Legislation and Its Effectiveness* (New York: Columbia University Press, 1929), p. 165.

68. Victor Von Borosin, "Our Recreation Facilities and the Immigrant," *Annals of the American Academy of Political and Social Science* 35 (January–June 1910): 357–67.

69. U.S. Department of Labor, Children's Bureau, *Facilities for Children's Play in the District of Columbia* (Washington, D.C.: Government Printing Office, 1917), pp. 17–18.

70. Fein, *Making of an American Jewish Community*, p. 165; George N. Caylor, "Memories of My Baltimore Childhood, 1885–1896," Md V.F. in Enoch Pratt Free Library, Baltimore; interviews with Nathan Cooper and Wilfred S.

71. Interview with Harry S., who was offered supper money as an inducement to continue his studies in Hebrew school after he reached thirteen. The money was regarded as compensation for lost earned income.

72. "We were typical gamins, who would leave our poor and cheerless homes, to spend as much time as possible in the street. . . . Earning money in our neighborhood was virtually impossible, people were too poor to employ us running errands, doing other chores, or performing little jobs that youngsters like us could perform. There seemed but two choices left—to beg or steal. . . . Virtually all of us had been petty pilferers. . . . A couple of our 'till hoppers' had recently been caught and sent to reformatory to stay until 21." Caylor, "Memories of My Baltimore Childhood," pp. 12–14.

73. Fein, *Making of an American Jewish Community*, p. 163, f. 97 (Fein quotes Dr. Pollack).

74. Ibid., pp. 217–19. Playgrounds were donated at school no. 43 by Mrs. Rayner Frank and school no. 40 by the Baltimore Association of Jewish Women, *Children's Playground Association of Baltimore* (Baltimore: Baltimore Association of Jewish Women, 1913).

75. Aaronsohn, *Broken Lights*, pp. 18, 19, 22, 24.

76. Meginnis, *Samuel Ready*, p. 30.

CHAPTER   FIVE

1. "On September 8, 1892, the [four] senior girls move to what was the sewing room." *Ready Record* (September 25, 1892): 4.

2. Rowe explained to a mother that since her daughter returned to school late after a vacation, she had exhausted her vacation credits (even though she brought doctors' certificates).

3. Certain girls' names appear over and over in the *Ready Record*. These girls were also excellent students. Among them are: Heidi Donaldson, Eveline Durant, and Cathy Sullivan. Not all of these girls were seniors. Heidi Donaldson, the editor of the *Ready Record*, was only fifteen in 1892, and there were seventeen- and eighteen-year-old girls at the school at that time.

4. In the *Ready Record*, for example, articles by good students whose fathers were a car driver, a painter, an undertaker, appear beside articles by students whose fathers were clerks, teachers, merchants. It seems that students who eventually became dressmakers rarely published anything in the newspaper.

5. At the McDonogh School, after which the Samuel Ready was modeled, in September 1907, "Several 'news boys' run away as a result of the current ferocity of hazing, and shortly thereafter two 'old boys' are dismissed for their treatment of the younger students." Hugh F. Burgess, Jr., and Robert C. Al Smoot, *McDonogh School: An Interpretive Chronology* (Columbus, Ohio: Charles E. Merrill, 1973), p. 110.

6. Ibid., pp. 64–68.

7. In the *Ready Record* and in their letters, the girls never used the term *orphanage* when they referred to the school, not even in their make-believe games.

8. Reformers believed that fresh air and country living were important for children's health and could cure lung diseases. Rudolph R. Reeder, *How Two Hundred Children Live and Learn* (New York: Charities Publication Committee, 1909), p. 19. The *Sunday Sun* organized a Fresh Air Fund in Baltimore "to send children from poor families out in the country." Interview with Nathan Cooper.

9. Interviews with Mr. Benjamin and Simon Z.; Michael Aaronsohn, *Broken Lights* (Cincinnati: Johnson and Hardin, 1946), p. 34.

10. "He remembered that Dr. and Mrs. Rice [pseudonym for Reizenstein] of the orphanage had taught that it was dangerous to associate with mem

bers of the opposite sex." Aaronsohn, *Broken Lights*, p. 47. Though he may have discouraged relationships between boys and girls, Reizenstein demanded that the children be given sexual education.

11. For example, the superintendent reported that "Bella C. was discharged to the custody of her grandfather because of habits harmful to the morals of the other girls in the home."

12. Interview with Bess Hammet.

13. Michael Aaronsohn, *That the Living May Know* (Cincinnati: Johnson and Hardin: 1973), p. 16.

14. "At the head of a privileged set of monitors was the chief monitor, usually the oldest, the strongest, and the fiercest of all the elite. The discipline imposed and enforced by the monitors was excruciating." Aaronsohn, *That the Living*, p. 16.

15. Aaronsohn, *Broken Lights*, p. 29.

16. "The Children's Republic of the Hebrew Orphan Asylum was declared in December 1916 during the Chanukah vacation." The residents of the republic, Reizenstein explained to the directors, "are organized in two 'Groups' of girls and three of boys. Each group consists of several 'families' under a chief Big Brother or a chief Big Sister. The Big Brothers and Big Sisters constitute the 'Council' or chief legislative body, presided over by a president, elected by all the citizens. . . . Offenders against the laws of the Republic are tried before a court of the chief Big Brothers or the chief Big Sisters."

17. LeRoy Ashby, *Saving the Waifs: Reformers and Dependent Children, 1890–1917* (Philadelphia: Temple University Press, 1984), pp. 21–22. A former graduate of the H.O.A., Henry B. Waskaw, described in the *Baltimore Sun Magazine* of June 8, 1980, the children's republic of the H.O.A.: "[Dr. Reizenstein] originated a student government, which, unfortunately, didn't work. 'Judges' were appointed among the children to give demerits after a 'hearing,' to other children for such offenses as untidiness. A lack of maturity resulted in injustices." The article's title is "I Remember: Two Different 'Rulers' at Jewish Orphan Home."

18. Burgess and Smoot, *McDonogh School*, p. 123.

19. Aaronsohn, *That the Living*, p. 16.

20. Ibid., p. 18; *Broken Lights*, p. 34.

21. Aaronsohn, *That the Living*, pp. 9–10.

22. Waskow, "I Remember."

23. The *Catholic Mirror* of June 28, 1890, p. 6, reports: "The closing exercises of St. Patrick's School for Boys [the school the Dolan Home children attended] . . . took place. . . . The gold medal for excellence in catechism was drawn by Charles Russel. . . . Martin Garrett won the silver medal for attendance."

24. Aaronsohn, *That the Living*, p. 17.

25. Of the forty-five children in my sample, only three were full orphans when admitted. These children were siblings, and even they had an uncle who was their guardian.

26. Although decisions in regard to vocation and education were subject to the board of directors' approval, it was the superintendent who recommended a vocation for each child, as Michael Aaronsohn's case indicates. When Freudenthal died in 1910, nobody knew what plans he had for the boy. Aaronsohn and four friends had to enroll in the commercial course at City College instead of the academic course he thought he would pursue. Aaronsohn, *Broken Lights*, p. 32.

27. "Stealthily 'going to the ball game' was a regular Saturday afternoon feature. . . . Only when a lad was 'caught' and punished did the boys and girls regard the adventurer as a wicked person." Aaronsohn, *Broken Lights*, p. 19. On Freudenthal's moralistic tone while administering these punishments, see ibid., p. 22.

28. "I have tried to teach you that success or happiness in a large measure depends upon individual exertion, not upon wishful thinking or outside interposition," Freudenthal said to the children, according to Aaronsohn, *That the Living*, p. 12.

29. "Rabbi Freudenthal constantly hammered away at the necessity to excel through the perpetual practice of such virtues as thrift, diligence, perseverance, high courage, faith, good manners, personal rectitude, love of country, an unquenchable thirst for knowledge, and preeminently the fear of the Holy Presence." Ibid., p. 17. Also *Broken Lights*, pp. 30, 72; interview with Mr. Benjamin, July 20, 1988.

30. Aaronsohn, *Broken Lights*, p. 23.

31. Merle Curti, "Dime Novels," *Yale Review* 26 (1937): 761, shows that working-class children were the main readers of literature. For the "crusade" of middle-class parents, librarians, and educators against dime novels see Dora V. Smith, *Fifty Years of Children's Books* (Champaign, Ill.: National Council of Teachers of English, 1963), p. 5.

32. *Jewish Encyclopedia*, 1903, 6: 104; *Encyclopedia Judaica*, Jerusalem, 1974, 12: 1478–79 (s.v. "orphans").

33. Aaronsohn, *Broken Lights*, pp. 20, 29; *That the Living*, p. 19.

34. Burgess and Smoot, *McDonogh School*, p. 108.

35. Interview with Simon Z.; Aaronsohn, *Broken Lights*, p. 19.

36. Discipline problems involving girls were rarely reported. Girls did not run away, as the records show and the interview with Ilene B. points out.

37. The atmosphere of bereavement and mouring was well remembered by Mr. Benjamin, who was a young boy then, and Simon Z., who was only six years old and entered the H.O.A. two months after Dr. Freudenthal's death. Also Aaronsohn, *That the Living*, p. 22.

38. Aaronsohn, *That the Living*, pp. 22–23.

39. "His voice was chilling. His smile was bridled by suspicion and egotism. His phrase was laconic. His manner was brusque. . . . The doctor of philosophy presented a remarkable contrast to Rabbi Fernal [Freudenthal]." Aaronsohn, *Broken Lights*, pp. 29–30. Also interviews with Ilene B., Mr. Benjamin, Simon Z., and Hyman Warsaw.

40. Aaronsohn, *Broken Lights*, pp. 30–31.

41. "The gentleness of his spirit, the beauty of his countenance, and the charm of his speech caused the discord among the children to melt like wax." This is Aaronsohn's description of the rabbi who was acting superintendent in the interim between Freudenthal's death and Reizenstein's appointment. *Broken Lights*, p. 29.

42. All four interviewees described Reizenstein more or less in this manner, although they did not come together in the period of the interviews and some did not even know the others. Mr. Benjamin lived under Reizenstein's regime for seven years, Simon Z. for eight years. Ilene B. and Hyman Warsaw lived under his superintendency only one year.

43. Dr. Milton Reizenstein further explained that his younger brother suffered immensely from their father's strictness and could not come to terms with it long after their father's death in 1939. He himself regarded his father's strictness as part of his German Jewish education and the standards of discipline that prevailed during his father's time.

44. Roy Lubove, *The Professional Altruist; The Emergence of Social Work As a Career, 1880–1930* (Cambridge, Mass.: Harvard University Press, 1965), p. 104.

45. Interviews with Ilene B., Jeanette Rosner Wolman (the social worker in Sharlitt's time), and Hyman Warsaw.

46. Michael Sharlitt, *As I Remember, The Home in My Heart* (Shaker Heights, Ohio: Bellefaire Jewish Children's Home, 1959), pp. 72–93.

47. Interviews with Ilene B. and Bess Hammet (the last secretary of the H.O.A.).

48. On Dr. Freudenthal, Michael Aaronsohn wrote: "The warmth of Rabbi Fernal's [Freudenthal's] personality had been infused into every nook and corner of the institution." *Broken Lights*, p. 28. On Michael Sharlitt, Henry B. Waskaw wrote: "Under Mr. Sharlitt's sensitive superintendency, the incidence of runaways declined markedly. He stressed the fun of group living and evoked among the children a high degree of personal pride in individual accomplishment and a spirit of greater cooperation among the sub-groups of the Home." "I Remember: Two Different 'Rulers' at Jewish Orphan Home," *Baltimore Sun Magazine*, June 8, 1980. Ilene B. said of Jacob Kepecs: "a wonderful dear man—I loved him."

49. Heidi Donaldson, "A Retrospect: Impressions of Three 'Old Girls,'" twenty-fifth anniversary of the Samuel Ready School.

50. Ibid.

51. Cathy Sullivan, "A Retrospect."

52. Most of those who were dismissed left in their first year. Four out of the five dismissed from the first forty girls at the Samuel Ready left after two, six, eight, and ten months at the school. One was expelled after three years. All were expelled for behavior, unclean habits, or misconduct.

53. Rudolph R. Reeder, *How Two Hundred Children Live and Learn* (New York: Charities Publication Committee, 1910), p. 169.

54. "Many are the advantages enjoyed by Ready girls today to which we of 1887 were strangers, but for these there were great compensations. In

those early days when the family numbered less than twenty, there was an intimacy in the family circle which could not be possible when the school had tripled the number of its pupils." Cathy Sullivan, "A Retrospect."

55. Both Rowe and Freudenthal talked to their orphans about their futures. Heidi Donaldson wrote: "Will any of us ever get away from the influence of these half-hours in the evening when Miss Rowe talked with us about our plans for the future?" "A Retrospect."

56. Almost all the girls ended their letters to Rowe with a request to send their love to Mrs. Agnes O. Tilghman (who was the cooking teacher and the Sunday school teacher as well as the housekeeper), Miss Mary S. Yeakle (the sewing teacher and nurse), and sometimes to Miss Clara H. Steiner (the general studies teacher). The fact that they specified names and did not send the same message in every letter indicates that the sentiment expressed was real and not just a polite form of ending letters.

57. "Studies were made so much more interesting than they had been in the public schools, that the pupils scarcely knew they were working. . . . As a teacher of history, literature and English composition, I am sure she had few peers." Miss Steiner's Record, January 1925, p. 3.

58. "An October 1892 issue of The Ready Record contained an article on Tennyson's death. . . . In November of that year there was an article on John Greenleaf Whittier." Meginnis, Samuel Ready, p. 30.

59. On the twenty-fifth anniversary of the Samuel Ready in 1912, the alumnae presented the school with an Agnes O. Tilghman memorial room.

60. The school had two musical clubs: the Beethoven Club, later renamed the Schumann Club, and the Mendelssohn Club. The students had classes in vocal music and mandolin instruction besides individual instruction in piano, pipe organ, violin, and alpha (alpenhorn). Of the forty girls in my sample, six studied instrumental music with the intention of teaching, but only four graduated as music teachers.

61. Clara Steiner taught at Samuel Ready from 1887 to 1922. She retired in that year and died in 1925. Mary Yeakle taught at the school from 1890 to her death in 1921. Beth Donaldson, a Samuel Ready School graduate, taught at the school until her death in 1910.

62. In the 1920s Mary E. Krekel was superintendent. "Helen J. Rowe, Clara H. Steiner, and Mary S. Yeakle had been known as the trio. . . . [Mary Krekel] had her own trio with Mary M. Hood and Dorothy E. Webb, both teachers who, like her, were true children of Samuel Ready School." Frances S. Meginnis, Samuel Ready . . . The Man and His Legacy (Baltimore: University of Baltimore, 1987), p. 32.

63. An alumna of the Samuel Ready School in the 1920s described Mary E. Krekel's attitude toward her students: "The girls were as sensitive to what she didn't say as to what she said. She seldom raised her voice, and her gaze could wither one or recharge the ego. She was affectionately called 'the Dean.'" Meginnis, Samuel Ready, p. 37.

64. "To Milton Stern [Michael Aaronsohn], John Crist was a superman. For a number of years Milton voluntarily served as John Crist's redoubtable helper." Aaronsohn, That the Living, p. 20.

65. "That evening Milton and his sister Dinah [Michael and Dora Aaronsohn] sat on the bench, which circled the broad sycamore. Dinah listened avidly to the tales her brother told her about his life at City College." Aaronsohn, *Broken Lights*, p. 34. The role Michael Aaronsohn's sister played in his life is described in his three autobiographical narratives: *Broken Lights, The Red Pottage* (Cincinnati: Johnson and Hardin, 1956), and *That the Living May Know*.

66. "My brother was six years older than I [and] 'conspicuously' played father in vigorous and solemn fashion. . . . During my adolescent years, my sister on her own, as a struggling member of society, found time and the means to be with me, graciously sharing with me what she could. I cannot recall a cross word or an angry look that ever passed between us." Michael Sharlitt's mother died when he was four years old, and his father, who remarried and moved to the West, placed him and his older brother and sister in a Jewish orphanage in New York. Sharlitt, *As I Remember*, p. 19.

67. When Abigail Blair graduated from the school at the age of eighteen, she returned home to her mother and apparently enjoyed the company of her family and friends. Susan Vault, who was a full orphan, enjoyed living with her aunt and uncle when she left school and seemed at home with them, although her frequent letters to Rowe also indicate her close relation with the superintendent and homesickness for the school. Nora Cooper wrote Rowe for a recipe for sherbet, which she wanted to make for her uncle, who did not like ice cream. The letters of these girls and others show that in many cases their relations with family outside the institution were good. But as shown in Chapter Six, that is not the whole picture.

68. Saul Ulenberg was released from the H.O.A. in 1899 upon his uncle's request and "placed in charge of his uncle." But a year later the 1900 U.S. Census—Maryland indicates that Saul Ulenberg was a resident of Boys' Home.

69. Register of Wills, 1893, v. 70, folio 7, p. 246, in Baltimore City Court.

70. Eileen Simpson, *Orphans: Real and Imaginary* (New York: New American Library, 1987), pp. 3–134.

71. Aaronsohn, *Broken Lights*, p. 33, describes the advantages for an H.O.A. boy of going to City College: "going to the City College also meant . . . opportunities to 'skip' away in the afternoon to visit one's parent."

72. Running away for a short visit was a weekly affair in the H.O.A., according to Mr. Benjamin, Michael Aaronsohn, and Simon Z. But when the same boy ran away frequently, the superintendent asked the board to release the child. "Dan S. who was admitted June 26, 1903 started this run away affair July 2nd 1903 and repeated the offence four different times always inducing [other] children to run away with him; Moshe Sn. ran away 3 times the last time March 12 when I went to his mother's home 1151 Low St. and brought him back in the following day March 18 he ran away again from the Public School and upon the order of our President I left him home with his mother. Simon K., ran away on March 20, 1904, had him apprehended by the Police and brought back to our 'Home.'" Freudenthal asked the Board in April 1904 to discharge the first two boys.

73. Mr. Benjamin and Michael Aaronsohn, for example, had family members who were interested in their welfare and also had strong relationships with their siblings. Ilene B., on the other hand, described her relationships with her outside relatives as "not close" and those with her siblings in the H.O.A. as equally "not close." The Samuel Ready School girls present the same pattern. The Sanderson sisters, the Delphy sisters, the Hullingood sisters had close relationships with relatives and also with each other.

74. The H.O.A. appeared frequently in the newspaper, the *Jewish Comment*, which was published in Baltimore. For example see the issue of February 13, 1903: "The Orphan Asylum benefit performances have always been well patronized, and they are made the occasion of an unusually interesting society gathering."

75. The two groups were known in Baltimore Jewry as the "Uptown"— the German Jews, and the "Downtown"—the Russian Jews. Isaac M. Fein, *The Making of an American Jewish Community* (Philadelphia: Jewish Publication Society of America), pp. 198–232.

76. My sample from the 1890s and the 1900 U.S. Census—Maryland Population both show that the majority of the H.O.A. population were Russian Jewish children. The annual reports of the H.O.A. show that the benefactors were mainly German Jews.

77. Until 1907, the superintendent and the directors, with the help of the Ladies Aid Society, solicited contributions and also maintained contact with the children's relatives. In 1907 the H.O.A. became part of Federated Jewish Charities, the central charity organization of the German Jews. Soliciting money then became that organization's responsibility.

78. Jewish orphanages might not have been common in Russia for political or economic reasons. Jews were restricted in their movements and were also very poor. Conditions, not ideology, might have forced them to care for their orphans at home. Pogroms at the end of the nineteenth century and at the beginning of the twentieth left many Jewish orphans without any relatives. Jewish communities in the West, including the Jewish community of Baltimore, took these children to their orphanages.

79. Bess Hammet, the H.O.A.'s secretary, did not eat at the institution because she thought that its food was not "kosher." When the "Russian" orphanage (the Betsy Levy Home) merged with the H.O.A. the "only friction occurred from feelings by the Broadwayites that their claims to greater religious orthodoxy were being threatened by the consolidation." Waskow, "I Remember." See also Aaronsohn, *Broken Lights*, p. 12.

80. Aaronsohn, *Broken Lights*, p. 18.

81. The three girls of the Dorfan family "were to be discharged to the care of their father and mother [who had applied for them and were able to provide for them] provided the father [a chronic deserter] would appear in court and pledge himself to remain with, and take care of his family. Instead of doing this, he took the children away, without permission. The mother was referred to Hon. J. M. Moses, as legal counsel of the H.O.A., with a written statement of the mother." Superintendent's report.

82. Jacob died some years ago. He was not rich but was well known among Baltimore Jewish people. His funeral, an acquaintance recalled, was one of the largest he had seen during a long life in Baltimore. Interview with Wilfred S.

83. "Last September," wrote Rowe to the school's secretary, "Ella Love, nine years old, under the care of the paternal grandmother, was admitted to our School. Her father called yesterday and said he wanted her, that he is able to provide for her. I told him I would consult the trustees and he could call on Saturday next; that we would be glad if he could take his daughter but we would require the grandmother's presence in order to deliver the child to the one who placed her here. Do you not think that under the circumstances it is best to let her go?" The girl was immediately released.

84. For example, Rowe in one instance granted a mother's request to take her child on a short vacation in order to meet the child's sibling, but denied the same request in another instance because the child had not exhibited deserving conduct. Her letters always explained her policy and her reasons for not respecting a parent's wish.

85. After two years of waiting to be admitted to the Ready School, Lynn Blain was finally accepted after her mother persuaded Dr. Daniel C. Gilman, a Ready trustee, to write a letter of recommendation for her daughter. This was the only instance found in which Rowe bowed to a parent's pressure.

86. "On Tuesday—a minister who is about to take charge of a boarding school in Graham, Virginia, accompanied by three ladies, visited our school." *Ready Record* (June 10, 1892): 4.

87. Meginnis, *Samuel Ready*, pp. 31, 33–34. Ann Graham Ross's will from April 15, 1897, left $26,470 for Samuel Ready School.

88. *Ready Record* 2 (June 30, 1893): 2. In 1894, Dr. Goucher asked Rowe if she had another student as talented and eager for an education as the one she had already sent. He could not promise a second scholarship, but he promised to make an effort for a worthy candidate.

89. Certain companies, like the U.S. Fidelity and Guaranty Company and the Fidelity and Deposit Company, regularly employed Samuel Ready School students.

90. "In publishing the within regulations, the Board of Trustees of the Dolan Children's Aid Society desire to call the attention of the Clergy and Laity to the fact that, not with standing the general impression that the charity, was sufficient in itself to make all his charities self-sustaining, the actual revenue . . . amounts to very little more than Seven Hundred Dollars per annum." Introduction to the Dolan Home minute book, p. 19.

91. For example: "Received during the quarter Fred, Charles, John, Edward and Sean (5). Taken by their parents Jeremy, Matthew, Jack (3) all boarders." Dolan Home minute book, p. 122. For the parents' residence and occupations, see Chapter Two.

92. In a sharp letter the Mother Superior of the Sisters of the Holy Cross complained of "Sisters being obliged to collect in market the necessary food for those children." Dolan Home minute book.

93. "It was a most friendly environment. The Jewish children furtively moved about the village streets, woods, and fields without any sign of curiosity or hostility on the part of the Christian denizens." Aaronsohn, *That the Living*, p. 21.

94. The orphanage moved to Mt. Washington, then a rural area. Jewish Family and Children's Bureau, *A Century of Understanding, 1856–1956* (Baltimore: 1956) (s.v. "Hebrew Orphan Asylum").

95. Meginnis, *Samuel Ready*, p. 38.

CHAPTER SIX

1. For example, Joanna Miller was released from the H.O.A. upon reaching eighteen. She boarded with Mr. B. and went to work at Mr. Solomon's. She had savings at the H.O.A., and asked the board to give her that money.

2. "The shift from the Calverton orphanage to the tenement district in East Baltimore was indeed a drastic change." It was a "radical transplantation from an environment of comparative elegance and refinement to that of a forbidding milieu." Michael Aaronsohn, *That the Living May Know* (Cincinnati: Johnson and Hardin, 1973), p. 34; *Broken Lights* (Cincinnati: Johnson and Hardin, 1946), pp. 40–42.

3. Simon Z.'s wife found the knowledge her husband acquired in the orphanage in electricity, plumbing, and gardening very useful; he did all the maintenance work in the house.

4. On the depressions during the 1890s see James B. Crooks, *Politics and Progress: The Rise of Urban Progressivism in Baltimore, 1895 to 1911* (Baton Rouge: Louisiana University Press, 1979), p. 167, and Charles Hirschfeld, *Baltimore, 1870–1900; Studies in Social History* (Baltimore: Johns Hopkins University Press, 1941), pp. 54–55.

5. Lucy Maud Montgomery, *Ann of Green Gables* (New York: Grosset and Dunlop, 1908).

6. Michael Aaronsohn wrote that the students of City College assimilated him "with perfect comradeship and unaffected grace." Moreover, no one ever questioned him about the orphanage (*That the Living*, p. 28). It is highly probable that he did not volunteer the information that he came from the H.O.A. because his classmate Wilfred S. did not know about it until recently.

7. David M. Katzman, *Seven Days A Week: Women and Domestic Service in Industrializing America* (New York: Oxford University Press, 1978), p. 49.

8. An indication of the school's success is "the fact that all those who last year finished their course and were honorably dismissed almost immediately obtained employment in the directions for which they had been fitted." In 1911 the trustees reported that the "girls leaving the institution have rarely to wait long for employment. Indeed there are sometimes applications for their service in advance of their graduation." Samuel Ready minute book.

9. Frances S. Meginnis, *Samuel Ready . . . The Man and His Legacy* (Baltimore: University of Baltimore, 1987), p. 27.

10. "At about six o'clock Friday evening Idaline Delphy one of our former girls came to see us and about seven o'clock Lauren Keller who just left us, came and we had a delightful time. Idaline spent the night and stayed until after dinner on Saturday. Lauren only stayed a short time." *Ready Record* 1 (January 27, 1892): 4.

11. *Ready Record* 19 (March 18, 1910): 5 had alumnae news and an "Alumnae Department" in which a graduate detailed the history of straw work in the United States.

12. "The Hebrew Orphan Asylum was not spared by the Spanish influenza epidemic. Beginning on October 2, the illness among the children lasted well-nigh through the month. There were forty-seven cases in all among the children. Happily, there were no fatalities and although the temperatures were high in some instances, no pneumonia or other complications. Two trained nurses with the assistance of Selma Milner a former ward of our institution, who volunteered her services in the crisis, attended to the patients from October 8, to October 20." Superintendent's report.

13. "Women with high school training basically faced a single opportunity: teaching, and the teaching job market was already overcrowded. For these women, clerical employment, particularly as stenographers and typists, quickly became 'the other thing they could do.'" Ileen A. Devault, "Sons and Daughters of Labor: Class and Clerical Work in Pittsburgh, 1870s–1910s" (Ph.D. diss., Yale University, 1985).

14. Def. Mina Nadler by Hanna M. Koehler 6-A/239/1897/3439-A., Hall of Records, State Archives, Annapolis.

15. In the "First Joint Report of the Federated Jewish Charities," 1907, Dr. Freudenthal stated that one girl was attending the Western Female High School and a boy and a girl the preparatory school (preparing for high school). In the "Ninth Joint Report of the Federated Jewish Charities," 1915, p. 82, Dr. Reizenstein declared that "no less than fifteen of our boys and girls were encouraged to continue their education during the past year beyond the elementary school. Six girls attended the Western High School, of whom three graduated last June, having completed the four years' course in three years. Two of them are now attending the Teachers' Training School and one the Nurses Training School of the Hebrew Hospital. Another girl entered the Nurses Training School in the summer and a third girl in the fall. Three girls attended business school during the year. . . . One of the boys is studying medicine at the University of Maryland. . . . Five boys are attending City College. Three girls are attending the Western High School." In 1915 there were 130 children in the H.O.A. and 11.5 percent of them attended high school.

16. In the summer Dr. Reizenstein organized classes for thirty-eight children who had difficulties being promoted to the next grade. Besides these children, there were also mentally retarded children.

17. In addition to students whose professions were identified by Mr. Ben-

jamin and Simon Z., superintendents' reports list the professions of four more girls on the prize winners' list: two graduated from the teachers' training school and two from the training school for nurses.

18. During the 1910s, Dr. Reizenstein complained about admitting boys who ought to be in a reform school. The policy did not change; the directors were reluctant to commit Jewish boys to the corrective institutions in Maryland.

CHAPTER SEVEN

1. William J. Doherty, "A Study of Results of Institutional Care," *Proceedings of the National Conference of Charities and Correction at the Forty-second Annual Session Held in Baltimore, Maryland, May 12–19, 1915* (Chicago: Hildmann Printing Co., 1915), pp. 174–93.

2. The struggle of Samuel Ready parents to retain their children at the school after they reached sixteen in order to complete their vocational education was an example of that attitude. At the H.O.A. single parents, like Aaronsohn's widowed mother, were willing to let their children graduate from high school even though they could legally work when they reached fourteen. A similar trend can be detected from the attempts of relatives of children at the Dolan Home to convince the orphanage's management to send them to St. Mary's Industrial School rather than to a farm in the county. Barbara Brenzel, in *Daughters of the State: A Social Portrait of the First Reform School for Girls in North America, 1865–1905* (Cambridge, Mass.: MIT Press, 1983), finds a similar trend.

3. A *Jewish Comment* editorial of December 16, 1910, reported: "Ten years ago and less, 65 to 70 Jewish children were taken charge of by the Orphan Asylum of this city. Now 215 are in our two institutions, and more clamoring for admittance. The Cleveland Asylum, which is a quasi-national institution, has sometimes over 500 children; it will not be long before Baltimore alone will need accommodations for two thirds of that number."

4. Eighth Biennial Report of the Board of State Aid and Charities to the Governor and the General Assembly of Maryland, 1914–1915, pp. 72–73, in Maryland Historical Society, Baltimore.

5. "It is noticeable that 46.3% of all societies for the protection and care of children, 45.6% of the hospitals and sanitariums and 39.8% of the institutions for the care of children receive public aid." Department of Commerce, U.S. Bureau of the Census, *Benevolent Institutions, 1910* (Washington, D.C.: Government Printing Office, 1914), p. 79.

6. In 1933, public appropriations in Maryland supported 45 percent of all children in institutions and in general 33.6 percent of all dependent children in the state. The word "institution" in 1933 included child care agencies that placed children as well as institutions for handicapped children. U.S. Department of Commerce, Bureau of the Census, *Children under Institutional Care and in Foster Homes, 1933* (Washington, D.C.: Government Printing Office, 1935), p. 83.

7. Doherty, "A Study of Results of Institutional Care," p. 175.

8. "The picture herein drawn is not all inviting and constitutes rather a sad commentary upon the efficiency of some of our New York institutions. . . . Proper social vision of the welfare of dependent children on the part of both staff and institution management gradually is replacing the gloom and haze of dreary decades of barren institutions" (ibid., p. 193).

9. In 1911, Dr. Hasting H. Hart, a social worker, backed away from his previous emphasis on the economy of foster care. "For the normal child needing care, [Hart] unequivocally advocated the boarding-home. In this connection he warned his hearers that care in private homes is not a cheap proposition. He confessed that at one time he was guilty of pressing the economical argument more than was wise. On the contrary, the supervision in the homes, requires the services of able men and women, whose salaries form an important part of the budget of a child-placing society." *Jewish Comment*, February 10, 1911.

10. Sophia Van Senden Theis and Constance Goodrich, *The Child in the Foster Home. Part 1. The Placement of Children in Free Foster Homes: A Study Based on the Work of the Child-Placing Agency of the New York State Charities Association* (New York: New York School of Social Work, 1921), pp. 79–105.

11. *Jewish Comment*, June 16, 1911. Editor Harry H. Levin, who reported the outcome of a conference on charity held in Baltimore, was also secretary of the H.O.A. Board of Directors.

12. Elias L. Trozkey wrote in 1930: "To speak plainly in the light of present-day experience, does it not seem odd that some Jewish communities, in their desire to be hyper-modern, are chasing after shibboleths that have been given up by our non Jewish friends a decade or so ago. The abolition in a large or medium sized community of all institutional work can hardly be hailed as a progressive step, indeed it must be considered a disservice to dependent childhood. The dual form of child care [foster home as well as institutional care] is unquestionably for many years to come, the right policy with regard to Jewish communities." *Institutional Care and Placing Out* (Chicago: Marks Nathan Jewish Orphan Home, 1930), p. 18.

13. "There are indeed some opportunities inherent in the institution which the average-family life misses altogether. It is easier to organize the life of the child as a whole, to co-ordinate formal teaching with recreation, work with play, in a way that may produce remarkable and excellent results. . . . It may be more expensive, and it may require greater intelligence and skill, but there are instances to show that is possible." Edward T. Devine, *Social Work* (New York: McMillan, 1922), p. 122.

14. Sharlitt refers to results of a 1942 study of fifty-four men and women who spent their formative years in foster care. Sharlitt, *As I Remember*, p. 275.

15. The Bureau of the Census, *Children under Institutional Care and in Foster Homes, 1933*, lists forty-six institutions in Maryland. Many were new institutions located in the counties. The real number of orphanages cannot

be established from the census because some institutions listed as "Aid Societies" or "Homes" were actually placing-out agencies. In 1910, as mentioned before, there were only thirty-six orphanages in Maryland.

16. Frances S. Meginnis, *Samuel Ready . . . The Man and His Legacy* (Baltimore: University of Baltimore, 1987), pp. 36–44.

DATE DUE

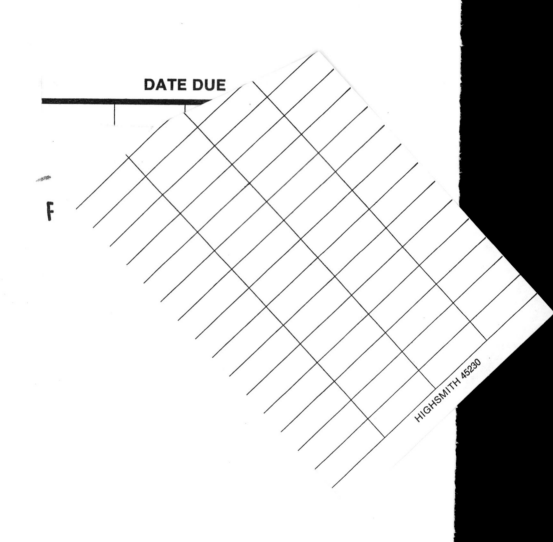

F